STEPS TO WRITING WELL

A CONCISE GUIDE TO COMPOSITION

THIRD EDITION

JEAN WYRICK Colorado State University

HOLT, RINEHART AND WINSTON, INC.
New York Chicago San Francisco Philadelphia
Montreal Toronto London Sydney Tokyo

This book is dedicated to DAVID
and to SARAH, KATE, and AUSTIN

Cover: Richard and Mary Magruder/Image Bank

Library of Congress Cataloging in Publication Data

Wyrick, Jean.
  Steps to writing well.

  Includes index.
  1. English language—Rhetoric.   I. Title.
PE1408.W93   1987   808'.042   86-14223
ISBN 0 03 004473 1

Published simultaneously in Canada
7 8 9 0   090   9 8 7 6 5 4 3 2

Holt, Rinehart and Winston, Inc.
The Dryden Press
Saunders College Publishing

To the Teacher

The third edition of *Steps to Writing Well* has been written and revised for teachers of composition who have had trouble finding a text that is accessible to their students. Too many texts on today's market, these teachers rightfully complain, are still unnecessarily complex, sophisticated, or massive for the majority of students. Written simply in an informal, straightforward style and addressed to the student, this text is designed to provide a clear step-by-step guide to writing a variety of 500-to-800-word essays. The combination of concise, practical advice, twenty student and professional essays, and a brief handbook should provide more than enough helpful information for students enrolled in a one-semester or one-quarter course without intimidating them with more material than they can possibly master.

Although many parts of the book have been revised or expanded for this edition, its organization remains essentially the same. Part One offers advice on "The Basics of the Short Essay"; Part Two discusses the "Modes and Strategies"; and Part Three presents "A Concise Handbook." The text still begins with the essay "To the Student," which not only argues that students can learn to write better with practice and dedication but also gives them a number of practical reasons why they *should* learn to write better.

Part One, containing seven chapters, moves students sequentially through the process of writing the short essay. Chapter 1, on prewriting, stresses finding the proper attitude ("the desire to communicate") and presents helpful suggestions for selecting a subject. Student samples illustrating two more prewriting techniques, clustering and cubing, have been added to this chapter, which now offers students a half-dozen methods for finding a significant focus for their essays. An expanded section on audience should also help student writers identify their particular readers and communicate more effectively with them. After finding a topic and identifying their audience, students are then ready for Chapter 2, devoted almost entirely to a discussion of the thesis statement. This chapter first explains the role of the "working thesis" in early drafts and then clearly outlines what a good thesis is and isn't by presenting over two dozen new examples to illustrate the advice. Also included in this chapter is explanation of the "essay map," an organizational tool that can help students outline their essays and plan their body paragraphs.

Chapter 3 discusses in detail the requirements of good body paragraphs: topic sentences, unity, order and coherence, adequate development, use of specific detail, and logical sequence. Over forty paragraphs—many of them new to this edition—illustrate both strengths and weaknesses of student writing. These paragraphs are not complex literary or professional excerpts but rather well-designed, precise examples of the principles under examination, written on subjects students can understand and appreciate. A new section in this chapter twice provides the opportunity for students to see how a topic may progress from a working thesis statement to an informal essay outline, which, in turn, helps produce well-developed paragraphs in the body of an essay. To complete the overview of the short essay, Chapter 4 explains, through a number of helpful samples, how to write good introductions, conclusions, and titles.

Chapter 5, "Revising Your Writing," has also been expanded in this edition. Because too many students still think of "revision" as merely proofreading their essays rather than as an integral part of composing, this chapter is devoted to explaining the revision process and to stressing the necessity of revision in all good writing. These pages guide the students through the various stages of revision, carefully cautioning novice writers against trying to analyze and revise too many parts of their papers at once. The chapter also includes hints for overcoming writer's block, a checklist for essays, and two student essays for revision practice.

Chapter 6, on effective sentences, emphasizes the importance of clarity, conciseness, and vividness, with nearly one hundred and fifty sample sentences illustrating the chapter's advice. Chapter 7, on word choice, presents practical suggestions for selecting accurate, appropriate words that are specific, memorable, and persuasive. This chapter also contains a new section on avoiding sexist language.

Each chapter in Part One contains numerous new samples and exercises. As before, the "Practicing What You've Learned" exercises follow each major section in each chapter so that both teacher and students may quickly discover if particular material needs additional attention. Moreover, by conquering small steps in the writing process, one at a time, the students should feel more confident and should learn more rapidly. Assignments, which also follow each major section in these chapters, suggest class activities and frequently emphasize "peer teaching," a useful method that asks students to prepare appropriate exercises for classmates and then to evaluate the results. Such assignments, operating under the premise that "you don't truly learn a subject until you teach it," provide engaging classroom activity for all the students and also remove from the teacher some of the burden of creating additional exercises.

Part Two concentrates on the four rhetorical modes: exposition, argumentation, description, and narration. Chapter 8 on exposition is divided into separate discussions of the expository strategies: example, process, comparison/contrast, definition, classification, and causal analysis. Each discussion in Chapter 8 and each of the chapters on argument, description, and narration follow a similar format by offering the students (a) a clear definition of the mode (or strategy), explained with familiar examples; (b) practical advice on developing each essay; (c) warnings against common problems; (d) suggested essay topics on subjects that appeal to students' interests and capabilities; (e) a sample student essay with marginal notes; (f) a professional essay followed by questions on content, structure, and style, and a vocabulary list; (g) a revision worksheet to guide student writers through their rough drafts. The advice on developing the essay and the section on common problems are both explained in easy-to-understand language accompanied by numerous examples. The ten student essays, some new to this edition, should encourage student writers by showing them that others in their situation can indeed compose organized, thoughtful essays. The student essays that appear here are not perfect, however; consequently, teachers may use them in class to generate suggestions for still more improvement. The ten professional essays were also selected to spur class discussion and to illustrate the rhetorical principles presented in this text. The four professional essays most popular with users of the second edition were retained in this revision; six new essays replace older readings.

Two important additions to Part Two bear noting. First, the chapter on argumentation has been greatly expanded to give students more help preparing and organizing their own persuasive points as well as developing effective counter-arguments. A sample topic is presented in various stages of the writing process and then in a completed student essay. Suggestions such as the pro-and-con sheet and the "although–because" thesis may also prove useful in the early writing stages. Finally, two professional essays arguing different sides of the same issue provide students with an opportunity to compare and contrast the effectiveness of two argumentative approaches.

The other most important change in this edition is the addition of

Chapter 12, "Writing the Research Paper." In this chapter students will learn how to use the library, take notes, and incorporate source material into their essays. Examples are provided to help students understand the difference between summary and paraphrase and between plagiarism in its various forms and proper documentation. The chapter also contains information on the current MLA parenthetical documentation format and samples of the most often used bibliographic entries, as well as a "problem-solving" student essay that uses research material to support its points.

Part Three contains a concise handbook with non-technical explanations and new, easy-to-understand examples showing how to correct the most common errors in grammar, punctuation, and mechanics. This edition also includes nine sets of exercises over the grammar and punctuation rules. Instead of following each and every rule with five or ten simplistic sentences containing the error in question, this text offers a series of exercises systematically placed so that the students may practice applying several rules at one sitting, just as they must do when they write their own prose.

Once again, readers of this edition may note an occasional attempt at humor. The lighthearted tone of some samples and exercises is the result of the author's firm belief that while learning to write is serious business, solemn composition classrooms are not always the most beneficial environments for anxious beginning writers. The author takes full responsibility (and all of the blame) for the bad jokes and even worse puns.

Finally, an updated and expanded Instructor's Manual with suggestions for teaching and answers to exercises and essay questions is available from the English Editor, Holt, Rinehart and Winston, 383 Madison Avenue, New York, NY 10017.

Although a third edition of this text has allowed its author to make a number of changes and additions, the book's purpose remains the same, as stated in the original preface: "While there are many methods of teaching composition, *Steps to Writing Well* tries to help inexperienced writers by offering a clearly defined sequential approach to writing the short essay. By presenting simple, practical advice directly to the students, this text is intended to make the demanding jobs of teaching and learning the basic principles of composition easier and more enjoyable for everyone."

Acknowledgments

I would like to express my deep appreciation to Developmental Editor Kate Morgan for her excellent work throughout every stage of this revision; without her unfailing support, patience, and good humor, there would be no third edition this year. I'm always grateful to English Editor Charlyce Jones Owen for her guidance and consistent encouragement. I am also indebted to my editorial production team: Jeanette Ninas Johnson, Annette Mayeski, Stefania Taflinska, and Louis Scardino. My appreciation to the following colleagues for their useful suggestions: Professors Philip Tetreault, Dean Junior College; Kathleen Dubs, University of San Francisco; Donnasue Farrell, Manatee Community College; Elizabeth Fifer, Lehigh University; Steve Flaherty, DeVry Institute of Technology; Mary Helen Halloran, University of Wisconsin; Sandra Hanson, La Guardia Community College; Mary Anne Hutchinson, Utica College; John Huxhold, St. Louis Community College; Hannah Laipson, Quinsigamond Community College; Jo Ann Little, Pima Community College; W. C. Truckey, Lewis and Clark Community College.

Finally, many thanks to my husband, David Hall, for his assistance and understanding, and to my three children for whom—even though none of them can read yet—"Mom's book" has special meaning.

JEAN WYRICK
Director of Composition
Colorado State University

To the Student

Finding the Right Attitude

If you agree with one or more of the following statements, we have some serious myth-killing to do before you begin this book:

1. I'm no good in English—never have been, never will be.
2. Only people with natural talent for writing can succeed in composition class.
3. My composition teacher is a picky, comma-hunting liberal/conservative/hippie freak/old fogey/whatever, who will insist I write just like him or her.
4. I write for myself, not for anyone else, so I don't need this class or this book.
5. Composition classes are designed to put my creativity in a strait jacket.

The notion that good writers are born, not made, is a widespread myth that may make you feel defeated before you start. But the simple truth is that good writers *are* made—simply because *effective writing is a skill that can be learned.* Despite any feelings of insecurity you may have about composition, you should realize that you already know many of the basic rules of good writing; after all, you've been writing since you were six years old. What you need now is some practical advice on composition, some coaching to sharpen your skills, and a strong dose of determination to practice those skills until you can consistently produce the results you want. Talent, as the French writer Flaubert once said, is nothing more than long patience.

Think about learning to write well as you might consider your tennis game. No one is born a tennis star. You first learn the basic rules and movements and then go out on the court to practice. And practice. No one's tennis will improve if he or she stays off the court; similarly, you must write regularly and receive feedback to improve your composition skills. Try to see your teacher not as Dr. Frankenstein determined to reproduce his or her style of writing in you, but rather as your coach, your loyal trainer who wants you to do the very best you can. Like any good coach, your teacher will point out your strengths and weaknesses; she or he will often send you to this text for practical suggestions for improvement. And while there are no quick, magic solutions for learning to write well, the most important point to remember is this: with this text, your own common sense, and determination, *you can improve your writing.*

Why Write?

"OK," you say, "so I can improve if I try—but why should I bother? Why should I write well? I'm not going to be a professional writer."

In the first place, writing helps us explore our own thoughts and feelings. Writing forces us to articulate our ideas, to discover what we really think about an issue. For example, let's suppose you're faced with a difficult decision and that the arguments pro and con are jumbled in your head. You begin to write down all the pertinent facts and feelings, and suddenly, you begin to see that you do, indeed, have stronger arguments for one side of the question than the other. Once you "see" what you are thinking, you may then scrutinize your opinions for any logical flaws or weaknesses and revise your argument accordingly. In other words, writing lays out our ideas for examination, analysis, and thoughtful reaction. Thus when we write, we (and the world at large) see who we are, and what we stand for, much more clearly. Moreover, writing can provide a record of our thoughts that we may study and evaluate in a way that conversation cannot. In short, writing well enables us to see and know ourselves—our feelings, ideas, and opinions—better.

On a more practical level, we need to write effectively to communicate with others. While a part of our writing is done solely for ourselves, the majority of it is created for others to share. In this world, it is almost impossible to claim that we write only for ourselves. We are constantly asked to put our feelings, ideas, and knowledge in writing for others to read. In four years of college, no matter what your major, you will repeatedly be required to write essays, tests, reports, and exercises (not to mention letters home). Later, you may need to write formal letters of application for jobs or graduate training. And on a job you may have to write numerous kinds of reports, proposals, analyses, and requisitions. To be successful in any field, you must make your correspondence with business associates and co-workers clearly understood; remember that enormous amounts of time, energy, and profit have been lost because of a single unclear office memo.

There's still a third—more cynical—reason for studying writing techniques. Once you begin to improve your ability to use language, you will become more aware of the ways others write and speak. Through today's mass media, we are continually bombarded with words from politicians, advertisers, scientists, preachers, and teachers. We need to understand and evaluate what we are hearing, not only for our benefit but also for self-protection. Language is frequently manipulated to manipulate us. For example, years ago some government officials on trial preferred us to see Watergate as an "intelligence information gathering mission" rather than as simple breaking and entering, and today some politicians claim to merely "misspeak themselves" when caught in lies. Similarly, military officers and CIA members may discuss the "neutralization" of their enemies, possibly through the use of weapons with names such as "Peacekeeper," designed to obscure their potential for our total destruction. Common household products are given lofty names and descriptions to increase sales—a new mother who opens an official-looking package labeled "infant sensory development material," for instance, may be disappointed to find only a baby pacifier inside. Advertisers frequently try to sell us "authentic art reproductions" that are, of course, fakes all the same; the television networks treat us to "encore presentations" that are the same old summer reruns.

By becoming better writers ourselves, we can learn to recognize and reject the irresponsible, cloudy, and dishonest language of others before we become victims of their exploitation.

A Good Place to Start

If improving writing skills is not only possible but important, it is also something else: hard work. H. L. Mencken, American critic and writer, once remarked that "for every difficult and complex problem, there is an obvious solution that is simple, easy and wrong." No composition text can promise easy formulas guaranteed to improve your writing overnight. Nor is writing always fun for anyone. But this text can make the learning process easier, less painful, and more enjoyable than you might anticipate. Written in plain, straightforward language addressed to you, the student, this book will suggest a variety of practical ways for you to organize and write clear, concise prose. Because each of your writing tasks will be different, this text cannot provide a single, simple blueprint that will apply in all instances. Later chapters, however, will discuss some of the most common methods of organizing essays, such as development by example, definition, classification, causal analysis, comparison/contrast, and argument. As you become more familiar with, and begin to master, these patterns of writing, you will find yourself increasingly able to assess, organize, and explain the thoughts you have about the people, events, and situations in your own life. And while it may be true that in learning to write well there is no free ride, this book, along with your own willingness to work and improve, can start you down the road with a good sense of direction.

J.W.

Contents

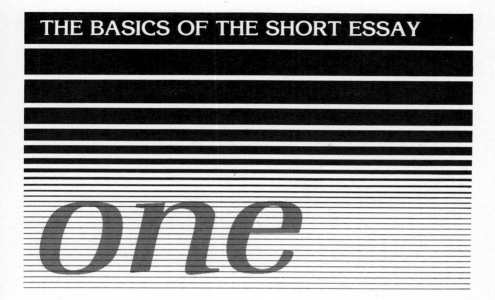

THE BASICS OF THE SHORT ESSAY

one

PART ONE

In the first section of this text, you will read about the main parts of the short essay, the kind you are most likely to encounter in composition class and in other college courses. Chapters 1 and 2, on prewriting and the thesis statement, will help you organize your thoughts and plan the design of your essay; Chapter 3, on paragraphs, will show you how to write the body or middle section; Chapter 4 will help you complete your essay. Chapter 5 will offer suggestions for revising your writing, and Chapters 6 and 7 will present additional advice on selecting the words and composing the sentences in your rough drafts.

Prewriting

GETTING STARTED, OR SOUP CAN LABELS CAN BE FASCINATING

For many writers getting started is the hardest part. You may have noticed that when it is time to begin a writing assignment, you suddenly develop an enormous desire to defrost your refrigerator, water your plants, or sharpen your pencils for the fifth time. If this situation sounds familiar, you may find it reassuring to know that many professionals undergo these same strange compulsions before they begin writing. Jean Kerr, author of *Please Don't Eat the Daisies*, admits that she often finds herself in the kitchen reading soup can labels—or anything—in order to prolong the moments before taking pen in hand. John C. Calhoun, vice-president under Andrew Jackson, insisted he had to plow his fields before he could write, and Joseph Conrad, author of *Lord Jim* and other novels, is said to have cried on occasion from sheer dread of sitting down to compose his stories.

In order to spare you as much hand-wringing as possible, this chapter presents some practical suggestions on how to begin writing your short essay. Although all writers must find the methods that work best for them, you may find some of the following ideas helpful.

But no matter how you actually begin putting words on paper, it is absolutely essential to maintain two basic ideas concerning your writing task. Before you write a single sentence, you should always remind yourself that

1. you have some valuable ideas to tell your reader, and
2. more than anything, you want to communicate those ideas to your reader.

3

These reminders may seem obvious to you, but without a solid commitment to your own opinions as well as to your reader, your prose will be lifeless and boring. If *you* don't care about your subject, you can't very well expect anyone else to. Have confidence that your ideas are worthwhile and that your reader genuinely wants, or needs, to know what you think.

Most importantly, however, you must have a strong desire to tell others exactly what you are thinking. The single most serious mistake inexperienced writers make is writing for themselves only. The very act of composing an essay demonstrates that you have ideas about your subject; the point is to communicate your opinions to others clearly and persuasively. Whether you wish to inform your readers, change their minds, or stir them to action, you cannot accomplish your purpose by writing so that only you understand what you mean. Remember that the burden of communicating your thoughts falls on *you*, not the reader, who is under no obligation at all to struggle through confused, unclear prose, paragraphs that begin and end for no apparent reason, sentences that come one after another with no more logic than lemmings following one another into the sea. Therefore, before you begin writing, commit yourself to becoming more sensitive to the feelings of your reader. Ask yourself as you revise your writing, "Am I making myself clear to others, or am I merely jotting down a conversation with myself?" Other chapters in this book will give you concrete advice on ways to make your writing clearer, but for now, at the jumping-off point in the writing process, the goal is to become *determined to communicate with your readers.*

SELECTING A SUBJECT

Once you have decided that communicating with others is your primary goal, you are ready to select the subject of your essay. Here are some suggestions on how to begin:

Start early. Writing teachers since the earth's crust cooled have been pushing this advice, and for good reason. It's not because teachers are egoists competing for the dubious honor of having the most time-consuming course; it's because few writers, even experienced ones, can do a good job when rushed. You need time to mull over ideas, organize your thoughts, revise and polish your sentences. Rule of thumb: always give yourself twice as much time as you think you'll need to avoid the two-A.M.-why-did-I-come-to-college panic.

Select something in which you currently have a strong interest. If the essay subject is left to you, think of something fun, fascinating, or frightening you've done or seen lately, something perhaps you've already told a friend about. The subject might be the pleasure of a new hobby, the challenge of a recent book or movie, or even the harassment of registration—anything in which you are personally involved. If you aren't enthusiastic enough about your subject to want to spread the word, pick something else. Bored writers write boring essays.

Don't feel you have nothing from which to choose your subject. Your days are full of activities, people, joys, and irritations. Essays do not have to be written on lofty intellectual or "poetic" subjects—in fact, some of the world's best essays have been written on such subjects as china teacups, roast pig, and chimney sweeps. Think: what have you been talking or thinking about lately? What have you been doing that you're excited about? Or what about your past? Reflect a few moments on some of your most vivid memories—special people, vacations, holidays, childhood hideaways, your first job or first date—all of which are possibilities. If a search of your immediate or past personal experience doesn't turn up anything inspiring, you might try looking in the campus newspaper for stories that arouse your strong feelings; don't skip the "Letters to the Editor" column. What are the current topics of controversy on your campus? How do you feel about open admissions? Dorm hours and restrictions? Compulsory class attendance? Consider the material you are studying in your classes—information on spies during the Civil War might lead to a thought-provoking essay comparing nineteenth-century espionage to the modern methods of the CIA or FBI. Finally, your local newspaper or national news magazine might suggest essay topics to you on local, national, or international affairs that affect your life. In other words, when you're stuck for an essay topic, take a closer look at your environment: your own life, past, present, and future; your hometown; your college town; your state; your country; and your world. You'll probably discover more than enough subjects to satisfy the assignments in your writing class.

Keep a journal or daybook. Many professional writers carry small notebooks so that they can jot down ideas and impressions for future use. You may find that keeping a brief journal will also help you find or develop essay topics.

Don't feel you must turn your journal into a diary of your secret thoughts. Instead, use it to record interesting topics or conversations you've heard or intriguing ideas that occur to you at odd times or places. You might wish to write down a quotation you've read or perhaps pose a question for yourself that might turn into the basis for a research paper. Descriptions of problems or gripes you have might also lead to good problem-solving essays later; a list of subjects you're an "authority" on might result in an informative "how-to" paper. A journal is also a useful place to record notes (or great lines) on possible essay topics already in your mind or observations you've made about particular classroom discussions or readings. In short, use the journal in a variety of ways that may help you begin the writing process. You may also find that a daily entry of fifteen minutes or so will not only help you find and develop essay topics but also help you overcome the almost universal dread of putting pen to paper that nearly all writers experience at one time or another.

Narrow a large subject. Once you've selected a general subject to write on, you may find that it is too broad for effective treatment in a short essay; therefore, you may need to narrow it somewhat. Suppose, for instance, you like to work with plants and have decided to make them the subject of your essay. The subject of "plants," however, is far too large and unwieldy for a short essay, perhaps even for a short book. Consequently, you must make your subject less general. "Houseplants" is more specific, but, again, there's too much to say. "Minimum-care houseplants" is better, but you still need to pare this large, complex subject further so that you may treat it in depth in your short essay. After all, there are many houseplants that require little attention. After several more tries, you might arrive at more specific, manageable topics such as "houseplants that thrive in dark areas" or "the easy-care Devil's Ivy."

Then again, let's assume you are interested in sports. A 500–800-word essay on "sports" would obviously be superficial, since the subject covers so much ground. Instead, you might divide the subject into such categories as "sports heroes," "my years on the high school tennis team," "the new role of women in sports," "my love of jogging," and so forth. Perhaps several of your categories would make good short essays, but after looking at your list, you might decide that your real interest at this time is jogging and that it will be the topic of your essay.

FINDING YOUR ESSAY'S FOCUS

Even after you've narrowed your large subject to a more manageable topic, you still must find a specific focus or direction for your essay. What is it, for example, that you want to say about jogging? Which particular aspects of jogging will you discuss? What's the point or purpose of your paper on jogging? Sometimes part of your problem may be solved by your assignment; your teacher may choose the direction of your essay for you by asking for certain specific information or by prescribing the method of development you should use (compare jogging to aerobics; explain the process of jogging properly; analyze the effects of daily jogging, and so forth). But if the purpose and development of your essay are decisions you must make, you should always allow your interest and knowledge to guide you. Often a direction or focus for your essay will surface as you narrow your subject, but don't become frustrated if you have to discard several ideas before you hit the one that's right. For instance, you might first consider writing on how to select running shoes and then realize that you know too little about the shoe market, or you might find that there's just too little of importance to say about jogging paths to make an interesting 500-word essay.

Let's suppose for a moment that you have decided on a topic for your essay, but now you're stuck—you simply don't know what you want to say about your topic or what your paper's purpose or main point might be.

At this point you may profit from trying more than one prewriting exercise designed to help you generate some ideas about your topic. The exercises described below are, in a sense, "pump-primers" that will get your creative juices flowing again. Since all writers compose differently, not all of those exercises will work for you—in fact, some of them may lead you nowhere. Nevertheless, try all of them at least once or twice; you may be surprised to discover that some pump-primer techniques work better with some topics than with others.

1. Listing

Try jotting down all the ideas that pop into your head about your topic. Free associate; don't hold back anything. Try to brainstorm for at least ten minutes.

A quick list on jogging might look like this:

fun	races
healthy	both sexes
relieves tension	any age group
no expensive equipment	running with friend or spouse
shoes	too much competition
poor shoes won't last	great expectations
shin splints	good for lungs
fresh air	improves circulation
good for heart	firming
jogging paths vs. streets	no weight loss
hard surfaces	warm-ups before run
muscle cramps	cooling-downs after
going too far	getting discouraged
going too fast	hitting the wall
sense of accomplishment	marathons

As you read over the list, look for connections between ideas or one large idea that encompasses several small ones. In this list you might first notice that many of the ideas focus on improving health (heart, lungs, circulation), but you discard that subject because a "jogging improves health" essay is too obvious; it's a topic that's been done too many times to say anything new. A closer look at your list, however, turns up a number of ideas that concern how *not* to jog or reasons why someone might get discouraged and quit a jogging program. You begin to think of friends who might have stuck with jogging as you have if only they'd warmed up properly beforehand, chosen the right places to run, paced themselves more realistically, and so on. You decide, therefore, to write an essay telling first-time joggers how to start a successful program, how to avoid a number of problems from shoes to track surfaces that might otherwise defeat their efforts before they've given the sport a chance.

2. Freewriting

Some people simply need to start writing to find a focus. Take out several sheets of blank paper, give yourself at least ten to fifteen minutes, and begin writing whatever comes to mind on your subject. Don't worry about spelling, punctuation, or even complete sentences. Don't change, correct, or delete anything. If you run out of things to say, write "I can't think of anything to say" until you can find a new thought. At the end of the time period you may discover that by continuously writing and writing you will have written yourself into an interesting, focused topic.

Here's a sample of freewriting from a student given ten minutes to write on the general topic of "Television Today."

Television is the pits. I can't stand to watch all the dumb sitcoms and police shows. So many of my friends are hooked on weekly programs that they can't study or go out or anything on those nights. Soap operas too—yeach. Even my little brother is hooked. After school he's glued to the tube watching these violent outer space cartoon fantasy shows where the characters change into supermen (and superwomen!) to fight evil forces. They always win, of course. One interesting thing though is that these shows often have a "moral" at the end that one of the characters talks to the kids about. Cartoons when I was growing up sure didn't have that. They were pretty much violence but it was the cat chases the mice and gets banged over the head by the mice or by their friend the bull dog or the coyote runs off the cliff for the hundredth time. Sort of sadistic, really. At least today's cartoons are putting the violence into some kind of good triumphs over evil story. People are always complaining about the effects of violence on T.V. on kids. I wonder if today's kids ———▶ out of time

This student quickly found himself thinking about the difference in the kinds of violence in today's cartoons as opposed to the cartoons of his childhood. More thinking (and maybe more freewriting) on this subject might lead him to an interesting argument paper (today's T.V. cartoons aren't harmful to children) or perhaps a research paper (studies on the effects of today's new brand of cartoon violence) or a contrast paper (changes in cartoon violence in the last ten years).

3. Looping[1]

Looping is a variation on freewriting that works amazingly well for many people, including those who are frustrated rather than helped by freewriting.

Let's assume you've been assigned that old standby "My Summer Vacation." Obviously you must find a focus, something specific and important to say. Again, take out several sheets of blank paper and begin to freewrite, as described above. Write for at least ten minutes. At the end of this period read over what you've written and try to identify a central idea that has emerged. This idea may be an important thought that occurred to you in the middle or at the end of your writing, or perhaps it was the idea you liked best for whatever reason. It may be the idea that was pulling you onward when time ran out. In other words, look for the thought that stands out, that seems to indicate the direction of your thinking. Put this thought or idea into one sentence called the "center-of-gravity sentence." You have now completed loop one.

To begin loop two, use your center-of-gravity sentence as a jumping-off point for another ten minutes of freewriting. Stop, read what you've written, and complete loop two by composing another center-of-gravity sentence. Use this second sentence to start loop three. You should write at least three loops and three center-of-gravity sentences. At the end of three loops, you may find that you have focused on a specific topic that might lead to a good essay. If you're not satisfied with your topic at this point, by all means try two or three more loops until your subject is sufficiently narrowed and focused.

Here's an example of one student's looping exercise:

SUMMER VACATION

Loop One   I think summer vacations are very important aspects of living. They symbolize getting away from daily routines, discovering places and people that are different. When I think of vacations I think mostly of traveling somewhere too far to go, say, for a weekend. It is a chance to get away and relax and not think about most responsibilities. Just have a good time and enjoy yourself. Vacations can also be a time of gathering with family and friends.

[1]This technique is suggested by Peter Elbow in *Writing Without Teachers* (New York: Oxford University Press, 1975).

Center-of-gravity
sentence

Vacations are meant to be used for traveling.

Loop Two

Vacations are meant for traveling. Last summer my family and I drove to Yellowstone National Park. I didn't want to go at first. I thought looking at geysers would be dumb and boring. I was really obnoxious all the way up there and made lots of smart remarks about getting eaten by bears. Luckily, my parents ignored me and I'm glad they did, because Yellowstone turned out to be wonderful. It's not just Old Faithful—there's lots more to see and learn about, like these colorful boiling pools and boiling patches of mud. I got interested in the thermodynamics of the pools and how new ones are surfacing all the time, and how algae make the pools different colors.

Center-of-gravity
sentence

Once I got interested in Yellowstone's amazing pools, my vacation turned out great.

Loop Three

Once I got interested in the pools, I had a good time, mainly because I felt I was seeing something really unusual. I knew I'd never see anything like this again unless I went to Iceland or New Zealand (highly unlikely!). I felt like I was learning a lot, too. I liked the idea of learning a lot about the inside of the earth without having to go to class and study books. I really hated to leave—Mom and Dad kidded me on the way back about how much I'd griped about going on the trip in the first place. I felt pretty dumb. But I was really glad I'd given the Park a closer look instead of holding on to my view of it as a boring bunch of water fountains. I would have had a terrible time, but now I hope to go back someday. I think the experience made me more open-minded about trying new places.

Center-of-gravity
sentence

My vacation this summer was special because I was willing to put aside my expectations of boredom and learn some new ideas about the strange environment at Yellowstone.

At the end of three loops, this student has moved from the general subject of "summer vacation" to the more focused idea that her willingness to learn about a new place played an important part in the enjoyment of her vacation. Although her last center-of-gravity sentence still contains some vague words ("special," "new ideas," "strange environment"), the thought stated here may eventually lead to an essay that will not only say something about this student's vacation but may also persuade the readers to reconsider their approach to taking trips to new places.

4. *Clustering*

Another excellent technique is clustering (sometimes called "mapping"). Place your general subject in a circle in the middle of a blank sheet of paper and begin to draw other lines and circles that radiate out from the original subject. Cluster those ideas that seem to fall together. At the end of ten minutes see if a topic emerges from any of your groups of ideas.

Ten minutes of clustering on the subject of "A Memorable Holiday" might look like the drawing on page 12.

This student may wish to brainstorm further on the Christmas he spent in the hospital with a case of appendicitis or perhaps the Halloween he first experienced a house of horrors. By using clustering, he has recollected some important details about a number of holidays that may help him focus on an occasion he wants to describe in his paper.

5. *Cubing*

Still another way to generate ideas is cubing. Imagine a six-sided cube that looks something like this:

Mentally, roll your subject around the cube and quickly freewrite your responses for fifteen minutes. If you had recently attended a Bruce Springsteen concert, your responses might look like this:

a. *Describe it:* The concert was at Red Rocks, an outdoor concert hall built into a natural setting. So beautiful as the sun went down behind the mountains. A real contrast to the trash we saw at the concert's ending. The backdrop on stage was a big American flag—appropriate for some of Springsteen's songs.

b. *Compare or contrast it:* The Springsteen concert was so different from the Willie Nelson concert a couple of weeks before. Willie's fans look mellow and fairly normal but the Boss's fans are louder and more excited and some are punker types with weird hairdos. More electricity at Springsteen's.

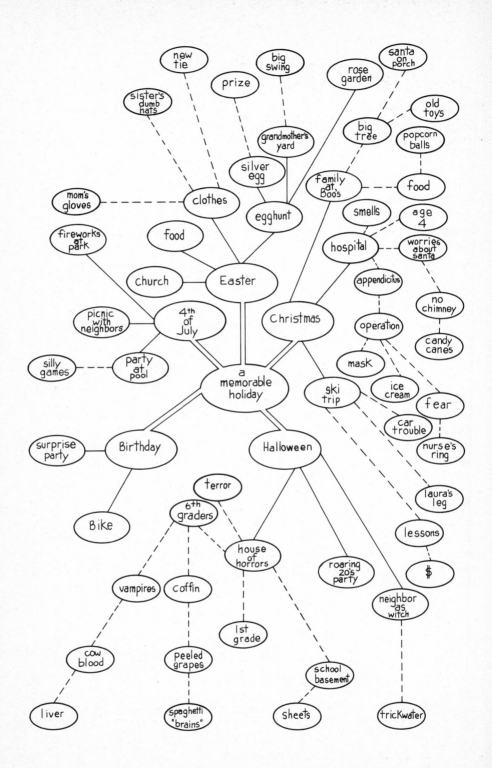

12

c. *Free associate it:* I guess I associate the concert with the Springsteen tapes I listen to. Often in the car. Makes me think of last summer's drive from Florida to Texas. Long stretches of highway, small towns, lots of fields. Driving too fast to match the beat of the music! Got to watch that.

d. *Analyze it:* What's Springsteen's appeal? He writes about regular people with everyday problems. No, he's sexy! So much energy, vitality, animal magnetism, whatever that is. He seems real, a likable guy, approachable by fans. Often donates money to needy groups.

e. *Argue for or against it:* I was so irritated with the stupid way the tickets were sold! First you had to camp out 48 hours in advance outside the Mall where the record store is located. It was freezing and we all had visions of being run over in the parking lot at night in our sleeping bags. Then the tickets didn't show up on time causing another delay. I missed a lot of work. You couldn't buy reserve seats either so that meant another wait and then crush at the concert. Then the big stampede through the gates—really dangerous. Must be a better way.

f. *Apply it:* How to use a concert? I'm not sure I can go anywhere with this one. Except to say that everyone needs to blow off some steam occasionally and a concert like Springsteen's is a great way to relax and party!

After you've written your responses, see if any one approach to your subject gives you an idea for a topic to write a paper on. The student who wrote about the Springsteen concert, for instance, decided she wanted to do an essay suggesting a better, safer way to distribute and sell the tickets for the rock concert series in her town. Cubing helped her realize that she had something to say about the concert that she might not have thought of otherwise.

6. The journal or daybook

If you have started to keep a journal (described on pp. 5–6), don't forget to read it over for essay topics. Quotations, comments, or observations you jotted down weeks ago might now help you decide on an idea to write about. Or you may wish to use something from your journal as the springboard for some freewriting, looping, clustering, and so on.

AFTER YOU'VE FOUND YOUR FOCUS

Once you think you've found the focus for your essay, you may be ready to compose a *working thesis statement*, an important part of your essay discussed in great detail in the next chapter. And if you've used one of the prewriting exercises outlined in this chapter, by all means hang onto it. The details and observations you generated as you focused your topic will almost certainly be useful to you as you begin to organize and develop your body paragraphs.

Practicing What You've Learned

A. Some of the subjects listed below are too broad for a 500–800-word essay. Identify those topics that might be treated in short papers and those that still need to be narrowed.

1. The role of the modern university
2. My first (and last) experience with cross-country skiing
3. The characters of William Shakespeare
4. Nuclear accidents
5. Collecting ugly dolls
6. Gun control laws
7. Down with throwaway bottles
8. Computers
9. The best teacher I've ever had
10. Selecting the right bicycle

B. Select two of the large subjects below and, through looping or listing details or another prewriting technique, find focused topics that would be appropriate for essays of 500–800 words.

1. music
2. cars
3. education
4. jobs
5. television commercials
6. politics
7. drugs
8. childhood
9. pollution
10. athletics

DISCOVER YOUR AUDIENCE

Once you have a focused topic and perhaps some ideas about developing your essay, you need to stop a moment and consider your *audience.* Before you can begin to decide what information needs to go in your essay and what should be omitted, you must know who will be reading your paper and why. Knowing your audience will also help you determine what *voice* you should use to achieve the proper tone in your essay.

Suppose, for example, you are attending a college organized on the quarter system, and you decide to write an essay arguing for a switch to the semester system. If your audience is composed of classmates, your essay will probably focus on the advantages to the student body, such as better opportunities for in-depth study in one's major, the ease of making better grades, and the benefits of longer mid-winter and summer vacations. On the other hand, if you address the Board of Regents, you might emphasize the power of the semester system to attract more students, cut registration costs, and use professors more efficiently. If your audience is composed of townspeople who know little about either system, you will have to devote more time to explaining the logistics of each one and then discuss the semester plan's advantages to the local merchants, realtors, restaurateurs, etc. *In other words, such factors as the age, education, profession, and interests of your audience can make a difference in determining which points of your argument to stress or omit, which ideas need additional explanation, and what kind of language to adopt.*

HOW TO IDENTIFY YOUR READERS

To help you analyze your audience before you begin writing your working thesis statement and rough drafts, here are some steps you may wish to follow:

1. First, check to see if your writing assignment specifies a particular audience (editors of a journal in your field or the Better Business Bureau of your town, for example) or a general audience of your peers (your classmates or readers of the local newspaper, for instance). Even if your assignment does not mention an intended audience, try to imagine one anyway. Imagining specific readers will help you stick to your goal of communicating with others. Forgetting that they have an audience of real people often causes writers to address themselves to their typing paper, a mistake that usually results in dull or unclear prose.

2. If a specific audience is designated, ask yourself some questions about their motivation or *reasons for reading* your essay.

- What do these readers want to learn?
- What do they hope to gain?
- Do they need your information to make a decision? formulate a new plan? design a new project?
- What action do you want them to take?

The answers to such questions will help you find both your essay's purpose and content. If, for example, you're trying to persuade an employer to hire you for a particular job, you certainly would write your application in a way that stresses the skills and training the company is searching for. You may have a fine hobby or wonderful family, but if your prospective employer-reader doesn't need to hear about that particular part of your life, toss it out of this piece of writing.

3. Next, try to discover what *knowledge* your audience has of your subject.

- What, if anything, can you assume that your readers already know about your topic?
- What background information might they need to know to clearly understand a current situation?
- What facts, explanations, examples will best present your ideas? how detailed should you be?
- What terms need to be defined? equipment explained?

Questions like those above should guide you as you collect and discard information for your paper. An essay written to your colleagues in electrical engineering, for instance, need not explain commonly used technical instruments; to do so might even insult your readers. But the same report read by your composition classmates would probably need more detailed explanation in order for you to make yourself understood. Always put yourself in your reader's place and ask: What else do I need to know to understand this point completely?

4. Once you have decided what information is necessary for your audience, dig a little deeper into your readers' identities. Pose some questions about their *attitudes* and emotional states.

- Are your readers already biased for or against your ideas in some way?
- Do they have positive or negative associations with your subject?
- Are they fearful or anxious, reluctant or bored?
- Do they have radically different expectations or interests?

It helps enormously to know the emotional attitudes of your readers toward your subject. Let's suppose you were arguing for the admission of a child with AIDS into a local school system, and your audience was the parent-teacher organization. Some of your readers might be frightened or even hostile; knowing this, you would wisely begin your argument with a disarming array of information showing that no cases of AIDS have developed from the casual contact of schoolchildren. In other words, the more you know about your audience's attitudes before you begin writing, the more convincing your prose, because you will make the best choices about both content and organization.

5. Last, think of any special qualities that might set your audience apart from any other.

- Are they older or younger than your peers?
- Do they share similar educational experiences or training?

- Are they from a particular part of the world or country that might color their perspective? urban or rural?
- Are they in positions of authority?

Knowing special facts about your audience makes a difference, often in your choice of words and tone. You wouldn't, after all, use the same level of vocabulary addressing a group of fifth-graders as you would writing to the children's teacher or principal. Similarly, your tone and word choice probably wouldn't be as formal in a letter to a friend as in a letter to the telephone company protesting your most recent bill.

Without question, analyzing your specific audience is an important step to take before you begin to shape your rough drafts. And before you move on to writing a working thesis, here are a few tips to keep in mind about *all* audiences, no matter who your readers are or what their reasons for reading your writing.

1. Readers don't like to be bored. Grab your readers' attention and fight to keep it. Remember the last dull movie you squirmed—or slept—through? How much you resented wasting not only your money but your valuable time as well? How you turned it off mentally and drifted away to someplace more exciting? As you write and revise your drafts, keep imagining readers who are as intelligent—and busy—as you are. Put yourself in their place: would you find this piece of writing stimulating enough to keep reading?

2. Readers hate confusion and disorder. Recall a time when you tried to find your way to a party only to discover that a friend's directions were so muddled you wound up hours later out of gas cursing in a cornfield? Or the afternoon you spent trying to follow a friend's notes for setting up a chemistry experiment, with explanations that twisted and turned like a wandering gypsy? Try to relive such moments of intense frustration as you struggle to make *your* writing clear and direct.

3. Readers want to think and learn (whether they realize it or not). Every time you write, you strike a bargain of sorts with your readers: in return for their time and attention, you promise to inform and interest them, to tell them something new or show them something familiar in a different light. You may enlighten them or amuse them or even try to frighten them—but they must feel, in the end, that they've gotten a fair trade. As you plan, write, and revise, ask yourself, "What are my readers learning?" If the honest answer is "nothing important," then you may be writing only for yourself. (If you yourself are bored re-reading your drafts, you're probably not writing for any-body at all.)

4. Readers want to see what you see, feel what you feel. Writing that is vague keeps your readers from fully sharing the information or expe-rience you're trying to communicate. Clear, precise language—full of concrete details and specific examples—lets your readers know that you understand your subject and that you want them to understand it, too. Even a potentially dull topic such as tuning a car can become engaging to a reader if the right details are provided in the right places: your terror as blue sparks leap under your nose when the wrong wire is touched, the depressing sight of the screwdriver squirming from your greasy fingers and disappearing into the oil pan, the sudden shoot-ing pain when the wrench slips and turns your knuckles to raw ham-burger. Get your readers involved and interested—and they'll listen to what you have to say. (Details also persuade your reader that you're an authority on your subject; after all, no reader likes to waste time listen-ing to someone whose tentative, vague prose style announces "I only sort-of know what I'm talking about here.")

5. Readers are turned off by writers with pretentious, phony voices. Too often inexperienced writers feel they must sound espe-cially scholarly, scientific, or sophisticated for their essays to be con-vincing. In fact, the contrary is true. When you assume a voice that is not yours, when you pretend to be someone you're not, you don't sound believable at all—you sound phony. Your readers want to hear what *you* have to say, and the best way to communicate with them is in a natural voice. You may also believe that to write a good essay it is necessary to use a host of unfamiliar, unpronounceable, polysyllabic words gleaned from the pages of your thesaurus. Again, the opposite is true. Our best writers agree with Mark Twain, who once said, "Never use a twenty-five-cent word when a ten-cent word will do." In other words, avoid pretension in your writing just as you do in everyday con-versation. Select simple, direct words you know and use frequently; keep your voice natural, sincere, and reasonable. (You'll find additional help on choosing the appropriate words and level of your diction in Chapter 7.)

Don't ever forget your readers!

Thinking about them both before and as you write will help you choose your ideas, organize your information effectively, and select the best words.

The Thesis Statement

AFTER SELECTING YOUR SUBJECT

The famous American author Thomas Wolfe had a simple formula for beginning his writing: "Just put a sheet of paper in the typewriter and start bleeding." For a few writers, the "bleeding" method works fine. Some of us, however, need a more structured approach. Without a clear notion of our essay's main purpose or a definite plan of how to begin and where to go, we may often find ourselves drifting aimlessly through ideas, starting with "x," trudging through "y," and concluding with several layers of wadded paper balls strewn about our feet. To avoid the problem of roaming from one unrelated idea to another, you first need to formulate a *working thesis statement.*

WHAT DOES A THESIS DO?

The thesis statement declares the main point or controlling idea of your entire essay. Frequently located near the beginning of a short essay, the thesis briefly answers the questions "What is my opinion on subject 'x'?" and "What am I going to argue (or illustrate or define or explain) in this essay?"

The essay on jogging discussed in Chapter 1, for instance, might contain the working thesis statement "Before beginning a successful jogging program, novice runners should learn a series of warm-up and cool-down exercises." The freewriting exercise on cartoons might lead to a working thesis such as "The television cartoons of today are less harmful to small children than the violent shows of ten years ago." Such a thesis states an opinion about the essay topic (less harmful to children) and suggests what the essay will do (show why modern car-toons are better than the earlier ones).

A working thesis statement, prepared if possible before you begin your first rough draft, is perhaps your single most useful organizational tool. Once you know your essay's main point, you can arrange the rest of your paper to explain and back up your thesis statement. In other words, *everything in your essay should support your thesis.* Conse-quently, if you write your thesis statement at the top of your first draft and refer to it often, your chances of drifting away from your purpose should be reduced.

What Is a "Working" Thesis?

It's important for you to notice at this point that there may be a differ-ence between the working thesis that appears in your rough drafts and your final thesis. As you begin your first rough draft, you may have one main idea in mind that surfaced from your prewriting activities. But as you write, you discover that what you really want to write about is slightly different. That's fine—*writing is an act of discovery*—and fre-quently we don't know exactly what we think or what to say until we write it. Don't hesitate to change or modify your working thesis if your rough draft has taken a new, better direction. A working thesis is there to help you focus and organize your essay, but it's not carved in stone. Just remember that if you do change your paper's topic or purpose, revise your thesis so that it is consistent with the body of your essay and so that it will guide your readers rather than confuse them.

What Is a Good Thesis?

To help you prepare a solid thesis statement, here are some guidelines.

A good thesis states the writer's clearly defined opinion on some subject. You must tell your reader what you think. Don't dodge the issue; present your opinion specifically and precisely. For example, if you were asked to write a thesis statement expressing your position on the national 55-mile-an-hour speed limit law, the first three theses listed below would not be acceptable:

Poor   Many people have different opinions on whether our country needs the 55-mile-an-hour speed limit law, and I only agree with some of them. [The writer's opinion is not clearly asserted.]

Poor   The question of whether we need a national law governing speed limits is a controversial issue. [This statement is closer to a lead-in than a thesis; the writer has still avoided presenting a clear opinion on the issue.]

Poor   I want to give my opinion on the 55-mile-an-hour law and the reasons I feel that way. [What *is* the writer's opinion? The reader still doesn't know.]

Better Sparsely populated states such as Wyoming should not be required to enforce the national 55-mile-an-hour speed limit law. [The writer clearly states an opinion.]

Better To continue the reduction of highway fatalities, our country needs to enforce the national 55-mile-an-hour speed limit law in every state. [Again, here is a clear position on the issue.]

A good thesis asserts one main idea. Many essays drift into confusion because the writer is trying to explain or argue two different, large issues in one essay. You can't effectively ride two horses at once; pick one main idea and explain or argue it in convincing detail.

Poor   The proposed no-smoking ordinance in our town will violate a number of our citizens' civil rights, and no one has proved secondary smoke is dangerous anyway. [This thesis contains two main assertions—the ordinance's violation of rights and secondary smoke's lack of danger— that require two different kinds of supporting evidence.]

Better The proposed no-smoking ordinance in our town will violate our civil rights. [This essay will show the various ways the ordinance will infringe on personal liberties.]

Better The most recent U.S. Health Department studies claiming that secondary smoke is dangerous to nonsmokers are based on faulty research. [This essay will also focus on one issue: the validity of the studies on secondary smoke danger.]

Poor   High school athletes shouldn't have to maintain a certain grade-point average to participate in school sports, and the value of sports is often worth the lower academic average. [Again, this essay moves in two different directions.]

Better High school athletes shouldn't have to maintain a certain grade-point average to participate in school sports. [This essay will focus on one issue: reasons why a particular average shouldn't be required.]

Better For some students, participation in sports is often more valuable than achieving a high grade-point average. [This essay will focus on why the benefits of sports sometime outweigh those of academics.]

Incidentally, at this point you may recall from your high school days a rule about always expressing your thesis in one sentence. Writing teachers often insist on this rule to help you avoid the double-assertion problem discussed above. While not all essays have one-sentence theses, many do, and it's a good habit to strive for at this early stage of your writing.

A good thesis has something worthwhile to say. Although it's true that almost any subject can be made interesting with the right treatment, some subjects are more predictable and therefore more boring than others. Before you write your thesis, think hard about your subject: does your position lend itself to trite, shallow, or overly obvious ideas? For example, most readers would find the theses below tiresome unless the writers had some original method of developing their essays:

Poor   Dogs have always been man's best friends. [This essay might be full of ho-hum clichés about dogs' faithfulness to their masters.]

Poor   Friendship is a wonderful thing. [Again, watch out for tired truisms that restate the obvious.]

Poor   Food in my dorm is horrible. [While this essay might be enlivened by some vividly repulsive imagery, the subject itself is ancient.]

In other words, try to select a subject that will interest, amuse, challenge, persuade, or enlighten your readers; if your subject itself is commonplace, try to find a unique approach or an unusual, perhaps even controversial, point of view. A good thesis should encourage the reader to read on with enthusiasm rather than invite a groan of "not this again" or a shrug of "so what."

A good thesis is limited to fit the assignment Your thesis should show that you've narrowed your subject matter to an appropriate size for your essay. Don't allow your thesis to promise more of a discussion than you can adequately deliver in a short essay. You want an in-depth treatment of your subject, not a superficial one. Certainly you may take on important issues in your essays; don't feel you must limit your topics to local or personal subjects. But one simply cannot re-fight Vietnam or effectively defend U.S. foreign policy in Central America in five to eight paragraphs. Focus your essay on an important part of a broader subject that interests you. (For a review of ways to narrow your subject, see pp. 6–7.)

Poor   Nuclear power should be banned as an energy source in this country. [Can the writer give the large subject of "nuclear power" a fair treatment in three to five pages?]

Better Because of its poor safety record over the past five years, the Collin County nuclear power plant should be closed. [This writer could probably argue this narrowed thesis in a short essay.]

Poor The parking permit system at this university should be completely revised. [An essay calling for the revision of the parking permit system would probably involve discussion of permits for various kinds of students, faculty, administrators, staff, visitors, delivery personnel, handicapped persons, and so forth. Therefore, the thesis is probably too broad for a short essay.]

Better Because of the complicated application process, the parking permit system at this university penalizes handicapped students. [This thesis is focused on a particular problem and could be argued in a short paper.]

Poor Black artists have contributed much to American culture. ["Black artists," "culture," and "much" cover more ground than can be dealt with in one short essay.]

Better Scott Joplin was a major influence in the development of the uniquely American music called ragtime. [This thesis is more specifically defined.]

A good thesis is clearly stated in specific terms. More than anything, a vague thesis reflects lack of clarity in the writer's mind and almost inevitably leads to an essay that talks around the subject but never makes a coherent point. Try to avoid words whose meanings are imprecise or those that depend largely upon personal interpretation, such as "interesting," "good," and "bad."

Poor The Women's Movement has been good for our country. [How is it good? For whom?]

Better The Women's Movement has worked to ensure the benefits of equal pay for equal work for both male and female Americans. [This tells who will benefit and how—clearly defining the thesis.]

Poor Registration is a big hassle. [No clear idea is communicated here. How much trouble is a "hassle"?]

Better Registration's alphabetical fee-paying system is inefficient. [The issue is specified.]

Poor My sister taught me many things about growing up. ["Things" and "growing up" are both too vague—what specific ideas does the writer wish to discuss?]

Better My sister taught me how to give and take criticism. [The thesis is clearly defined.]

A good thesis is clearly located, usually in the first or second paragraph. Many students are hesitant to spell out a thesis at the beginning of an essay. To quote one student, "I feel as if I'm giving everything away." Although you may feel uncomfortable "giving away" the main point so soon, the alternative of waiting until the last page to present your thesis can seriously weaken your essay. Without an assertion of what you are trying to prove, your reader does not know how to assess the supporting detail your essay presents. For example, if your roommate comes home one afternoon and points out that the roof on your apartment leaks, the rent is too high, and the closet space is too small, you may agree but you may also be confused. Does your roommate want you to call the owner, or is this merely a gripe session? How should you respond? On the other hand, if your roommate first announces that he or she wants to move to a new place, you can put the discussion of the roof, rent, and closets into its proper context and react accordingly. Similarly, you write an essay to have a specific effect on your readers. You won't have a chance of producing this effect unless the readers understand what you are trying to do.

Granted, there are some essays whose position is unmistakably obvious from the outset that can get by with a strongly *implied thesis*, and it's true that some essays, often those written by professional writers, are organized to build dramatically to a climax. But if you are still an inexperienced writer, the best choice at this point is to give a clear statement of your main idea. It is, after all, your responsibility to make your purpose clear, with as little expense of time and energy on the readers' part as possible. Readers should not be forced to puzzle out your essay's main point—it's your job to tell them. Remember: an essay is not a detective story, so don't keep your readers in suspense until the last minute. Until you feel comfortable with more sophisticated patterns of organization, plan to put your clearly worded thesis statement near the beginning of your essay. (Sometimes writers "discover" their thesis at the end of their first draft. That's fine—consider that draft a prewriting or focusing exercise and begin another draft using the newly discovered thesis as a starting point.)

AVOIDING COMMON ERRORS IN THESIS STATEMENTS

Here are five mistakes to avoid when forming your thesis statements:

1. Don't make your thesis merely an announcement of your subject matter or a description of your intentions. State an attitude toward the subject.

> **Poor**   The subject of this theme is my experience with a pet boa constrictor. [This is an announcement of the subject, not a thesis.]

Poor   I'm going to discuss boa constrictors as pets. [This represents a statement of intention, but not a thesis.]

Better   Boa constrictors do not make healthy indoor pets. [The writer states an opinion that will be explained and defended in the essay.]

Better   My pet boa constrictor, Sir Pent, was a much better friend than my dog, Fang. [The writer states an opinion that will be explained and illustrated in the essay.]

2. Don't clutter your thesis with expressions such as "in my opinion," "I believe," and "in this essay I'll argue that . . ." These unnecessary phrases weaken your thesis statement because they often make you sound timid or uncertain. This is your essay; therefore, the opinions expressed are obviously yours. Be forceful; speak directly, with conviction.

Poor   My opinion is that the federal government should devote more money to solar energy research.

Poor   My thesis states that the federal government should devote more money to solar energy research.

Better   The federal government should devote more money to solar energy research.

Poor   In this essay I will give you lots of reasons why horse racing should not be legalized in Texas.

Better   Horse racing should not be legalized in Texas.

3. Don't be unreasonable. Making irrational or oversimplified claims will not persuade your reader that you have a thorough understanding of the issue. Don't insult any reader; avoid irresponsible charges, name-calling, and profanity.

Poor   Radical religious fanatics across the nation are trying to impose their right-wing views by censoring high school library books. [Words such as "radical," "fanatics," "right-wing," and "censoring" will antagonize many readers immediately.]

Better   Only local school board members—not religious leaders or parents—should decide which books high school libraries should order.

Poor   Too many corrupt books in our high school libraries selected by liberal or atheistic educators are undermining the morals of our youth. [Again, some readers will be offended.]

Better   In order to ensure that high school libraries contain books that reflect community standards, parents should have a voice in selecting new titles.

4. Don't merely state a fact. A thesis is an assertion of opinion that leads to discussion. Don't select an idea that is self-evident or dead-ended.

Poor	Child abuse is a terrible problem in our country. [Yes, of course; who wouldn't agree that child abuse is terrible?]
Better	Child-abuse laws in this state are too lenient for repeat offenders. [This thesis will lead to a discussion in which supporting arguments and evidence will be presented.]
Poor	Advertisers often use sex in their ads to sell products. [True. But how could this essay be turned into something more than a description of one ad after another?]
Better	A number of liquor advertisers, well known for using pictures of sexy models to sell their products, are now using special graphics to send subliminal sexual messages to their readers. [This claim is controversial and will require persuasive supporting evidence.]
Better	Although long criticized for their sexist portrayal of women in television commercials, the auto industry is just as often guilty of stereotyping men as brainless idiots unable to make a decision. [This thesis makes a point that may lead to an interesting discussion.]

5. Don't express your thesis in the form of a question, unless the answer is already obvious to the reader.

Poor	Why should every college student have to take two years of foreign language?
Better	Math majors should be exempt from the foreign language requirement.

Practicing What You've Learned

A. Identify each of the following thesis statements as adequate or inadequate. If the thesis is weak or insufficient in some way, explain the problem.

1. I think *Star Wars* was the most interesting movie of its decade.
2. Which car is a better value, the Chevy or the Ford?
3. Some people think that college entrance examinations are biased against women and minorities.
4. My essay will tell you how to apply for a college loan with the least amount of trouble.

5. During the fall term, final examinations should be given before the Christmas break, not after the holidays as they are now.
6. Raising the drinking age to 21 is a terrible idea and won't help prevent traffic accidents.
7. Bicycle riding is good exercise for your legs.
8. Defeat of this year's nuclear test-ban treaty will lead to the world's ultimate destruction.
9. Persons over 75 should be required to renew their driver's licenses every year.
10. Having a close friend you can talk to is very important.

B. Rewrite the sentences below so that each one is a clear thesis statement. Be prepared to explain why you changed the sentences as you did.

1. Applying for a job can be a negative experience.
2. Skiing is good for your body, but it can be expensive and dangerous.
3. There are many advantages and disadvantages to the county's new voting machines.
4. The deregulation of the telephone system has been one big headache.
5. In this paper I will debate the pros and cons of the controversial motorcycle helmet law.
6. We need to do something about the billboard clutter on the main highway into town.
7. The gun control laws in this country need to be rewritten.
8. Prayer in the schools is a hot issue today.
9. In my opinion, Santa Barbara is a fantastic vacation spot.
10. The Civil Rights Movement of the 1960s had a tremendous effect on this country.

Assignment

Narrow the subject and write one good thesis sentence for each of the following topics:

1. capital punishment
2. high school
3. a recent movie or book
4. fast-food restaurants
5. parents
6. a hobby
7. grades
8. vacations
9. football
10. a current fashion

USING THE ESSAY MAP[1]

Many thesis sentences will benefit from the addition of an *essay map*, a brief statement in the introductory paragraph introducing the major points to be discussed in the essay. Consider the analogy of beginning a trip by checking your map to see where you are headed. Similarly, an essay map allows the readers to know in advance where you, the writer, will be taking them in the essay.

Let's suppose you have been assigned the task of praising or criticizing some aspect of your campus. You decide that your thesis will be "The campus bookstore is the worst place in town to buy textbooks." While your thesis does take a stand ("worst place"), your reader will not know why the bookstore is so poor or what points you will cover in your argument. With an essay map added, the reader will have a brief but specific idea where the essay is going and how it will be developed:

Essay map
(underlined)

> Thesis: The campus bookstore is the worst place in town to buy textbooks. <u>The unreasonable prices, the lack of qualified employees, and the constant book shortages discourage all but the most loyal customers.</u>

Thanks to the essay map, the reader knows that the essay will discuss the store's prices, employees, and book shortages.

Here's another example: this time let's assume you decided to praise your school's Study Skills Center:

Essay map
(underlined)

> Thesis: The University's Study Skills Center is an excellent place for freshmen to receive help with basic courses. <u>The Center's numerous free services, well-trained tutors, and variety of supplementary learning materials can often mean the difference between academic success and failure for many students.</u>

After reading the introductory paragraph, the reader knows the essay will discuss the center's services, tutors, and supplementary learning aids. In other words, the thesis statement defines the main purpose of your essay, and the essay map indicates the route you will take to accomplish that purpose.

The essay map is often inserted after the thesis, but it can also appear before it. It is, in fact, frequently tacked onto the thesis statement itself, as illustrated in the following examples:

Thesis with
underlined essay
map

> <u>Unreasonable prices, unqualified employees, and constant shortages</u> make the Campus Bookstore a terrible place to buy texts.

[1] I am indebted to Professor Susan Wittig for this useful concept, introduced in *Steps to Structure: An Introduction to Composition and Rhetoric* (Cambridge, Mass.: Winthrop Publishers, Inc., 1975), pp. 125–126.

Thesis with underlined essay map

Because of its free services, well-trained tutors, and <u>useful learning aids,</u> the Study Skills Center is an excellent place for freshmen seeking academic help.

Thesis with underlined essay map

For those freshmen who need extra help with their basic courses, the Study Skills Center is one of the best resources <u>because of its numerous free services, well-trained tutors, and variety of useful learning aids.</u>

In addition to suggesting the main points of the essay, the map provides two other benefits. It will provide a set of guidelines for organizing your essay, and it will help keep you from wandering off into areas only vaguely related to your thesis. A clearly written thesis statement and essay map provide a skeletal outline for the sequence of paragraphs in your essay, with one body paragraph frequently devoted to each main point mentioned in your map. (Chapter 3, on paragraphs, will explain in more detail the relationships among the thesis, the map, and the body of your essay.) Note that the number of points in the essay map may vary, although three or four may be the number found most often in 500–800-word essays. (More than four main points in a short essay may result in underdeveloped paragraphs; see pp. 41–44 for additional information.)

One important warning: avoid a tendency to make your essay map sound too repetitive or mechanical; try to link the thesis and map as smoothly as possible.

Poor The Campus Bookstore is a bad place to buy texts for three reasons. The reasons are high prices, unqualified employees, and book shortages.

Better Unreasonable prices, unqualified employees, and book shortages combine to give the Campus Bookstore its well-deserved reputation of the worst place in town to buy texts.

If you feel your essay map is too obvious or mechanical, try using it only in your rough drafts to help you organize your essay. Once you're sure it isn't necessary to clarify your thesis or to guide your reader, you might consider dropping it out of your final draft.

Practicing What You've Learned

Identify the thesis and the essay map in the following sentences by underlining the map.

1. *Citizen Kane* deserves to appear on a list of "Top Movies of All Times" because of its excellent ensemble acting, its fast-paced script, and its innovative editing.

2. Our state should double the existing fines for first-offense

      drunk drivers. Such a move would lower the number of accidents, cut the costs of insurance, and increase the state revenues for highway maintenance.

3. To guarantee sound construction, lower costs, and personalized design, more people should consider building their own log cabin home.

4. Apartment living is preferable to dorm living because it's cheaper, quieter, and more luxurious.

5. Not everyone can become an astronaut. To qualify, a person must have intelligence, determination, and training.

6. Through unscrupulous uses of propaganda and secret assassination squads, Hitler was able to take control of an economically depressed Germany.

7. Because it builds muscles, increases circulation, and burns harmful fatty tissue, weight lifting is a sport that benefits the entire body.

8. The new tax bill will not radically reform the loophole-riddled revenue system: deductions on secondary residences will remain, real estate tax shelters are untouched, and nonprofit health organizations will be taxed.

9. Avocados make excellent plants for children. They're inexpensive to buy, easy to root, quick to sprout, and fun to grow.

10. His spirit of protest and clever phrasing blended into unusual musical arrangements have made Bob Dylan a recording giant for over twenty years.

Assignment

Review the thesis statements you wrote for the Practice exercise on page 27. Write an essay map for each thesis statement. You may place the map before or after the thesis, or you may attach it to the thesis itself. Identify which part is the thesis and which is the essay map by underlining the map.

The Body Paragraphs

PLANNING THE BODY OF YOUR ESSAY

The middle or *body* of your essay is composed of paragraphs that support the thesis statement. By presenting details, explaining causes, offering reasons, and citing examples in these paragraphs, you supply enough specific evidence to persuade your reader that the opinion expressed in your thesis is a sensible one. Each paragraph in the body usually presents and develops one main point in the discussion of your thesis. Generally, but not always, a new body paragraph signals another major point in the discussion.

To plan the body of your essay, look at your introduction. The main points mentioned in your essay map will frequently provide the basis for the body paragraphs of your essay.

For example, recall the thesis and essay map praising the Study Skills Center (p. 29): "Because of its free services, well-trained tutors, and useful learning aids, the Study Skills Center is an excellent place for freshmen seeking academic help." Your plan for developing the body of your essay might look like this:

Body paragraph one: discussion of free services
Body paragraph two: discussion of tutors
Body paragraph three: discussion of learning aids

At this point you may wish to sketch in some of the supporting examples and details you will include in each paragraph. You might find it helpful to go back to your prewriting activities (listing, looping, freewriting, mapping, cubing, and so on) to see what ideas surfaced then. Adding some examples and supporting details might make the outline appear this way:

I. Free Services
   A. Mini-course on improving study skills
   B. Tutoring — composition / math
   C. Weekly seminars — stress management / test anxiety / building vocabulary
   D. Testing for learning disabilities
II. Tutors
   A. Top graduate students in their fields
   B. Experienced teachers
   C. Some bilingual
   D. Have taken training course at Center
III. Learning Aids
   A. Supplementary texts
   B. Workbooks
   C. Audiovisual aids

Notice that the sketch above is an *informal* rather than a *formal outline*—that is, it doesn't have strictly parallel parts nor is it expressed in complete sentences. Unless your teacher requests a formal sentence or topic outline, don't feel you must make one at this early stage. Just use the outline to plot out a tentative plan that will help you start your first draft.

Here's another sample outline, this time for the thesis and essay map on the campus bookstore: "Unreasonable prices, unqualified employees, and book shortages combine to give the Campus Bookstore its well-deserved reputation of the worst place in town to buy texts."

I. Unreasonable Prices
   A. Too expensive compared to other stores
   B. Sudden mark-ups
   C. Cheap buy-back policy
II. Unqualified Personnel
   A. Clerks with little knowledge of prices or book orders
   B. Untrained cashiers
III. Book Shortages
   A. Too few books ordered
   B. Wrong books ordered
   C. Wrong edition ordered
   D. Late orders

Of course, you may have more than three points to make in your essay. And, on occasion, you may need more than one paragraph to discuss a single point. For instance, you might discover that you need two paragraphs to explain fully the services at the Study Skills Center (for advice on splitting the discussion of a single point into two or more paragraphs, see p. 45). At this stage you needn't bother trying to guess whether you'll need more than one paragraph per point; just use the outline to get going. Most writers don't know how much they have to say before they begin writing—and that's fine because writing itself is an act of discovery and learning.

ORGANIZING THE BODY PARAGRAPHS

There are many ways to develop body paragraphs. Paragraphs developed by such common patterns as example, comparison, definition, and so forth will be discussed in specific chapters in Part Two; at this point, however, here are some comments about the general nature of all good paragraphs that should help you write the first draft of your essay.

> Most of the body paragraphs you will write require a *topic sentence*. In addition, every paragraph should have adequate *development, unity, and coherence.*

THE TOPIC SENTENCE

Most body paragraphs present one main point in your discussion, expressed in a *topic sentence.* The topic sentence of a body paragraph has three important functions:

1. It supports the thesis by clearly stating a main point in the discussion.
2. It announces what the paragraph will be about.
3. It controls the subject matter of the paragraph. The entire discussion—the examples, details, explanations—in a particular paragraph must directly relate to and support the topic sentence.

Think of a body paragraph (or a single paragraph) as a kind of mini-essay in itself. The topic sentence is, in a sense, a smaller thesis. It too asserts one main idea on a limited subject that the writer can explain or argue in the rest of the paragraph. And, like the thesis, the topic sentence should be stated in as specific language as possible.

To see how a topic sentence works in a body paragraph, study this sample:

Essay Thesis: The Study Skills Center is an excellent place for freshmen who need academic help.

Topic Sentence

1. The topic sentence supports the thesis by stating a main point (one reason why the Center provides excellent academic help).
2. The topic sentence announces the subject matter of the paragraph (a variety of free services that improve basic skills).
3. The topic sentence controls the subject matter (all the examples—the mini-course, the tutoring, the seminars, and the testing—support the claim of the topic sentence).

The Center offers students a variety of free services designed to improve basic skills. Freshmen who discover their study habits are poor, for instance, may enroll in a six-week mini-course in study skills that offers advice on such topics as how to read a text, take notes, and organize material for review. Students whose math or writing skills are below par can sign up for free tutoring sessions held five days a week throughout each semester. In addition, the Center presents weekly seminars on special topics such as stress management and overcoming test anxiety for those students who are finding college more of a nerve-wracking experience than they expected; other students can attend evening seminars in such worthwhile endeavors as vocabulary building or spelling tips. Finally, the Center offers a series of tests to identify the presence of any learning disabilities, such as dyslexia, that might prevent a student from succeeding academically. With such a variety of free services, the Center could help almost any student.

Here's another example from the essay on the bookstore:

Essay Thesis: The Campus Bookstore deserves its reputation as the worst place in town for students to buy their texts.

Topic Sentence

1. The topic sentence supports the thesis by stating a main point (one reason why the store is a bad place to buy texts).
2. The topic sentence announces the subject matter of the paragraph (unreasonable pricing policies).
3. The topic sentence controls the subject matter (all the examples—the high prices, the mark-ups, and the refund problems—support the claim of the topic sentence).

The Campus Bookstore's unreasonable pricing policies discourage potential customers. In the first place, the store's prices are, on the average, far higher than those of the other two bookstores that carry college texts. For instance, while the basic text required for Intro to Biology costs $18.95 at both other stores, it's marked up to $21.98 at the campus store. Similarly, the required freshman math book is $16.95 at the campus store whereas it's $14.50 elsewhere. Moreover, the prices at the store don't remain constant during the book-buying period. One day a book might be $11.95 and the next day it's $13.95. The campus store management defends this policy by noting it reflects "shifting overhead costs," but it's bothersome for the students who are trying to plan their tight budgets. And if high, fluctuating prices aren't bad enough, the campus store's buy-back policy is terrible. The refund on returned books is ten percent lower than that at the other stores, and the semester's refund period is but three days, often too brief a time for students to finish arranging their class schedule. Policies such as these often drive customers to the store's competitors.

Always be sure your topic sentences actually support the particular thesis of your essay. For example, the second topic sentence listed below doesn't belong in the essay promised by the thesis:

Thesis Elk hunting should be permitted because it financially aids people in our state.

Topic Sentences

1. Fees for hunting licenses help pay for certain free, state-supported social services.
2. Hunting helps keep the elk population under control.
3. Elk hunting offers a means of obtaining free food for those people with low incomes.

While topic sentence 2 is about elk and while it may be true, it doesn't support the thesis's emphasis on financial aid and therefore should be tossed out of this essay.

Here's another example:

Thesis In the past fifty years, movie stars have often tried to change the direction of America's politics.

Topic Sentences

1. During World War II stars sold liberty bonds to support the country's war effort.
2. Many stars refused to cooperate with the blacklisting of the 1950s.
3. Some stars were actively involved in protests against the Vietnam War.
4. More recently, stars have appeared in Congress criticizing the lack of legislative help for struggling farmers.

Topic sentences 2, 3, and 4 all show how stars have tried to effect a change. But topic sentence 1 only says that stars sold bonds to support, not change, the political direction of the nation. Although it does show stars involved in politics, it doesn't illustrate the claim of this particular thesis.

Sometimes a topic sentence needs only to be rewritten or slightly recast to fit:

Thesis The recent tuition hike will discourage students from attending our college.

Topic Sentences

1. Students already pay more here than at other in-state schools.
2. Out-of-state students would have to pay an additional "penalty" to attend.
3. Tuition funds should be used to give teachers raises.

As written, topic sentence 3 doesn't show why students won't want to attend the school. However, a rewritten topic sentence does support the thesis:

3. Because the tuition money will not be used for teachers' salaries, many top professors may take job offers elsewhere, and their best students may follow them there.

In other words, always check carefully to make sure that *all* your topic sentences clearly support your thesis's assertion.

Focusing Your Topic Sentence

A vague, fuzzy, or unfocused topic sentence most often leads to a paragraph that touches only on the surface of its subject or that wanders away from the writer's main idea. On the other hand, a topic sentence that is tightly focused and stated precisely will not only help the reader to understand the point of the paragraph but will also help you select, organize, and develop your supporting details.

Look, for example, at these unfocused topic sentences and their revisions:

Unfocused Too many people treat animals badly in experiments. (What people? Badly how? What kinds of experiments?)

Focused The cosmetic industry often harms animals in unnecessary experiments designed to test their products.

Unfocused Grades are an unfair pain in the neck. (Again, the focus is so broad: all grades? Unfair how?)

Focused Course grades based solely on one term paper don't accurately measure a student's knowledge of the subject.

Unfocused Getting the right job is important and can lead to rewarding experiences. (Note both vague language and a double focus—"important" and "can lead to rewarding experiences.")

Focused Getting the right job can lead to an improved sense of self-esteem.

Before you practice writing focused topic sentences, you may wish to review pages 20–26, the advice on composing good thesis statements, as the same rules generally apply.

Placing Your Topic Sentence

While the topic sentence most frequently occurs as the first sentence in the body paragraph, it also often appears as the second or last sentence. A topic sentence that directly follows the first sentence of a paragraph usually does so because the first sentence provides an introductory statement or some kind of a "hook" to the preceding paragraph. A topic sentence frequently appears at the end of a paragraph that first presents particular details and then concludes with its central point. Here are two paragraphs in which the topic sentences do not appear first:

Introductory
Sentence

Topic Sentence

Millions of Americans have watched the elaborate Rose Bowl Parade televised nationally each January from Pasadena, California. *Less well known, but growing in popularity, is Pasadena's Doo Dah Parade, an annual parody of the Rose Bowl spectacle, that specializes in wild-and-crazy participants.* Take this year's Doo Dah Precision Drill Team, for instance. Instead of marching in unison, the members cavorted down the avenue displaying—what else—a variety of precision electric drills. In heated competition with this group was the Synchronized Briefcase Drill Team, whose male and female members wore gray pinstripe suits and performed a series of tunes by tapping on their briefcases. Another crowd-pleasing entry was the Citizens for the Right to Bare Arms, whose members sang while carrying aloft unclothed mannequin arms. The zany procession, led this year as always by the All-Time Doo Dah Parade Band, attracted more than 40,000 fans and is already preparing for its tenth anniversary celebration next January 1.

In the previous paragraph, the first sentence serves as an introduction leading into the topic sentence; in the following paragraph, the writer places the topic sentence last to make a general comment about the importance of VCRs.

Because of VCRs, we no longer have to miss a single joke on our favorite sitcom. Sporting events can be recorded in their entirety even though we may have to go to work or class after the fifth inning or second quarter. Even our dose of television violence does not have to be postponed forever just because a popular special is on another channel at the same time. Moreover, events of his-

Topic Sentence

torical significance can be captured and replayed for future generations even if Aunt Tillie keeps us eating tacos until after the show begins. *In but a few years, VCRs have radically changed America's television viewing habits.*

As you can see, the position of topic sentences largely depends on what you are trying to do in your paragraph. However, if you are a beginning writer, you may want to practice putting your topic sentences first for a while in order to help you organize and unify your paragraphs.

Some paragraphs with a topic sentence near the beginning also contain a concluding sentence that makes a final general comment based on the supporting details. The last sentence below, for example, sums up and restates the main point of the paragraph.

Topic Sentence

Of all nature's catastrophes, tornadoes cause the most bizarre destruction. Whirling out of the sky at speeds up to three hundred miles per hour, tornadoes have been known to drive broom handles through brick walls and straws into tree trunks. In one extreme case, a Kansas farmer reported that his prize rooster had been sucked into a two-gallon distilled-water bottle. More commonly, tornadoes lift autos and deposit them in fields miles away, or uproot trees and drop them on lawns in neighboring towns. One tornado knocked down every wall in a house but one—luckily, the very wall shielding the terrified family.

Concluding Sentence

Wherever a tornado touches the earth, spectacular headlines are sure to follow.

Practicing What You've Learned

A. Point out the topic sentences in the following paragraphs; identify those paragraphs that also contain concluding sentences.

Denim is one of America's most widely used fabrics. It was first introduced during Columbus's voyage, when the sails of the Santa Maria were made of the strong cloth. During our pioneer days, denim was used for tents, covered wagons, and the now-famous blue jeans. Cowboys found denim an ideal fabric for protection against sagebrush, cactus, and saddle sores. World War II also gave denim a boost in popularity when sailors were issued jeans as part of their dress code. Today, denim continues to be in demand as more and more casual clothes are cut from the economical fabric. In 1981, for example, a record 612 million jeans were sold in the U.S., averaging nearly three pairs per person. Because of its low cost and durability, manufacturers feel that denim will continue as one of America's most useful fabrics.

Cooking in a microwave oven has simplified my hectic life. Instead of having to wait the interminable ten minutes for my morning coffee, I can place my cup in the micro and have hot coffee in seconds. I no longer have to decide in the foggy morning what ingredients must be defrosted for the evening meal. I can now come home at 5 p.m., decide what I feel like eating, and have it defrosted in a matter of minutes. The shortened cooking time means I can have full-course meals that once took me hours to cook. The microwave also makes cleanup much easier because the dish I cook in is the dish I eat in. Microwaves may be expensive, but the time and effort they save is worth a million to those of us with too-busy lives.

You always think of the right answer five minutes after you hand in the test. You always hit the red light when you're already late for class. The one time you skip class is the day of the pop quiz. Back-to-back classes are always held in buildings at opposite ends of campus. The one course you need to graduate will not be offered your last semester. If any of these sound familiar, you've obviously been a victim of the "Murphy's Laws" that govern student life.

Want to win a sure bet? Then wager that your friends can't guess the most widely sold musical instrument in America today. Chances are they won't get the answer right—not even on the third try. In actuality, the most popular instrument in the country is neither the guitar nor the trumpet, but the lowly kazoo. Last year alone, some three and one-half million kazoos were sold to music lovers of all ages. Part of the instrument's popularity arises from its availability, since kazoos are sold in variety stores and music centers nearly everywhere; another reason is its inexpensiveness—it ranges from the standard thirty-nine-cent model to the five-dollar gold-plated special. But perhaps the main reason for the kazoo's popularity is the ease with which it can be played by almost anyone—as can testify the members of the entire Swarthmore College marching band, who have now added a marching kazoo number to their repertoire. Louie Armstrong, move over!

Wearing jogging shoes was once restricted to serious runners, but now people from all walks of life wear this comfortable footwear. Secretaries spring along in jogging shoes on their way to and from work. Elderly people find much comfort from the support and padding in this type of shoe. Even dentists and hairstylists wear jogging shoes while standing for long hours on the job. Long-accustomed to wearing heavy-duty work boots, truck drivers and delivery people now enjoy the comfort of these shoes. Just after learning the fine art of walking, many children don their very first pair. Jogging shoes are a regular part of today's wardrobe.

B. Rewrite these topic sentences so that they are clear and focused rather than fuzzy or too broad.
   1. My personality has changed a lot in the last year.
   2. His blind date turned out to be really great.
   3. The movie's special effects were incredible.
   4. The Memorial Day celebration was more fun than ever before.
   5. The evening with her parents was an unforgettable experience.

C. Add topic sentences to the following paragraphs:

Famous inventor Thomas Edison, for instance, did so poorly in his first years of school that his teachers warned his parents that he'd never be a success at anything. Similarly, Henry Ford, the father of the auto industry, had trouble in school with both reading and writing. But perhaps the best example is Albert Einstein, whose parents and teachers suspected that he was retarded because he responded to questions so slowly and in a stuttering voice. Einstein's high school record was poor in everything but math, and he failed his college entrance exams the first time. Even out of school the man had trouble holding a job—until he announced the theory of relativity.

The divorced are twice as likely to develop lung cancer or suffer a stroke; divorced white males develop cirrhosis of the liver seven times more often and tuberculosis ten times more often. The heart attack rate among widows between twenty-five and thirty-four is five times higher than among married women of the same age.

A 1950s felt skirt with Elvis's picture on it, for example, now sells for $150, and Elvis scarves go for as much as $200. Elvis handkerchiefs, originally 50 cents or less, fetch $150 on today's market as do wallets imprinted with the singer's face. Posters from the Rock King's movies can sell for $50, and cards from the chewing gum series can run $30 apiece. Perhaps one of the most expensive collectors' items is the Emene Elvis guitar that can cost a fan from $500 to $700, regardless of musical condition.

When successful playwright Jean Kerr once checked into a hospital, the receptionist asked her occupation and was told, "Writer." The receptionist said, "I'll just put down 'housewife.'" Similarly, when a

British official asked W. H. Auden, the late award-winning poet and essayist, what he did for a living, Auden replied, "I'm a writer." The official jotted down "no occupation."

D. Write a focused topic sentence for five of the following subjects:
   1. job interviews
   2. friends
   3. airplanes
   4. money
   5. selecting a major
   6. clothes
   7. space exploration
   8. dreams
   9. dentists
   10. childhood

Assignment

Review the thesis statements with essay maps you wrote for the practice exercise on page 30. Choose two, and from each thesis create at least three topic sentences for possible body paragraphs.

PARAGRAPH DEVELOPMENT

Possibly the most serious—and most common—weakness of all essays by novice writers is *the lack of adequately developed body paragraphs.* The information in each paragraph must effectively explain, exemplify, persuade, define, or in some other way support your topic sentence. In the first place, you must include enough information in each paragraph to make your readers understand your topic sentence. Secondly, you must make the information in the paragraph clear and specific enough for the readers to understand and accept your ideas.

The next paragraph is underdeveloped. Although the topic sentence promises a discussion of Jesse James as a Robin Hood figure, the paragraph does not provide enough specific examples to explain this unusual view of the gunfighter.

Although he was an outlaw, Jesse James was considered a Robin Hood figure in my hometown in Missouri. He used to be generous to the poor, and he did many good deeds like giving away money. People in my hometown still talk about how lots of the things James did weren't all bad.

Rewritten, the paragraph might read as follows:

Although he was an outlaw, Jesse James was considered a Robin Hood figure in my hometown in Missouri. Jesse and his gang chose my hometown as a hiding place, and they set out immediately to make friends with the local people. Every Christmas for four years, the legend goes, he dumped bags of toys on the doorsteps of poor children. The parents knew the toys had been bought with money stolen from richer people, but they were grateful anyway. On three occasions, Jesse gave groceries to the dozen neediest families—he seemed to know when times were toughest—and once he supposedly held up a stage to pay for an old man's operation. In my hometown, some people still sing the praises of Jesse James, the outlaw who wasn't all bad.

The topic sentence promises a discussion of James's generosity and delivers just that by citing specific examples of his gifts to children, the poor, and the sick. The paragraph is, therefore, better developed.

Similarly, this paragraph offers supporting reasons but no specific examples or details to support those reasons:

Living with my ex-roommate was unbearable. First, she thought everything she owned was the best. Secondly, she possessed numerous filthy habits. Finally, she constantly exhibited immature behavior.

The writer might flesh out the paragraph this way:

Living with my ex-roommate was unbearable. First, she thought everything she owned, from clothes to cosmetics, was the best. If someone complimented my pants, she'd point out that her designer jeans looked better and would last longer because they were made of better material. If she borrowed my shampoo, she'd let me know that it didn't get her hair as clean and shiny as hers did. My hand cream wasn't as smooth; my suntan lotion wasn't as protective; not even my wire clothes hangers were as good as her padded ones! But despite her pickiness about products, she had numerous filthy habits. Her dirty dishes remained in the room for ages before she got the incentive to wash them. Piles of the "best" brand of tissues were regularly discarded from her upper bunk and strewn about the floor. Her desk and closets overflowed with heaps of dirty clothes, books, cosmetics, and whatever else she owned, and she rarely brushed her teeth (when she did brush, she left oozes of toothpaste on the sink). Finally, she constantly acted immaturely by throwing tantrums when things didn't go her way. A poor grade on an exam or paper, for example, meant ashtrays, shoes, or any other small object within her reach would hit the wall flying. Living with such a person taught me some valuable lessons about how not to win friends or keep roommates.

Having a well-developed paragraph is more than a matter of adding length, however. The information in each paragraph must effectively explain or support your topic sentence. *Vague generalities or repetitious ideas are not convincing.* Look, for example, at the following paragraph in which the writer offers only generalities:

Bicycles, popular for years in Europe, are becoming popular in America. Traveling by bicycle is better and easier than traveling by car. Bicycle riding is good for you, too, and it lets you get close to nature.

The paragraph is weak because none if its general statements are explained or supported with specific details. Why is travel by bicycle "better" than travel by car? "Better" in what ways? Why "easier"? "Good for you" in what ways? And what is the importance of getting "close to nature"? The writer obviously had some ideas in mind, but these ideas are not clear to the reader because they are not adequately developed in specific terms. By adding examples and details, the writer might revise the paragraph this way:

With the price of gasoline skyrocketing every year and with parking places becoming more and more scarce, an increasing number of Americans are discovering an Old World secret: bicycling. Bicycles have long been a common sight in Europe, where gasoline has always been expensive. Now bicyclists in America are learning that bicycles not only save gasoline and costly repairs, but also provide a pleasant, even exhilarating, way to exercise flabby muscles and clear clogged respiratory systems. In addition, cyclists are happily discovering a whole new way of looking at the world around them. Instead of spending their time and energy battling traffic jams and fighting for nonexistent parking spaces, they quickly sail along to their destinations, calm and relaxed, closer to the trees, flowers, and birds than any car has allowed them to be.

The reader now knows that bicycling is "better" because it improves mental and physical health and because it saves money and time.

After examining the two paragraphs below, decide which explains its point more effectively.

#1

Competing in an Ironman triathlon is one of the most demanding feats known to amateur athletes. First, they have to swim many miles and that takes a lot of endurance. Then they ride a bicycle a long way, which is also hard on their bodies. Last, they run a marathon, which can be difficult in itself but is especially hard after the first two events. Competing in the triathlon is really tough on the participants.

#2

Competing in an Ironman triathlon is one of the most demanding feats known to amateur athletes. During the first stage of the triathlon, the competitors must swim 2.4 miles in the open ocean. They have to battle the constantly choppy ocean, the strong currents, and the frequent swells. The wind is often an adversary, and stinging jellyfish are a constant threat. Once they have completed the ocean swim, the triathletes must ride 112 miles on a bicycle. In addition to the strength needed to pedal that far, the bicyclists must use a variety of hand grips to assure the continued circulation in their fingers and hands as well as to ease the strain on the neck and shoulder muscles. Moreover, the concentration necessary to steady the bicycle as well as the attention to the inclines on the course and the consequent shifting of gears causes mental fatigue for the athletes. After completing these two grueling segments, the triathletes must then run 26.2 miles, the length of a regular marathon. Dehydration is a constant concern as is the prospect of cramping. Even the pain and swelling of a friction blister can be enough to eliminate a contestant at this late stage of the event. Finally, disorientation and fatigue can set in and distort the athlete's judgment. Competing in an Ironman triathlon takes incredible physical and mental endurance.

The first paragraph contains, for the most part, repetitious generalities; it repeats the same idea (the triathlon is hard work) and gives few specific details to illustrate the point presented in the topic sentence. The second paragraph, on the other hand, does offer many specific examples and details—the exact mileage figures, the currents, jellyfish, inclines, grips, blisters, and so forth—that help the reader understand why the event is so demanding.

Joseph Conrad, the famous British novelist, once remarked that a writer's purpose was to use "the power of the written word to make you hear, to make you feel . . . before all, to make you *see.* That—and no more, and it is everything." By using specific details instead of vague, general statements, you can write an interesting, convincing essay. Ask yourself as you revise your paragraphs, "Have I provided enough clear, precise details to make my readers *see* what I want them to?" In other words, a well-developed paragraph effectively presents its point with *an appropriate amount of specific supporting detail.* (Remember that the handwritten paragraph in your rough draft will look much shorter when it is typed. Therefore, if you don't know much specific information about a particular idea, perhaps you should abandon it as a major point in your essay.)

PARAGRAPH LENGTH

"How long is a good paragraph?" is a question novice writers often ask. Like a teacher's lecture or a preacher's sermon, paragraphs should be long enough to accomplish their purpose and short enough to be interesting. In truth, there is no set length, no prescribed number of lines or sentences, for any of your paragraphs. In a body paragraph, your topic sentence presents the main point, and the rest of the paragraph must give enough supporting evidence to convince the reader. While too much unnecessary or repetitive detail is boring, too little discussion will leave the reader uninformed, unconvinced, or confused.

Although paragraph length varies, beginning writers should try to avoid the one- or two-sentence paragraph frequently seen in newspapers or magazine articles. (Journalists have their own rules to follow; paragraphs are shorter in newspapers, for one reason, because large masses of print in narrow columns are hard to read quickly.) Essay writers do occasionally use the one-sentence paragraph, most often to produce some special effect, when the statement is especially dramatic or significant and needs to call attention to itself. For now, however, you may wish to practice working on paragraphs of at least five sentences.

One more note on paragraph length: sometimes you may discover that a particular point in your essay is so complex that your paragraph is growing far too long—well over a typed page, for instance. If this problem occurs, look for a logical place to divide your information and start a new paragraph. For example, you might see a convenient dividing point between a series of actions you're describing or a break in the chronology of a narrative or between explanations of arguments or examples. Just make sure you begin your second paragraph with some sort of transition phrase or key words to let the reader know you are still discussing the same point as before ("Still another problem caused by the computer's faulty memory circuit is . . . ").

Practicing What You've Learned

A. Analyze the following paragraphs. Explain how you might improve the development of each one.

1. Professor Wilson is the best teacher I've ever had. His lectures are interesting, and he's very concerned about his students. He makes the class challenging but not too hard. On tests he doesn't expect more than one can give. I think he's a great teacher.

2. Newspaper advice columns are pretty silly. The problems are generally stupid or unrealistic, and the advice is out of touch with today's world. Too often the columnist just uses the letter to make a smart remark about some pet peeve. The columns could be put to some good uses, but no one tries very hard.

3. Driving tests do not adequately examine a person's driving ability. Usually the person being tested does not have to drive very far. The test does not require the skills that are used in

      everyday driving situations. Supervisors of driving tests tend to be very lenient.

4. Old-age homes are sad places. They are usually located in ugly old houses unfit for anyone. The people there are lonely and bored. What's more, they're often treated badly by the people who run the homes. It's a shame something better can't be done for the elderly.

5. There is a big difference between acquaintances and friends. Acquaintances are just people you know slightly, but friends give you some important qualities. For example, they can help you gain self-esteem and confidence just by being close to you. By sharing intimate things, they also help you feel happy about being alive.

Assignment

A. Select two of the paragraphs from Practice A and rewrite them, adding enough specific details to make well-developed paragraphs.

B. Write a paragraph composed of generalities and vague statements. Exchange this paragraph with a classmate's, and turn each other's faulty paragraph into a clearly developed one.

C. Find at least two well-developed paragraphs in an essay or book; explain why you think the two paragraphs are successfully developed.

PARAGRAPH UNITY

Every sentence in a body paragraph should directly relate to the main idea presented by the topic sentence. A paragraph must stick to its announced subject; it must not drift away into another discussion. In other words, a good paragraph has *unity*.

      Examine the unified paragraph below; note that the topic sentence clearly states the paragraph's main point and that each sentence thereafter supports the topic sentence.

   [1]Frank Lloyd Wright, America's leading architect of the first half of the twentieth century, believed that his houses should blend naturally with their building sites. [2]Consequently, he designed several "prairie houses," whose long, low lines echoed the flat earth plan. [3]Built of brick, stone, and natural wood, the houses shared a similar texture with their backgrounds; [4]large windows were often used to blend the interior and exterior of the homes. [5]Wright also punctuated the lines and spaces of the houses with greenery in planters to further make the buildings look part of nature.

The first sentence states the main idea, that Wright thought houses should blend with their location; the other sentences support this assertion:

Topic sentence: Wright's houses blend with their natural locations
2. long, low lines echo flat prairie
3. brick, stone, wood provide same texture as location
4. windows blend inside with outside
5. greenery in planters imitates the natural surroundings

Now look at the next paragraph in which the writer strays from his original purpose:

[1]Cigarette smoke is unhealthy even for people who don't have the nicotine habit themselves. [2]Secondhand smoke can cause asthmatics and sufferers of sinusitis serious problems; [3]doctors regularly advise heart patients to avoid confined smoky areas because coronary attacks might be triggered by the lack of clean air. [4]Moreover, having the smell of smoke in one's hair and clothes is a real nuisance. [5]Even if a person is without any health problems, exhaled smoke doubles the amount of carbon monoxide in the air, a fact that may cause lung problems in the future.

Sentence four refers to smoke as a nuisance and therefore does not belong in a paragraph that discusses smoking as a health hazard to nonsmokers.

Sometimes a large portion of a paragraph will drift into another topic. In the paragraph below, did the writer wish to focus on her messiness or on the beneficial effects of her engagement?

I have always been a very messy person. As a child, I was a pack rat, saving every little piece of insignificant paper that I thought might be important when I grew up. As a teenager, my pockets bulged with remnants of basketball games, candy bars, gum wrappers, and other important articles from my high school education. As a college student, I became a boxer—not a fighter, but the kind who cannot throw anything away and therefore it winds up in a box in my closet. But my engagement has changed everything. I'm really pleased with the organization in my life, and I owe it all to my fiancé. My overall outlook on life has changed because of his influences on me. I'm much much more cheerful, and I'm even getting places on time like I never did before. It's truly amazing what love can do.

Note shift from the topic of messiness

This writer may wish to discuss the changes her fiancé has inspired and then use her former messiness, tardiness, and other bad habits as examples illustrating those changes; however, as presented here, the paragraph is not unified around a central idea. On the contrary, it first seems to promise a discussion of her messiness but then wanders into comments on "what love can do."

Also beware a tendency to end your paragraph with a new idea. A new point calls for an entirely new paragraph. For example, the paragraph below focuses on the origins of Muzak; the last sentence, on Muzak's effects on workers, should be omitted or moved to a following paragraph on Muzak's uses in the workplace.

Muzak, the ever-present sound of music that pervades elevators, office buildings, and reception rooms, was created over 50 years ago by George Owen Squier, an army general. A graduate of West Point, Squier was also an inventor and scientist. During World War I he headed the Signal Corps where he began experimenting with the notion of transmitting simultaneous messages over power lines. When he retired from the army in 1922, he founded Wired Radio, Inc., and later in 1934 the first Muzak medley was heard in Cleveland, Ohio, for homeowners willing to pay the great sum of $1.50 a month. That year he struck upon the now-famous name, which combined the idea of music with the brand name of the most popular camera of the day, Kodak. Recent experiments show that workers get more done if they listen to Muzak.

Think of paragraph unity in terms of the diagram below:

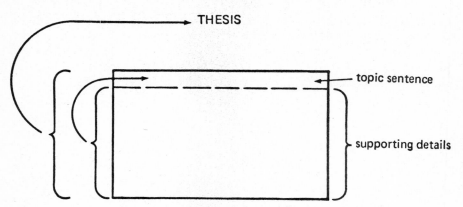

The sentences in the paragraph support the paragraph's topic sentence; the paragraph, in turn, supports the thesis statement.

Practicing What You've Learned

In each of the following examples, delete or rewrite any information that interferes with the unity of the paragraph:

In the Great Depression of the 1930s, American painters suffered severely because few people had the money to spend on the luxury of owning art. To keep our artists from starving, the government ultimately set up the Federal Art Project, which paid then little-known painters such as Jackson Pollock, Arshile Gorky, and Willem de Kooning to paint murals in post offices, train stations, schools, housing projects, and other public places. During this period, songwriters were also affected by the depression, and they produced such memorable songs as "Buddy, Can You Spare a Dime?" The government-sponsored murals, usually depicting familiar American scenes and historical events, gave our young artists an opportunity to develop their skills and new techniques; in return, our country obtained thousands of elaborate works of art in over one thousand American cities. Sadly, many of these art works were destroyed in later years, as public buildings were torn down or remodeled.

After complaining in vain about the quality of food in the campus restaurant, University of Colorado students are having their revenge after all. The student body recently voted to rename the grill after Alferd Packer, the only American ever convicted of cannibalism. Packer was a Utah prospector trapped with an expedition of explorers in the southwest Colorado mountains during the winter of 1874; the sole survivor of the trip, he was later tried by a jury and sentenced to hang for dining on at least five of his companions. Colorado students are now holding an annual "Alferd Packer Day" and have installed a mural relating the prospector's story on the main wall of the restaurant. Some local wits have also suggested a new motto for the bar and grill: "Serving our fellow man since 1874." Another incident of cannibalism occurred in the winter of 1846, when the Donner party, a wagon train of eighty-seven California-bound immigrants, became trapped by ice and snow in the mountains south of the Great Salt Lake.

Smoking a cigar was my grandfather's favorite pastime. I remember how he would stroll across the living room to his wooden cigar box and carefully select just the right cigar from several in the box. Next, the cellophane wrapper was removed and the end of the cigar was snipped off. My grandfather would then light the cigar by holding a wooden match an inch from the tip. After smoking for a while, with just the right flick, he would tip the ashes into his familiar glass ashtray. My grandmother never smoked and hated emptying that ashtray. But my grandfather's long, slow smoke rings are what I remember best, along with the paper cigar ring I always got to wear on my finger.

Inventors of food products often name their new creations after real people. In 1896 Leo Hirschfield hand-rolled a chewy candy and named it after his daughter Tootsie. In 1920 Otto Schnering gave the world the Baby Ruth candy bar, named after the daughter of former President Grover Cleveland. To publicize his new product, Schnering once dropped the candy tied to tiny parachutes from an airplane flying over Pittsburgh. And one of our most popular soft drinks was named by a young suitor who sought to please his sweetheart's physician father, none other than old Dr. Pepper. Despite the honor, the girl's father never approved of the match and the young man, Wade Morrison, married someone else.

Living in a college dorm is a good way to meet people. There are activities every weekend such as dances and parties, where one can get acquainted with all kinds of students. Even just sitting by someone in the cafeteria during a meal can start a friendship. Making new friends from foreign countries can teach students more about international relations. A girl on my dorm floor, for example, is from Peru, and I've learned a lot about the customs and culture in her country. She's also helping me with my study of Spanish.

COHERENCE

In addition to unity, *coherence* is essential to a good paragraph. Coherence means that all the sentences and ideas in your paragraph flow together to make a clear, logical point about your topic. Your paragraph should not be a confusing collection of ideas set down in random order. The readers should be able to follow what you have written and see easily and quickly how each sentence grows out of, or is related to, the preceding sentence. To achieve coherence, you should have a smooth connection or transition between the sentences in your paragraphs.

There are five important means of achieving coherence in your paragraphs:

1. a natural or easily recognized order
2. transition words and phrases
3. repetition of key words
4. substitution of pronouns for key nouns
5. parallelism

These transition devices are similar to the couplings between railroad cars; they enable the controlling engine to pull the train of thought along as a unit.

A Recognizable Ordering of Information

Without consciously thinking about the process, you may often organize paragraphs in easily recognized patterns that give the reader a sense of logical movement and order. Discussed below are four common patterns of ordering sentences in a paragraph:

The order of time

Some paragraphs are composed of details arranged in chronological order. You might, for example, explain the process of changing an oil filter on your car by beginning with the first step, draining the old oil, and concluding with the last step, installing the new filter. Here is a paragraph on black holes in which the writer chronologically orders her details:

A black hole in space, from all indications, is the result of the death of a star. Scientists speculate that stars were first formed from the gases floating in the universe at the beginning of time. In the first stage in the life of a star, the hot gas is drawn by the force of gravity into a burning sphere. In the middle stage—our own sun being a middle-aged star—the burning continues at a regular rate, giving off enormous amounts of heat and light. As it grows old, however, the star eventually explodes to become what is called a nova, a superstar. But gravity soon takes over again, and the exploded star falls back in on itself with such force that all the matter in the star is compacted into a mass no larger than a few miles in diameter. At this point, no heavenly body can be seen in that area of the sky, as the tremendous pull of gravity lets nothing escape, not even light. A black hole has thus been formed.

The order of space

When your subject is a physical object, you should select some orderly means of describing it: from left to right, top to bottom, inside to outside, and so forth. For example, you might describe a sculpture as you walk around it from front to back. Below is a paragraph describing a goalie in which the writer has ordered the details of his description in a feet-to-head pattern.

Hockey goalies must take ample time prior to a game to be sure their protective equipment is properly fitted. They start by lacing on their steel toe skates that include extra thick tongue pads and arch guards. Then, the outside leg pads are strapped on top of an inner set of shin and knee protectors. These are clumsy and wide but absorb the bulk of the shots the goalies will deflect during a game. Loose-fitting hockey pants come next. These must allow for ample flexibility and protection of the hips. The leather gloves used both for catching and deflecting pucks are also large and flexible. They protect the wrist area as well as the hands. The upper arms, shoulders, and chest are guarded by a single unit body pad that resembles the armor knights wore generations ago; however, the pad is made of a lightweight synthetic. The throat protector is attached to the goalie's mask, a wirecage or molded piece of fiberglass. Finally, the hockey helmet holds the face mask in place while assuring total head protection.

Deductive order

A paragraph ordered deductively moves from a generalization to particular details that explain or support the general statement. Perhaps the most common pattern of all paragraphs, the deductive paragraph begins with its topic sentence and proceeds to its supporting details, as illustrated in the example below:

If 111 ninth graders in Honolulu are typical of today's teenagers, spelling and social science teachers may be in for trouble. In a recent experiment, not one of the students tested could write the Pledge of Allegiance correctly. In addition, the results showed that the students apparently had little understanding of the pledge's meaning. For example, several students described the United States as a "nation under guard" instead of "under God," and the phrase "to the Republic for which it stands" appeared in several responses as "of the richest stand" or "for Richard stand." Many students changed the word "indivisible" to the phrase "in the visible," and over nine percent of the students, all of whom are Americans from varying racial and ethnic backgrounds, misspelled the word "America."

Inductive order

An inductive paragraph begins with an examination of particular details and then concludes with a larger point or generalization about those details. Such a paragraph often ends with its topic sentence, as does the following paragraph on Little League baseball:

At almost every Little League baseball game, one or another adult creates a minor scene by yelling obscenely at an umpire or a coach. Similarly, it is fairly common to see such adults arguing loudly with each other in the stands over whose child should have caught a missed ball. Perhaps the most astounding spectacle of all, however, is an irate father or mother yanking a child off the field after a bad play for a humiliating lecture in front of the whole team. Sadly, Little League baseball today often seems intended more for childish parents than for the children who actually play it.

Transition Words and Phrases [Harbrace p. 324-325]

Some paragraphs may need transition words to help you move smoothly from one thought to the next so that your ideas do not appear choppy or jerky.

Here is a list of common transition words and phrases and their uses:

giving examples	for example, for instance, specifically, in particular, namely
comparison	similarly, not only . . . but also, in comparison
contrast	although, but, while, in contrast, however, though, on the other hand

markers

sequence	first . . . second . . . third, and finally, moreover, also, in addition, next, then, after, furthermore
results	therefore, thus, consequently, as a result

Notice the difference the use of transition words makes in the paragraphs below:

Working in the neighborhood grocery store as a checker was one of the worst summer jobs I've ever had. In the first place, I had to wear an ugly, scratchy uniform cut at least three inches too short. My schedule of working hours was another inconvenience; because my hours were changed each week, it was impossible to make plans in advance, and getting a day off was out of the question. In addition, the lack of working space bothered me. Except for a half-hour lunch break, I was restricted to three square feet of room behind the counter and consequently felt as if I were no more than a cog in the cash register.

The same paragraph rewritten without transition words sounds choppy and childish:

Working in the neighborhood grocery store as a checker was one of the worst summer jobs I've ever had. I had to wear an ugly, scratchy uniform. It was cut at least three inches too short. My schedule of working hours was inconvenient. My hours changed each week. It was impossible to make plans in advance. Getting a day off was out of the question. The lack of working space bothered me. Except for a half-hour break, I was restricted to three square feet of room behind the counter. I felt like a cog in the cash register.

While transition words and phrases are useful in bridging the gaps between your ideas, don't overuse them. Not every sentence needs a transition phrase, so use one only when the relationship between your thoughts needs clarification. It's also a mistake to place the transition word in the same position in your sentence each time. Look at the paragraph below:

It's a shame that every high school student isn't required to take a course in first aid. *For example*, you might need to treat a friend or relative for drowning during a family picnic. Or, *for instance*, someone might break a bone or receive a snakebite on a camping trip. *Also*, you should always know what to do for a common cut or burn. *Moreover*, it's important to realize when someone is in shock. *However*, very few people take the time to learn the simple rules of first aid. *Thus*, many injured or sick people suffer more than they should. *Therefore*, everyone should take a first aid course in school or at the Red Cross Center.

As you can see, a series of sentences each beginning with a transition word quickly becomes repetitious and boring. To hold your read-

er's attention, use transition words only when necessary to avoid chop-
piness, and vary their placement in your sentences.

Repetition of Key Words

Important words or phrases (and their synonyms) may be repeated
throughout a paragraph to connect the thoughts into a coherent
statement:

> One of the most common, and yet most puzzling, phobias is the *fear* of
> *snakes*. It's only natural, of course, to be afraid of a poisonous *snake,* but many
> people are just as frightened of the harmless varieties. For such people, a tiny
> green grass *snake* is as terrifying as a cobra. Some researchers say this
> unreasonable *fear* of any and all *snakes* is a legacy left to us by our tree-dwelling
> ancestors, for whom these *reptiles* were a real and constant danger. Others
> maintain that the *fear* is a result of our associating the *snake* with the notion of
> evil, as in the Garden of Eden. Whatever the reason, the fact remains that for
> many otherwise normal people, the mere sight of a *snake* slithering through the
> countryside is enough to keep them city dwellers forever.

The repeated words "fear," "snake," and the synonym "reptile"
help tie one sentence to another so that the reader may follow the ideas
easily.

Pronouns Substituted for Key Nouns

A pronoun is a word that stands for a noun. In your paragraph you
may use a key noun in one sentence and then use a pronoun in its place
in the following sentences. The pronoun "it" often replaces "shark" in
the description below:

> [1]The great white shark is perhaps the best equipped of all the ocean's
> predators. [2]*It* can grow up to twenty-one feet and weight three tons, with two-
> inch teeth that can replace themselves within twenty-four hours when damaged.
> [3]The shark's sense of smell is so acute *it* can detect one ounce of fish blood in a
> million ounces of water. [4]In addition, *it* can sense vibrations from six hundred
> feet away.

Sentences two, three, and four are tied to the topic sentence by the
use of the pronoun "it."

Parallelism

Parallelism in a paragraph means using the same grammatical structures in several sentences to establish coherence. The repeated use of
similar phrasing helps tie the ideas and sentences together. Next, for
example, is a paragraph predominantly unified by its use of grammatically parallel sentences:

The weather of Texas offers something for everyone. If you are the kind who likes to see snow drifting onto mountain peaks, a visit to the Big Bend area will satisfy your eye. If, on the other hand, you demand a bright sun to bake your skin a golden brown, stop in the southern part of the state. And for hardier souls, who ask from nature a show of force, the skies of the Panhandle regularly release ferocious springtime tornadoes. Finally, if you are the fickle type, by all means come to central Texas, where the sun at any time may shine unashamed throughout the most torrential rainstorm.

The parallel structures of sentences 2, 3, and 5 ("If you" + verb) keep the paragraph flowing smoothly from one idea to the next.

Using a Variety of Transition Devices

Most writers use a combination of transition devices in their paragraphs. In the following example, three kinds of transition devices are circled. See if you can identify each one.

Transitions are the glue that holds a paragraph together. These devices lead the reader from sentence to sentence, smoothing over the gaps between by indicating the relationship between the sentences. If this glue is missing, the paragraph will almost inevitably sound choppy or childish, even if every sentence in it responds to a single topic commitment. However, transitions are not substitutes for topic unity: like most glue they are most effective when joining similar objects, or, in this case, similar ideas. For example, in a paragraph describing a chicken egg, no transition could bridge the gap created by the inclusion of a sentence concerned with naval losses in the Civil War. In other words, transitions can call attention to the topic relationships between sentences, but they cannot create those relationships.

transition words	repetition of pronouns	repetition of key words

Practicing What You've Learned

A. Identify each of the following paragraphs as ordered by time, space, or parallelism:

My apartment is so small that it will no longer hold all my possessions. Every day when I come in the door, I am shocked by the clutter. The wall to my immediate left is completely obscured by art and movie posters that have become so numerous they often overlap, hiding even each other. Along the adjoining wall is my stereo equipment: records and tapes are stacked several feet high on two long, low tables. The big couch that runs across the back of the room is always piled so high with schoolbooks and magazines that a guest usually ends up sitting on the floor. To my right is a large sliding glass door that opens onto a balcony—or at least it used to, before it was permanently blocked by my tennis gear, golf clubs, and ten-speed bike. Even the tiny closet next to the front door is bursting with clothes, both clean and dirty. I think the time has come for me to move.

In the early part of this century, tennis was almost exclusively a pastime of the wealthy. Rich young men in long white pants and young women in long dresses gathered at country clubs to amuse themselves with the new sport. This trend continued into the fifties, when Americans suddenly found themselves with more money and time than ever before and not enough ways to spend them. As more and more people began to realize the fun and physical benefits of tennis, public courts became numerous and sporting goods manufacturers began turning out better tennis equipment and tennis clothing. In the eighties, tennis is more popular than ever and has made the significant move from being primarily a participatory sport to a spectator sport, with televised tennis matches netting the best professionals thousands of dollars. Tennis, in short, has finally arrived.

Students have diverse ways of preparing for final exams. Some stay up the night before, trying to cram into their brains what they avoided all term. Others pace themselves, spending a little time each night going over the notes they took in class that day. Still others cross their fingers and hope they absorbed enough from lectures. A dishonest few pray that their fellow students will give them the answers. In the end, though, everyone hopes the tests are easy.

B. Circle and identify the transition devices in the following paragraphs:

Each year I follow a system when preparing firewood to use in my stove. First, I hike about a mile from my house with my bow saw in hand. I then select three good size oak trees and mark them with orange ties. Next, I saw through the base of each tree about two feet from the ground. After I fell the trees, not only do I trim away the branches, but I also sort the scrap from the usable limbs. I find cutting the trees into manageable length logs is too much for one day; however, I roll them off the ground so they will not begin to rot. The next day I cut the trees into eight-foot lengths, which allows me to handle them more easily. Once they are cut, I roll them along the fire lane to the edge of the road where I stack (them) neatly but not too high. The next day I borrow my uncle's van, drive to the pile of logs, and load as many logs as I can, thus reducing the number of trips. (When) I finally have all the logs in my backyard, I begin sawing (them) into eighteen-inch lengths. I create large piles that (consequently) have to be split and finally stacked. The logs will age and dry until winter (when) I will make daily trips to the woodpile.

Fans of professional baseball and football argue continually over which is America's favorite spectator sport. (Though) the figures on attendance for each vary with every new season, certain arguments remain the same, spelling out both the enduring appeals of each game and something about the people who love to watch. Football (for instance) is a quicker, more physical sport, and football fans enjoy the emotional involvement (they) feel while watching. Baseball (on the other hand) seems more mental, like chess, and attracts those fans who prefer a quieter, more complicated game. (In addition) professional football teams usually play no more than fourteen games a year, providing fans with a whole week between games to work themselves up to a pitch of excitement and expectation. Baseball teams, (however) play almost every day for six months, so that the typical baseball fan is not so crushed by missing a game, knowing there will be many other chances to attend. (Finally) football fans seem to love the half-time pageantry, the marching bands, and the pretty cheerleaders, (whereas) baseball fans are more content to concentrate on the game's finer details and spend the breaks between innings filling out their own private scorecards.

C. These paragraphs lack common transition devices. Fill in each blank with the appropriate transition word or key word.

#1

Scientists continue to debate the cause of the dinosaurs' disappearance. One group claims the _dinosaurs_ vanished after a comet smashed into the Earth; dust and smoke _soon_ blocked the sun for a long time. _Deprived_ of no direct sunlight, the Earth underwent a lengthy "winter," far too cold for the huge _dinosaurs_ to survive. A University of Berkeley paleontologist, _however_, disputes this claim. He argues that _although_ we generally think of _dinosaurs_ living in swampy land, fossils found in Alaska show that _dinosaurs_ could live in cold climates _as well as_ warm ones.

Another
_____One_____ group claims that the _dinosaurs_ became extinct following an intense period of global volcanic activity. _In addition_ to killing the _dinosaurs_ themselves, these scientists _also_____ believe the volcanic activity killed much of the plant life that the _dinos_____ate and, ___that_____, many of the great _beasts_____ who survived the volcanic eruptions starved to death. Still

Paleontologists
_other_____ groups of _scientists_ claim the _dinos_____ were destroyed by acid rain, _____or_____ by a passing "death star," _____or_____ even by visitors from outer space.

#2

A recent study by the National Center for Health Statistics has revealed some fascinating information for those of us interested in living longer lives. The _____study_____ shows, for _instance_____, that people live longest in Hawaii, where the average _life span_____ is 77.02 years. _However_____ in Washington, D.C., the expected span is the lowest: only 69.2 years. _____Next_____ to Hawaii, states that boast long expectancies include Minnesota, Iowa, and Utah, _whereas_____ residents of Louisiana, South Carolina, Mississippi are on the lower end of the scale._Furthermore_, according to the _____ research, women can expect to live almost seven years longer than men. _Therefore_____, congratulations to those Hawaiian women who will see us well into the twenty-first century!

D. The sentences in each of the following exercises are out of order. By noting the various transition devices, you should be able to arrange each group of sentences into a coherent paragraph.

Paragraph One: How To Purchase a New Car

6 • If you're happy with the car's performance, find out about available financing arrangements.

3 • Later, at home, study your notes carefully to help you decide which car fits your needs.

7 • After you have discussed various loans and interest rates, you can negotiate the final price with the salesperson.

5. • A visit to the showroom also allows you to test-drive the car.
8 • Once you have agreed on the car's price, feel confident you
     have made a well-chosen purchase.
4 • Next, a visit to a nearby showroom should help you select the
     color, options, and style of the car of your choice.
1 • First, take a trip to the library to read the current auto
     magazines.
2 • As you read, take notes on models and prices.

Paragraph Two: Henry VIII and the Problems of Succession

8 • After Jane, Henry took three more wives, but all these marriages
     were childless.
7 • Jane did produce a son, Edward VI, but he died at age fifteen.
2 • The problem of succession was therefore an important issue
     during the reign of Henry VIII.
6 • Still hoping for a son, Henry beheaded Anne and married Jane
     Seymour.
9 • Thus, despite his six marriages, Henry failed in his attempts to
     secure the succession.
1 • In sixteenth-century England it was considered essential for a
     son to assume the throne.
3 • Henry's first wife, Catherine of Aragon, had only one child, the
     Princess Mary.
5 • But Anne also produced a daughter, the future Queen
     Elizabeth I.
4 • Consequently, he divorced Catherine and married Anne Boleyn.

Assignment

Use one of the quotations below to help you think of a topic for a
paragraph of your own. Feel free to use facts, personal experiences,
improvised material, experiences of friends, etc., to develop your
paragraph. Be sure to narrow your topic, focus your topic sentence,
and double check your rough drafts for adequate development, unity,
and coherence.

1. "Few things are harder to put up with than the annoyance of
   a good example"—Mark Twain, writer and humorist
2. "Genius is one per cent inspiration and ninety-nine per cent
   perspiration"—Thomas Edison, inventor
3. "There is no picking the rose without being pricked by the
   thorns"—Arabic proverb
4. "Nobody ever went broke underestimating the intelligence of
   the American public"—H. L. Mencken, writer and critic
5. "Family jokes are the bond that keeps most families alive"—
   Stella Benson, writer

6. "Nobody can make you feel inferior without your consent"—
   Eleanor Roosevelt, stateswoman
7. "In real love you want the other person's good. In romantic
   love you want the other person"—Margaret Anderson,
   publisher
8. "Women have served all these centuries as looking glasses
   possessing the magic and delicious power of reflecting the
   figure of man at twice its natural size"—Virginia Woolf,
   novelist
9. "When a person declares that he's going to college, he's
   announcing that he needs four more years of coddling before
   he can face the real world"—Al Capp, creator of the *Li'l
   Abner* cartoon
10. "The mass of men lead lives of quiet desperation"—Henry
    Thoreau, writer and naturalist
11. "The mass of Americans lead lives of diet desperation"—J. C.
    Wheeler, writer
12. "Hollywood stars are America's royalty"—Andy Warhol,
    artist
13. "Heroes today are not born. They are packaged"—Mark
    Gerzon, writer
14. "Even if you are on the right track, you will get run over if
    you just sit there"—Will Rogers, humorist and author
15. "I hear and I forget; I see and I remember; I do and I
    understand"—Chinese proverb

PARAGRAPH SEQUENCE

The order in which you present your paragraphs is another decision
you must make. In some essays, the subject matter itself will suggest its
own order.[1] For instance, in an essay designed to instruct a beginning
jogger, you might want to discuss the necessary equipment—good jogging shoes, loose-fitting clothing, sweatband, etc.—before moving to a
discussion of where to jog and how to jog. Other essays, however, may
not suggest a natural order, in which case you yourself must decide
which order will most effectively reach and hold the attention of your
audience. Frequently, writers withhold their strongest point until last.
(Lawyers often use this technique; they first present the jury with the
weakest arguments, then pull out the most damning evidence—the
"smoking pistol." Thus the jury members retire with the strongest
argument freshest in their minds.) Sometimes, however, you'll find it
necessary to present one particular point first, so that the other points
make good sense. Study your own major points and decide which

---

[1]For more information on easily recognized patterns of order, see pp. 50–52.

order will be the most logical, successful way of persuading your reader to accept your thesis.

TRANSITIONS BETWEEN PARAGRAPHS

As you already know, each paragraph usually signals a new major point in your discussion. These paragraphs should not appear as isolated blocks of thought, but rather as parts of a unified, step-by-step progression. To avoid a choppy essay, link each paragraph to the one before it with *transition devices.* Just as the sentences in your paragraphs are connected, so are the paragraphs themselves; therefore, you can use the same transition devices suggested on pages 52–53.

The first sentence of most body paragraphs frequently contains the transition device. To illustrate this point, here are some topic sentences lifted from the body paragraphs of a student essay criticizing a popular sports car, renamed the 'Gator to protect the guilty and to prevent lawsuits. The transition devices are italicized.

Thesis: The 'Gator is one of the worst cars on the market.

- When you buy a *'Gator,* you buy physical inconvenience. [repetition of key word from thesis]
- *Another* reason the 'Gator is a bad buy is the cost of insurance. [transition word, key word]
- You might overlook the *inconvenient* size and exorbitant *insurance* rates if the 'Gator were a strong, reliable car, *but* this automobile constantly needs repair. [key words from preceding paragraphs, transition word]
- When you decide to sell this *car,* you face *still another* unpleasant surprise: the extremely low resale value. [key word, transition word]
- *But* perhaps the most serious drawback is the 'Gator's safety record. [transition word, key word]

Sometimes, instead of using transition words or repetition of key words or their synonyms, you can use an *idea hook.* The last idea of one paragraph may lead you smoothly into your next paragraph. Instead of repeating a key word from the previous discussion, find a phrase that refers to the entire idea just expressed. If, for example, the previous paragraph discussed the highly complimentary advertising campaign for the 'Gator, the next paragraph might begin, "This view of the 'Gator is ridiculous to anyone who's pumped a week's salary into this gas guzzler." The phrase "this view" connects the idea of the first paragraph with the one that follows. Idea hooks also work well with transition words: "This view, however, is ridiculous . . . "

If you do use transition words, don't allow them to make your essay sound mechanical. For example, a long series of paragraphs beginning "first . . . second . . . third . . . " quickly becomes boring. Vary the type and position of your transition devices so that your essay has a subtle but logical movement from point to point.

CHAPTER SUMMARY

Here is a brief restatement of what you should know about the paragraphs in the body of your essay:

1. Each body paragraph usually contains one major point in the discussion promised by the thesis statement.
2. Each major point is presented in the topic sentence of a paragraph.
3. Each paragraph should be adequately developed with clear supporting detail.
4. Every sentence in the paragraph should support the topic sentence. (Unity)
5. All sentences in the paragraph should be smoothly linked by transition devices. (Coherence)
6. The sequence of your essay's paragraphs should be logical and effective.
7. There should be a smooth flow from paragraph to paragraph.
8. The body paragraphs should successfully persuade your reader that the opinion expressed in your thesis is valid.

Completing the Essay

To complete your rough draft, you should think of an essay as a coherent, unified whole composed of three main parts: the introduction (lead-in, thesis, and essay map), the body (paragraphs with supporting evidence), and the conclusion (final address to the reader). These three parts should flow smoothly into one another, presenting the reader with an organized, logical discussion. The following pages will suggest ways to begin, end, and name your essay effectively.

HOW TO WRITE A GOOD LEAD-IN

The first few sentences of your essay are particularly important; first impressions, as you know, are often lasting ones. The beginning of your essay, then, must catch the readers' attention and make them want to keep reading. Recall the way you read a magazine: if you are like most people, you probably skim the magazine, reading a paragraph or two of each article that looks promising. If the first few paragraphs hold your interest, you read on. When you write your own introductory paragraph, assume that you have only a few sentences to attract your reader. Consequently, you must pay particular attention to making those first lines especially interesting and well written.

In some essays, your thesis statement alone may be controversial or striking enough to capture the readers.[1] At other times, however, you

---

[1]Do note that for some writing assignments, such as certain kinds of technical reports, attention-grabbing lead-ins are not appropriate. Frequently, these reports are directed toward particular professional audiences and have their own designated format; they often begin, for example, with a statement of the problem under study or with a review of pertinent information or research.

will want to use the introductory device called a *lead-in*. The lead-in (1) catches the readers' attention, (2) announces the subject matter and tone of your essay (humorous, satiric, serious, etc.), and (3) sets up, or leads into, the presentation of your thesis and essay map.

Here are some suggestions and examples of lead-ins:

1. A paradoxical or intriguing statement

"Eat two chocolate bars and call me in the morning," says the psychiatrist to his patient. Such advice sounds like a sugar fanatic's dream, but recent studies have indeed confirmed that chocolate positively affects depression and anxiety.

2. An arresting statistic or shocking statement

One of every seven women living in Smith County will be raped this year, according to a recent report prepared by the Country Rape Information and Counseling Services.

3. A question

It is twice the number of people who belong to the Southern Baptist Convention, eight times the number who serve in the U.S. armed forces, and just one million short of the number who voted for Barry Goldwater for President in 1964. What is it? It's the number of people in the U.S. who have smoked marijuana: a massive 26 million.

4. A quotation or literary allusion

"I think onstage nudity is disgusting, shameful, and damaging to all things American," says actress Shelley Winters. "But if I were twenty-two with a great body, it would be artistic, tasteful, patriotic, and a progressive religious experience."

5. A relevant story, joke, or anecdote

A group of young women were questioning Saturday afternoon shoppers about their views on the 1982 defeat of the Equal Rights Amendment. One old man in overalls answered, "ERA? Well, I like it just fine. But you know, I can't pick it up on my darned old radio after dark." That was the problem—too few people knew what the ERA really stood for.

6. A description, often used for emotional appeal

With one eye blackened, one arm in a cast, and third-degree burns on both her legs, the pretty, blond two-year-old seeks corners of rooms, refuses to speak, and shakes violently at the sound of loud noises. Tammy is not the victim of a war or a natural disaster; rather, she is the helpless victim of her parents, one of the thousands of children who suffer daily from America's hidden crime, child abuse.

7. A factual statement or a summary who-what-where-when-and-why lead-in

Texas's first execution of a woman in 22 years is scheduled for September 17 at the Huntsville Unit of the state's Department of Correction, despite the protests of various human rights groups around the country.

8. An analogy or contrast

The Romans kept geese on their Capitol Hill to cackle alarm in the event of attack by night. Modern Americans, despite their technology, have hardly improved on that old system of protection. According to the latest Safety Council report, almost any door with standard locks can be opened easily with a common plastic credit card.

9. A personal experience

I realized times were changing for women when I overheard my six-year-old nephew speaking to my sister, a prominent New York lawyer. As we left her elaborate, luxurious office one evening, Tommy looked up at his mother and queried, "Mommy, can little boys grow up to be lawyers, too?"

10. A catalogue of relevant examples

A two-hundred-pound teenager quit school because no desk would hold her. A three-hundred-pound chef who could no longer stand on his feet was fired. A three-hundred-fifty-pound truck driver broke furniture in his friends' houses. All these people are now living better, happier, and thinner lives, thanks to the remarkable intestinal bypass surgery first developed in 1967.

11. Statement of a problem or a popular misconception

Some people believe that poetry is written only by aging beatniks or solemn, mournful men and women with suicidal tendencies. The Poetry in the Schools Program is out to correct that erroneous point of view.

Thinking of a good lead-in is often difficult when you sit down to begin your essay. Many writers, in fact, skip the lead-in until the first draft is written. They compose their thesis and essay map first and then write the body of the essay, saving the lead-in and conclusion for last.

As you write the middle of your essay, you may discover an especially interesting piece of information you might want to save to use as part of your lead-in.

AVOIDING ERRORS IN LEAD-INS

In addition to the previous suggestions, here is some advice to help you avoid common lead-in errors:

Make sure your lead-in introduces your thesis. A frequent weakness in introductory paragraphs is an interesting lead-in but no smooth or clear transition to the thesis statement. To avoid a gap or awkward jump in thought in your introductory paragraph, you may need to add a connecting sentence or phrase between your lead-in and thesis. Study the paragraph below, which uses a comparison as its lead-in. The italicized transition sentence takes the reader from a general comment on all handicapped Americans to information about those in Smallville, smoothly preparing the reader for the thesis that follows.

In the 1950s black Americans demanded and won the right to sit anywhere they pleased on public buses. Today, another large group of Americans—the handicapped confined to wheelchairs—is fighting for the simple right to board those same buses. *Here in Smallville, as well as in other cities, the lack of proper boarding facilities often denies handicapped citizens basic transportation to jobs, grocery stores, and medical centers.* In order to give persons confined to wheelchairs the same opportunities as those given to other residents, the Smallville City Council should vote the funds necessary to convert the public transportation system so that it may be used by handicapped citizens.

Make your lead-in brief. Long lead-ins in short essays often give the appearance of a tail wagging the dog. Use a brief, attention-catching hook to set up your thesis; don't make your introduction the biggest part of your essay.

Don't begin with an apology or complaint. Statements such as "I don't know much about coin collecting, but . . . " and "This assignment is boring, but . . . " do nothing to entice your reader.

Don't assume your audience already knows your subject matter. Identify the pertinent facts even though you know your teacher knows the assignment. ("The biggest flaw in this experiment occurred in the last step." What experiment?) If you are writing about a particular piece of literature, identify the title of the work and its author, using the writer's full name in the first reference.

Stay clear of overused lead-ins. If composition teachers had a nickel for every essay that began with a dictionary definition, they could all retire to Bermuda. Leave *Webster's* alone and find a livelier way to begin. Using a question for your lead-in is becoming overused, too, so use it only when it is obviously the best choice for your opener.

Practicing What You've Learned

Find three good lead-ins from essays, magazine articles, or newspaper feature stories. Identify the kinds of lead-ins you found, and tell why you think each effectively catches the reader's attention and sets up the thesis.

HOW TO WRITE A GOOD TITLE

As in the case of lead-ins, your title may be written at any time, but many writers prefer to finish their essays before naming them. A good title is similar to a good newspaper headline in that it attracts the readers' interest and makes them want to investigate the essay. Like the lead-in, the title also helps announce the tone of the essay. An informal or humorous essay, for instance, might have a catchy, funny title. Some titles show the writer's wit and love of wordplay; a survey of recent magazines revealed these titles: "Bittersweet News about Saccharin," "Coffee: New Grounds for Concern," and "The Scoop on the Best Ice Cream."

On the other hand, a serious, informative essay should have a more formal title that suggests its content as clearly and specifically as possible. Let's suppose, for example, that you are doing research on the meaning of color in dreams, and you run across an essay listed in the library's *Readers' Guide* titled merely "Dreams." You don't know whether you should read it. To avoid such confusion in your own essay and to encourage readers' interest, always use a specific title: "Animal Imagery in Dreams," "Dream Research in Dogs," and so forth. Moreover, if your subject matter is controversial, let the reader know which side you're on (e.g., "The Advantages of Solar Power"). Never substitute a mere label, such as "Football Games" or "Euthanasia," for a meaningful title. And never, never label your essays "theme one" or "comparison and contrast essay." In all your writing, including the title, use your creativity to attract the readers' attention and to invite their interest in your ideas.

If you're unsure about how to present your title, here are two basic rules:

1. Your own title should *not* be underlined or put in quotation marks. It should be written at the top of page one of your essay or on an appropriate cover sheet with no special marks of punctuation.

2. Only the first word and the important words of your title should be capitalized. Generally, we do not capitalize words such as "an," "and," "a," or "the," or prepositions, unless they appear as the first word of the title.

HOW TO WRITE A GOOD CONCLUDING PARAGRAPH

Like a good story, a good essay should not stop in the middle. It should have a satisfying conclusion, one that gives the reader a sense of completion on the subject. Don't allow your essay to drop off or fade out at the end—instead, use the concluding paragraph to emphasize the validity of your argument. Remember that the concluding paragraph is your last chance to convince the reader. (As one cynical but realistic student pointed out, the conclusion is that last part of your essay the teacher reads before putting a grade on your paper.) Therefore, make your conclusion count.

Here are some suggestions for ending your essays and some samples:

1. A restatement of both the thesis and the essay's major points (for long essays only)

As much as we may dislike the notion, it's time to reinstate the military draft. With the armed services' failure to meet its recruitment goals, the rising costs of defense, and the racism and sexism inherent in our volunteer system, we have no other choice if we wish a protected future.

2. An evaluation of the importance of the essay's subject

These amazing, controversial photographs of the comet will continue to be the subject of debate because, according to some scientists, they yield the most important clues yet revealed about the origins of our universe.

3. A statement of the essay's broader implications

Because these studies of feline leukemia may someday play a crucial role in the discovery of a cure for AIDS in human beings, the experiments, as expensive as they are, must continue.

4. A call to action

The fate of Raoul Wallenberg is still unknown. While Congress has awarded him honorary citizenship, such a tribute is not enough. We must write our Congressional representatives today to voice our demand that the Soviets either release him or cite proof of his death. No hero deserves less.

5. A prophecy or warning based on the essay's thesis

Understanding the politics that led up to Hiroshima is essential for all Americans—indeed, for all the world's peoples. Without such knowledge, the frightful possibility exists that somewhere, sometime, someone may drop the bomb again.

6. A witticism that emphasizes or sums up the point of the essay

No one said dieting was easy. But for some of us who have struggled long, the cliché "Half a loaf is better than none" has taken on new meaning!

7. A quotation, story, or joke that emphasizes or sums up the point of the essay

Bette Davis's role on and off the screen as the catty, wisecracking woman of steel helped make her an enduring star. After all, no audience, past or present, could ever resist a dame who drags on a cigarette and then mutters about a passing starlet, "There goes a good time that was had by all."

(For a longer joke that emphasizes its essay's point, see the ending of "Gobbledygook," p. 181 in this text.)

8. An image or description that lends finality to the essay

As the last of the Big Screen's giant ants are incinerated by the army scientist, one can almost hear the movie audiences of the 1950s breathing a collective sigh of relief, secure in the knowledge that once again the threat of nuclear radiation had been vanquished by the efforts of the U.S. military.

(For another brief image that captures the essence of an essay, see also the "open house" scene that concludes "To Bid the World Farewell," p. 156.)

9. A rhetorical question that makes the readers think about the essay's main point

No one wants to see hostages put in danger. But what nation can afford to let terrorists know they can get away with murder?

10. An emphatic summary of the essay's thesis, stated in fresh terms

Soap operas are popular not because they're mindless drivel formulated to distract us from our daily chores, but because they present life as many of us want it to be: fast-paced, glamorous, and full of exciting characters.

AVOIDING ERRORS IN CONCLUSIONS

Try to omit the following common errors in your concluding paragraphs:

Avoid a mechanical ending. One of the most frequent weaknesses in student essays is the conclusion that rigidly restates the thesis and its main points. A short essay of 500–750 words rarely requires a summary conclusion—in fact, such an ending often insults the readers' intelligence by implying that their attention spans are extremely short. Only after reading very long essays do most readers need a precise recap of the writer's ideas.

Don't introduce new points. Treat the major points of your essay in separate body paragraphs rather than in your exit.

Don't tack on a conclusion. There should be a smooth flow from your last body paragraph into your concluding statements.

Don't change your stance. Sometimes writers who have been critical of something throughout their essays will soften their stance or offer apologies in their last paragraph. For instance, someone complaining about the poor quality of a particular college course might abruptly conclude with statements that declare the class wasn't so bad after all, maybe he or she should have worked harder, maybe he or she really did learn something after all, etc. Such reneging may seem polite, but in actuality it undercuts the thesis and confuses the reader who has taken the writer's criticisms seriously. Instead of contradicting themselves, writers should stand their ground, forget about puffy clichés or "niceties," and find an empathetic way to conclude that is consistent with their thesis.

Avoid trite expressions. Don't begin your conclusions by declaring, "in conclusion," "in summary," or "as you can see, this essay proves my thesis that. . . . " End your essay so that the reader clearly senses completion; don't merely announce that you're finished.

Practicing What You've Learned

Find three good concluding paragraphs. Identify each kind of conclusion and tell why you think it is an effective ending for the essay or article.

Assignment

Select any three of the student or professional essays in this text; give the first one a better title; the second, a more interesting lead-in; the third, a more emphatic or smoother conclusion. Why are your choices more effective than those of the original writers?

5

Revising Your Writing

"There is no good writing, only rewriting"—James Thurber
"When I say writing, O, believe me, it is rewriting that I have chiefly in mind"—Robert Louis Stevenson

The absolute necessity of revision cannot be overemphasized. All good writers rethink, rearrange, and rewrite large portions of their prose. The French novelist Colette, for instance, wrote everything over and over. In fact, she often spent an entire morning working on a single page. Hemingway, to cite another example, rewrote the ending to *A Farewell to Arms* thirty-nine times. While no one expects you to make thirty-nine drafts of each essay, the point is clear: revision is an essential part of good writing. It is part of your commitment to your reader. Therefore, plan to spend at least a third to a half of your overall writing time revising and polishing your essay.

Try not to think of revision as an activity that is begun only after you've finished your last rough draft. Nor is revision merely proofreading for errors before you hand in your paper. Revision is a *thinking process* that can occur while you are writing the first draft, or in between drafts, or at the end of a draft. In other words, you can revise a word, sentence, or paragraph as soon as you've written it or you can revise an entire essay; most writers, in fact, do both. But whenever you revise, remember that you are not merely editing for style or correcting surface errors—rather, you are making important decisions about the best ways to organize, develop, and clarify your information.

While each of us has an individual approach to revising, here are some suggestions for composing and rethinking your drafts that you may find helpful.

PREPARING THE FIRST DRAFT

1. Once you have a focused topic, a working thesis, and perhaps an essay map or rough outline to guide you, begin your first draft. One of the most important points to remember now is that no part of your rough draft is sacred or permanent. No matter what you have written, you can always change it.

2. Always write on one side of your paper only, in case you want to cut and tape together portions of your first and/or subsequent drafts rather than recopying the entire essay over and over. Leave big margins on all sides of your rough drafts so you can add information or jot down minor corrections. If you are typing, double or triple space for the same reason.

3. As you write, you may find yourself deciding to delete a sentence or an entire passage here and there. If so, mark a single "X" or line through the material; don't scratch it out completely—you might decide later you want to reinsert the material or use it elsewhere.

4. If you cannot think of a word you want, put down a word close to the one you want, circle it, and go on. Keep writing; don't agonize over every word. Similarly, put a check in the margin by sentences that don't quite hit the mark. The important point now is to keep going, to keep the ideas flowing.

5. If you experience Writer's Block, read the suggestions on pages 76–77 of this chapter.

REVISING THE FIRST DRAFT

1. Two thousand years ago, the Roman author Horace advised a young writer, "Put all your manuscript away and keep it for nine years. You can always destroy what you have not published; there is no art to unsay what you have once let go of." Of course, you won't often have the time to follow this wise advice, but it is still a good idea, after you've written the first draft, to go away for several hours—overnight, if possible. All writers become tired, and if you push yourself too hard, the fatigue will show in your prose. You're also much more aware of the weak spots in your essay when you have had some distance from your prose than when it's still hot from the pen.

2. When you do return to your draft, don't try to look at all the parts of your paper, from organization to word choice to mechanics, at the same time. Doing so is impossible and will only overload and frustrate you. At this point, reread your paper for *purpose* and *audience* only, thinking over such questions as

- Has your essay fulfilled the purpose of your assignment? (For example, if you were asked to analyze a book's character, did you or did you merely summarize plot?)

- Did you follow directions carefully? (If you were given a three-part assignment, did you treat all the parts as requested?)
- If you were asked to address a particular audience, did you do so or did you begin writing to someone else (or to yourself)?
- Did your discussion contain the information pertinent for your particular readers? (For other questions regarding audience, see pp. 14–18.)

3. Once you're satisfied with your commitment to your essay's purpose and audience, look closely at your essay's *focus* and *organization*. Ask yourself such questions as

- Is your thesis sufficiently focused and expressed in clear, specific terms?
- Do your major points in your body paragraphs support your thesis? (If you discover that after you've written your rough draft, your body paragraphs do not support the thesis, don't despair. See if the thesis can be rewritten to fit the essay; you may have had a slightly different thesis in mind all along, or a better one may have evolved as you organized your thoughts in writing.)
- Have you included all the points you wanted to cover?
- Are your paragraphs arranged in a logical order or a pattern that's easy to follow?
- Are your ideas within each paragraph ordered sensibly?
- Is any part of your paper out of proportion? Too long or short?
- Does your paper begin or end abruptly?

If you are like most writers, you will almost certainly need to prepare a second draft to untangle some of the organizational snags.

REVISING THE SECOND DRAFT

Once you are happy with the organization of the paper, look closely at the *development* of your ideas.

- Do you have enough supporting evidence to make your points clear and convincing?
- Is each of your ideas explained through use of specific details rather than fuzzy generalities?
- Which ideas need additional information or details to make them completely clear to your readers?
- Which ideas or comments should be deleted because they're off the subject or merely padding?
- Are any ideas repetitious? Any that should be combined?

Remember that for many beginning writers, underdeveloped or overly general ideas are often the biggest problems, so spend as much time as you can revising your prose to ensure that, first, you have provided enough information and, second, that the information has been expressed in enough specific detail (for more help with development, see pp. 41–45).

REVISING THE THIRD DRAFT

Revision at this point should focus on *clarity, conciseness,* and *vividness.*

1. Read each sentence carefully. Is each one as clear and precise as possible? Are there any that run on for too long or any that contain misplaced words or phrases that might cause confusion? Are your words and their connotations accurate and appropriate?

2. Almost every writer has a wordiness problem. Scrutinize your writing for ways to cut excess words. Search out and destroy deadwood phrases, circumlocutions, "to be" and other space-wasting verb-and-noun combinations (review pp. 96–97 for some specific phrases to guard against). Combine choppy or repetitive sentences wherever possible. (To help you decide if you need to combine sentences, you might try this experiment. Select a body paragraph and count the number of words it contains. Then count the number of sentences; divide the number of words by the number of sentences to discover the average number of words per sentence. If your score is less than 15–18, you may need to combine some sentences.)

3. After pruning your essay to the essentials, work on making your writing as vivid and pleasing as possible. Replace bland or passive verbs with active, vigorous ones; change blah surface descriptions into more fascinating ones by adding specific details. Delete unnecessary jargon or "officialese," and substitute original, arresting words for clichés and predictable phrases. Try to put yourself in the reader's place by thinking of the Johnny Carson Show. Carson: "The lake was so beautiful today." Audience: "How beautiful was it?" Help the reader, your audience, see how "it" was by selecting the best words to describe it. (For additional advice on word choice, see Chapter 7.)

THE FINAL TOUCHES

1. Review your essay for errors in spelling, grammar, and punctuation. If these are major problems for you, keep a list of the mistakes you make in each essay. Read your rough draft for one of these errors at a time: once for fragments, once for comma splices, once for spelling errors, and so on. In addition, while you are looking for grammar and punctuation errors, you may find it helpful to read your essay one sen-

tence at a time—starting at the *end* of the essay and working toward the beginning. This way you are less likely to begin thinking about the content of your essay and wander off the job of looking for errors in mechanics.

2. Go over the checklist on page 78. Revise (yes, again!) any part of your essay that seems weak.

3. Try to type your final draft. Not only will your essay look better, but you will also be able to catch more errors yourself before you hand in the paper. Misspelled words and underdeveloped paragraphs, for example, are much more obvious to a writer once the essay is typed. Avoid typing paper that smears easily or that is too slick to mark with a ball-point pen—leave onionskin to onions.

4. Proofread your final draft at least twice, preferably several hours after you have typed it.

5. Make a copy of your final draft—or at least save your rough drafts—in case your essay is accidentally lost. If you are asked to rewrite parts of your essay, referring to the early drafts may suggest some worthwhile options.

SOME LAST ADVICE: HOW TO PLAY WITH YOUR MENTAL BLOCKS

Every writer, sooner or later, suffers from some form of Writer's Block, the inability to think of and/or organize ideas. Symptoms may include sweaty palms, pencil chewing, and a pronounced tendency to sit in corners and weep. While not every "cure" works for everyone, below are a few suggestions to help minimize your misery:

Try to give yourself as much time as possible to write your essay. Don't try to write the entire paper in one sitting. By doing so, you may place yourself under too much pressure. Writer's Block often accompanies the "up against the wall" feeling that strikes at two A.M. the morning your essay is due at nine. Rome wasn't constructed in a day, and neither are most good essays.

When an irresistible force meets an immovable object, something's gotta give. Conquer the task: break the paper into manageable bits. Instead of drooping with despair over the thought of a twenty-five-page research paper, think of it as a series of small parts (explanation of the problem, review of current research, possible solutions, or whatever). Then tackle one part at a time and reward yourself when that section's done.

Get the juices flowing and the pen moving. Try writing the easiest or shortest part of your essay first. A feeling of accomplishment may give you the boost of confidence you need to undertake the other, more difficult sections. If no part looks easy or inviting, try more prewriting exercises, like the ones described on pages 7–13, until you feel prepared to begin the essay itself.

Since most of you have had more experience talking than writing, try verbalizing your ideas. Sometimes it's helpful to discuss your ideas with a friend or classmate. Their questions and comments (not to mention their sympathy for your temporary block) will often trigger the thoughts you need to begin writing again. Or you might want to talk into a tape recorder so you can hear what you want to say.

If Writer's Block does hit, remember that it is a temporary bogdown, not a permanent one. Other writers have had it—and survived to write again. Try leaving your papers and taking a walk outdoors or at least into another room. Think about your readers—what should they know or feel at this point in your essay? As you walk, try to complete the sentence "What I am trying to say is. . . ." Keep repeating this phrase and your responses aloud until you find the answer you want.

Sometimes while you're blocked at one point, a bright idea for another part of your essay will pop into your head. If possible, skip the section that's got you stuck and start working on the new part. (At least jot down the new idea somewhere so it won't be lost when you need it later.)

Change partners and dance. If you're thoroughly overcome by the vast white wasteland on the desk before you, get up and do something else for a while. Exercise, do the dishes, put on music and dance. Give your mind a break and refresh your spirit. When you come back to the paper, you may be surprised to discover that your subconscious writer has been working while the rest of you played.

Here's the single most important piece of advice to remember: relax. No one—not even the very best professional writer—produces perfect prose every time pen hits paper. If you're blocked, you may be trying too hard; if your expectations of your first draft are too high, you may not be able to write at all for fear of failure. You just might be holding yourself back by being a perfectionist at this point. You can always revise and polish your prose in another draft—the first important step is jotting down your ideas. Remember that once the first word or phrase appears on your blank page, a major battle has been won.

A CHECKLIST FOR YOUR ESSAY

If you have written an effective essay, you should be able to answer ''yes'' to the following questions:

1. Do I feel I have something important to say to my reader?
2. Am I sincerely committed to communicating with my reader and not just with myself?
3. Have I considered my audience? (See Chapter 1.)
4. Do my title and lead-in attract the reader's attention and help set up my thesis? (See Chapter 4.)
5. Does my thesis statement assert one clearly focused idea? (See Chapter 2.)
6. Does my thesis and/or essay map give the reader an indication of what points the essay will cover? (See Chapter 2.)
7. Does each of my body paragraphs contain a main point in the essay's discussion, and is that point expressed in a clear topic sentence? (See Chapter 3.)
8. Does each body paragraph have unity, coherence, and adequate development? (See Chapter 3.)
9. Does each body paragraph have sufficient specific details to prove or explain my essay's main points? (See Chapter 3.)
10. Are all the paragraphs in my essay smoothly linked in an effective order? (See Chapter 3.)
11. Does my concluding paragraph provide a suitable ending for the essay? (See Chapter 4.)
12. Are all my sentences clear, concise, and emphatic? (See Chapter 6.)
13. Are my words accurate, necessary, and meaningful? (See Chapter 7.)
14. Have I proofread for errors in grammar, punctuation, spelling, or typing? (See Part Three.)

And most important:

15. Has my essay been effectively revised so that I am proud of this piece of writing?

Practicing What You've Learned

Applying what you know about effective essay writing, identify the strengths and weaknesses of the following two student themes. Use the checklist above to help you evaluate parts of the essays. What changes would you recommend to improve the quality of these essays?

DORM LIFE

Dorm life is not at all what I had expected it to be. I had anticipated meeting friendly people, quiet hours for studying, eating decent food, and having wild parties on weekends. My dreams, I soon found out, were simply illusions, erroneous perceptions of reality.

My roommate, Kathy, and I live in Holland Hall on the third floor. The people on our dorm floor are about as unfriendly as they can possibly be. I wonder whether or not they're just shy and afraid or if they are simply snobs. Some girls, for example, ignore my roommate and me when we say "hello." Occasionally, they stare straight ahead and act like we aren't even there. Other girls respond, but it's as if they do it out of a sense of duty rather than being just friendly. The guys seem nice, but some are just as afraid or snobby as the girls.

I remember signing up for "quiet hours" when I put in my application for a dorm room last December. Unfortunately, I was assigned to a floor that doesn't have any quiet hours at all. I am a person who requires peace and quiet when studying or reading. The girls in all the rooms around us love to stay up until early in the morning and yell and turn up their stereos full blast. They turn their stereos on at about eight o'clock at night and turn them off early in the morning. There is always at least one girl who has a record playing at maximum volume. Now, I am very appreciative of music, but listening to "acid rock" until three in the morning isn't really my idea of what music is. The girls right across from us usually play Neil Diamond or Simon and Garfunkel and I enjoy that. On the other hand, though, the girls on either side of our room love to listen to Z. Z. Top or Bachman-Turner Overdrive into the wee hours of the morning. It is these girls who run up and down the hall, yell at each other, laugh obnoxiously, and try to attract attention. All this continuous racket makes it nearly impossible to study, read, or get any sleep. Kathy and I usually end up going to the library or student cafeteria to study. As far as sleep goes, it doesn't matter what time we go to bed, but rather it depends on how noisy it is, and how late the stereos are on. Sometimes the noise gets so loud and rambles on for so long that even when it stops, my ears are ringing and my stomach keeps churning. It is on nights like this that I never go to sleep. I wish the people here were a little more considerate of the people around them.

Parties, on weekends, are supposedly the most important part of dorm life. Parties provide the opportunity to meet others and have a good time. Holland Hall has had two parties that are even worth mentioning. One of them was a Fifties dance held in the courtyard approximately three weeks ago. Unfortunately, all the other dormitories, the fraternities, and the sororities heard about it, and by eight o'clock at night there were masses of people. It was so packed that it was hard to move around. The other party, much to my dismay, turned out to be a luau party. I do not really care for roast pig, and my stomach turned from the scent of it when I entered the room. Our floor never has parties. Everyone leaves their doors open, turns up the stereo, yells back and forth. I suppose that there will be more dorm parties once everyone becomes adjusted to this life and begins to socialize.

Dorm food is what I anticipated it would be, terrible, and I was right, it is awful. Breakfast is probably the hardest meal to digest. The bacon and sausage are cold, slightly uncooked, and very greasy. Sometimes, it's as though I am eating pure grease. The eggs look and taste like nothing I ever had before. They look like plastic and they are never hot. I had eggs once and I vowed I would never have another one as long as I lived in Holland Hall. The most enjoyable part of breakfast is the orange juice. It's always cold and it seems to be fresh. No one can say dorm food is totally boring because the cooks break up the monotony of the same food by serving "mystery meat" at least once every two weeks. This puts a little excitement in the student's day because everyone cracks jokes and wonders just what's in this "mystery meat." I think a lot of students are afraid to ask, fearful of the answer, and simply make snide remarks and shovel it in.

All in all, I believe dorm life isn't too great, even though there are some good times. Even though I complain about dorm food, the people, the parties, and everything else, I am glad I am here. I am happy because I have learned a lot about other people, responsibilities, consideration, and I've even learned a lot about myself.

MAYBE YOU SHOULDN'T GO AWAY TO COLLEGE

Going away to college is not for everyone. There are good reasons why a student might choose to live at home and attend a local school. Money, finding stability while changes are occurring, and accepting responsibility are three to consider.

Money is likely to be most important. Not only is tuition more expensive, but extra money is needed for room and board. Whether room and board is a dorm or an apartment, the expense is great.

Most students never stop to consider that the money that could be saved from room and board may be better spent in future years on graduate school, which is likely to be more important in their careers.

Going to school is a time of many changes anyway, without adding the pressure of a new city or even a new state. Finding stability will be hard enough, without going from home to a dorm. Starting college could be an emotional time for some, and the security of their home and family might make everything easier.

When students decide to go away to school, sometimes because their friends are going away, or maybe because the school is their parents' alma mater, something that all need to decide is whether or not they can accept the responsibility of a completely new way of life.

Everyone feels as if they are ready for total independence when they decide to go away to college, but is breaking away when they are just beginning to set their futures a good idea?

Going away to school may be the right road for some, but those who feel that they are not ready might start looking to a future that is just around the corner.

Assignment

Select a paragraph from one of the preceding student essays and rewrite it, making any changes in organization, development, sentence construction, word choice, or anything else you feel is necessary. Feel free to elaborate on, eliminate, or change the content in order to improve the paragraph's organization and development.

6

Effective Sentences

A welfare worker once broke up a staff meeting when he reported on one of his clients: "Mrs. Smith hasn't had any clothes for a year and has been visited regularly by the clergy." And students at the University of Delaware may have been similarly surpised when they learned from their Student Directory that the Office of Women's Affairs was "available for confidential advice, including sexual harassment."

Certainly the social worker didn't mean to imply anything obscene about local religious leaders, nor did the writers of the Student Directory mean to suggest that sexual harassment was a service of the Office of Women's Affairs. But the implications (and humor) are nevertheless present—solely because of the faulty way the sentences are constructed.

To improve your own writing, you must express your thoughts in clear, coherent sentences that produce precisely the reader response you want. Effective sentences are similar to the threads in a piece of knitting or weaving: each thread helps form the larger design; if any one thread becomes tangled or lost, the pattern becomes muddled. In an essay, the same is true: if any sentence is fuzzy or obscure, the reader may lose the thread of your argument and in some cases never bother to regain it. Therefore, to persuade your reader, you must concentrate on writing informative, effective sentences that consistently clarify the purpose of your essay.

Many problems in sentence clarity involve errors in grammar, usage, and word choice; the most common of these errors are discussed in Chapter 7 and Part Three of this text. In this chapter, however, you'll find some general suggestions for writing clear, concise, engaging sentences. However, *don't try to apply all the rules at one time to the first draft of your essay.* Trying to do so will probably result in panic or writer's block. Work first on your essay's content and general organization; then, in a later draft, rework your sentences so that each one is informative and persuasive. Your reader reads only the words on the page, not those in your mind—so it's up to you to make sure the sentences in your essay approximate the thoughts in your head as closely and vividly as possible.

Remember: All good writers revise their sentences.

DEVELOP A CLEAR STYLE

When you are ready to revise the sentences in your rough draft for clarity, try to follow the next five rules:

Give Your Sentences Content

Fuzzy sentences are often the result of fuzzy thinking. When you examine your sentences, ask yourself, "Do I know what I'm talking about here? Or are my sentences vague or confusing because I'm really not sure what my point is or where it's going?" Look at this list of content-poor sentences taken from student essays; how could you reword and put more information into each one?

If you were to view a karate class, you would become familiar with the aspects that make it up.

The meaning of the poem isn't very clear the first time you read it, but after several readings, the poet's meaning comes through.

One important factor that is the basis for determining a true friend is the ability that person has for being a real human being.

Listening is important because we all need to be able to sit and hear all that is said to us.

Don't pad your paragraphs with sentences that run in circles, leading nowhere; rethink your ideas and revise your writing so that every sentence—like each brick in a wall—contributes to the construction of a solid argument. In other words, commit yourself to a position and make each sentence contain information pertinent to your discussion; leave the job of padding to mattress manufacturers.

Sometimes, however, you may have a definite idea in mind but still continue to write "empty sentences"—statements that alone do not contain enough information to make a specific point in your discussion. Frequently, an "empty sentence" may be revised by combining it with the sentence that follows, as shown in the examples below. The "empty" or overly general sentences are underlined.

Poor   There are many kinds of beautiful tropical fish. The kind most popular with aquarium owners is the angelfish.

Better   Of the many kinds of beautiful tropical fish, none is more popular with aquarium owners than the angelfish.

Poor   D. W. Griffith introduced many new cinematic techniques. Some of these techniques were contrast editing, close-ups, fade-outs, and the freeze-frame shot.

Better   D. W. Griffith made movie history by introducing such new cinematic techniques as contrast editing, close-ups, fade-outs, and the freeze-frame shot.

Poor   There is a national organization called The Couch Potatoes. The group's 8,000 members are devoted television watchers.

Better   The Couch Potatoes is a national organization whose 8,000 members are devoted television watchers.

For more help on combining sentences, see pp. 102–105.

Make Your Sentence Specific

In addition to containing an informative, complete thought, each of your sentences should provide the readers with enough clear details for them to "see" the picture you are creating. Sentences full of vague words produce blurry, boring prose and drowsy readers. Remember your reaction the last time you asked a friend about a recent vacation? If the only response you received was something like, "Oh, it was great—a lot of fun," you probably yawned and proceeded quickly to a new topic. But if your friend had begun an exciting account of a recent wilderness rafting trip, with detailed stories about narrow escapes from freezing white water, treacherous rocks, and uncharted whirlpools, you'd probably have stopped and listened. The same principle works in your writing—clear, specific details are the only sure way to attract and hold the reader's interest. Therefore, make each sentence contribute something new and interesting to the overall discussion.

The examples below first show sentences far too vague to sustain anyone's attention. Rewritten, these sentences contain specific details that add clarity and interest:

Vague   She went home in a bad mood. [What kind of a bad mood? How did she act or look?]

Specific She stomped home, hands jammed in her pockets, angrily kicking rocks, dogs, small children, and anything else that crossed her path.

Vague My neighbor bought a really nice old desk. [Why nice? How old? What kind of desk?]

Specific My neighbor bought a solid oak, roll-top desk made in 1885 that contains a secret drawer triggered by a hidden spring.

Vague He was an attractive man. [Attractive in what ways—his appearance, personality, or both? Again, do you "see" this man?]

Specific He had Paul Newman's eyes, Robert Redford's smile, Sylvester Stallone's body, and Howard Hughes's money.

Keep Your Sentences Simple

Because our society is becoming increasingly specialized and highly technical, we tend to equate complexity with excellence and simplicity with simplemindedness. This assumption is unfortunate, because it often leads to a preference for unnecessarily complicated and even contorted writing. In a recent survey, for example, a student chose a sample of bureaucratic hogwash over several well-written paragraphs, explaining his choice by saying that it must have been better since he didn't understand it.

Our best writers have always worked hard to present their ideas simply and specifically, so that their readers could easily understand them. Mark Twain, for instance, once praised a young author this way: "I notice that you use plain simple language, short words, and brief sentences. This is the way to write English. It is the modern way and the best way. Stick to it." And when a critic asked Hemingway to define his theory of writing, he replied, "[I] put down what I see and what I feel in the best and simplest way I can tell it."

In your own writing, therefore, work for a simple, direct style. Avoid sentences that are overpacked (too many ideas or too much information at once) as in the following example on racquetball:

John told Phil that to achieve more control over the ball, he should practice flicking or snapping his wrist, because this action is faster in the close shots and placing a shot requires only a slight change of the wrist's angle instead of an acute movement of the whole arm, which gives a player less reaction time.

To make the overpacked sentence easier to understand, try dividing the ideas into two or more sentences:

John told Phil that to achieve more control over the ball, he should practice flicking or snapping his wrist, because this action is faster in the close shots.

Placing a shot requires only a slight change of the wrist's angle instead of an acute movement of the whole arm, which gives a player less reaction time.

Don't ever run the risk of losing your reader in a sentence that says too much to comprehend in one bite. Try too for a straightforward construction; President Reagan's sentence below, for example, takes far too many twists and turns for anyone to understand it easily on the first reading:

My goal is an America where something or anything that is done to or for anyone is done neither because of nor in spite of any difference between them, racially, religiously or ethnic-orgin-wise.

If the sentences in your rough draft are contorted, try rephrasing your meaning in short sentences and then combining thoughts where most appropriate.

Pay Attention to Word Order

The correct word order is crucial for clarity. Always place a modifier near the word it modifies. The position of a modifier can completely change the meaning of your sentence; for example, each sentence below presents a different idea because of the placement of the modifier "only."

A. Naomi can communicate *only* in sign language. [The phrase "only in sign language" implies that Naomi cannot communicate in any way except sign language, that it is her sole means of communication.]

B. *Only* Naomi can communicate in sign language. ["Only Naomi" implies that Naomi is the sole person in the group who can communicate in sign language.]

To avoid confusion, therefore, place your modifiers close to the words or phrases they modify.

A modifier that seems to modify the wrong part of a sentence is called "misplaced." Not only can misplaced modifiers change or distort the meaning of your sentence, they can also provide unintentional humor as well, as illustrated by the following excerpt from the 1929 Marx Brothers' movie *Coconuts:*

Woman: There's a man waiting outside to see you with a black mustache.

Groucho: Tell him I've already got one.

Of course, the woman didn't mean to imply that the man outside was waiting with (that is, accompanied by) a mustache; she meant to say, "There's a man with a black mustache who is waiting outside. . . ."

A poster advertising a lecture on campus provided this opportunity for humor: "Professor Elizabeth Sewell will discuss the latest appearance of Halley's Comet in room 104." Under the announcement a local wit had scribbled, "Shall we reserve room 105 for the tail?"

Here are some other examples of misplaced modifiers:

Misplaced   Because she is thoroughly housebroken, Sarah can take her dog almost anywhere she goes. [Did the writer mean that Sarah—or the dog—was housebroken?]

Revised   Because she is thoroughly housebroken, Sarah's dog can accompany her almost anywhere she goes.

Misplaced   Now that it's flu season, learn how to protect yourself from your family doctor. [Did the writer mean that you should protect yourself from your doctor—or from the flu?]

Revised   Now that it's flu season, learn from your family doctor how to protect yourself.

Misplaced   Three family members were found bound and gagged by the grandmother. [Did the writer mean that the grandmother had tied up the family?]

Revised   The grandmother found the three family members who had been bound and gagged.

Misplaced   Paula Smith became a mother for the third time today, completing her work for a Master of Arts degree in drama at Harvard. [Did the writer mean that having a baby completed Smith's degree work at Harvard?]

Revised   Paula Smith, now completing her work for a Master of Arts degree in drama at Harvard, became a mother for the third time today.

In each of the preceding examples the writer forgot to place the modifying phrase so that it modifies the correct subject. In most cases, a sentence with a misplaced modifier can be corrected easily by moving the word or phrase closer to the word that should be modified.

In some sentences, however, the object of the modifying phrase is missing entirely. Such a phrase is called a "dangling modifier." Most of these errors may be corrected by adding the missing subject. Here are some examples followed by their revisions:

Dangling   Waving farewell, the plane began to roll down the runway. [Did the writer mean that the plane was waving farewell?]

Revised   Waving farewell, we watched as the plane began to roll down the runway.

Dangling While telling a joke to my roommate, a cockroach walked across my soufflé. [Did the writer mean that the cockroach was telling the joke?]

Revised While telling a joke to my roommate, I saw a cockroach walking across my soufflé.

Dangling Having tucked the children into bed, the cat was put out for the night. [Did the writer mean that the cat tucked the children into bed?]

Revised Having tucked the children into bed, Mother and Father put the cat out for the night.

Dangling After studying for only two weeks, the course showed how to turn old curtains into beautiful bed sheets. [Did the writer mean that the course itself hit the books?]

Revised After studying the course for only two weeks, I learned how to turn old curtains into beautiful bed sheets.

Misplaced and dangling modifiers frequently occur when you think faster than you write; a careful reading of your rough drafts will help you weed out any confused or unintentionally humorous sentences. (For additional examples of misplaced and dangling modifiers, see pp. 298–299 in Part Three.)

Avoid Mixed Constructions and Faulty Predication

Sometimes you may begin with a sentence pattern in mind and then shift, mid sentence, to another pattern—a change that often results in a generally confusing sentence. In many of these cases, you will find that the subject of your sentence simply doesn't fit with the predicate. Look at the following examples and note their corrections:

Faulty Financial aid is a growing problem for many college students. [Financial aid itself isn't a problem; rather, it's the lack of aid.]

Better College students are finding it harder to obtain financial aid.

Faulty The reason their football team plays on artificial turf is because their coach doesn't want the players to graze during halftime. ["The reason . . . is because" is both wordy and ungrammatical. If you have a reason, you don't need a "reason because."]

Better Their football team plays on artificial turf because their coach doesn't want the players to graze during halftime.

Faulty Love is when you start rehearsing dinner-date conversation before breakfast. [A thing is never a "when" or a "where"; rewrite all "is when" or "is where" constructions.]

Better You're in love if you start rehearsing dinner-date conversation before breakfast.

Many mixed constructions occur because the writer is in too much of a hurry; check your rough drafts carefully to see if you have included sentences in which you started one pattern and switched to another. (For more help on faulty predications and mixed constructions, see pp. 304–305 in Part Three.)

DEVELOP A CONCISE STYLE

Almost all writing suffers from wordiness—the tendency to use more words than necessary. When useless words weigh down your prose, the meaning is often lost, confused, or hidden. Flabby prose calls for a reducing plan; put those obese sentences on a diet by cutting out unnecessary words, just as you avoid fatty foods to keep yourself trim. Mushy prose is ponderous and boring; crisp, to-the-point writing, on the other hand, is both accessible and pleasing. Beware, however, a temptation to overdiet; you don't want your prose to become so thin or brief that your meaning disappears completely. Therefore, cut out only the *unessential* words and phrases.

Wordy prose is frequently the result of using one or more of the following: (1) deadwood constructions (2) redundancies (3) pretentiousness.

Avoid Deadwood Constructions

Always try to cut empty "deadwood" from your sentences. Having a clear, concise style does not mean limiting your writing to choppy, childish Dick-and-Jane sentences; it only means that all unnecessary words, phrases, and clauses should be deleted. Below are some sentences containing common deadwood constructions and ways they may be pruned:

Poor *The reason why* the painter wasn't happy despite his first-prize award was because the judges had hung his painting upside down.

Better The painter was unhappy despite his first-prize award because the judges had hung his painting upside down.

Poor The land settlement *was an example where* the Indians did not receive fair treatment.

Better The land settlement was unfair to the Indians.

Poor Because *of the fact that* his surfboard business failed after only a month, my brother decided to leave Minnesota.

Better Because his surfboard business failed after only a month, my brother decided to leave Minnesota.

Other notorious deadwood construction include:

regardless of the fact that	(use "although")
due to the fact that	(use "because")
the reason is that	(omit)
as to whether or not to	(omit "as to" and "or not")
at this point in time	(use "now" or "today")
it is believed that	(use a specific subject and "believes")
concerning the matter of	(use "about")
by means of	(use "by")
these are the kinds of . . . that	(use "these" plus a specific subject)

Watch a tendency to tack on empty "fillers" that stretch one word into an awkward phrase:

Wordy Each candidate should be evaluated *on an individual basis.*

Concise Each candidate should be evaluated *individually.*

Wordy Television does not portray violence *in a realistic fashion.*

Concise Television does not portray violence *realistically.*

Wordy The New York blackout produced a *crisis-type situation.*

Concise The New York blackout produced a *crisis.*

To retain your reader's interest and improve the flow of your prose, trim all the fat from your sentences.

"There are," "It is." These introductory phrases are often space wasters. When possible, omit them or replace them with specific subjects, as shown in the following:

Wordy *There are* thirty thousand students attending this university.

Revised Thirty thousand students attend this university.

Wordy *There is* a good reason why I do not eat liver.

Revised I do not eat liver for a good reason.

Wordy *It is* impossible for some people to learn to relax.

Revised Some people never learn to relax.

"Who" and "which" clauses. Some "who" and "which" clauses are unnecessary and may be turned into modifiers placed before the noun:

Wordy The getaway car, *which was* stolen, turned the corner.

Revised The stolen getaway car turned the corner.

Wordy The chef, *who was* depressed, ordered his noisy lobsters to simmer down.
Revised The depressed chef ordered his noisy lobsters to simmer down.

When adjective clauses are necessary, the words "who" and "which" may sometimes be omitted:

Wordy Tinsel Tony, who was a big-time wrestler, challenged every grandmother in the arena.
Revised Tinsel Tony, a big-time wrestler, challenged every grandmother in the arena.

"To be." Most "to be's" are inessential and ought not to be. Delete them every time you can.

Wordy She seems *to be* angry.
Revised She seems angry.

Wordy The freeze-dried facelift proved *to be* unsuccessful.
Revised The freeze-dried facelift proved unsuccessful.

Wordy The new mayor wanted his archenemy, the local movie critic, *to be* arrested.
Revised The new mayor wanted his archenemy, the local movie critic, arrested.

"Of" and infinitive phrases. Many "of" and infinitive ("to" plus verb) phrases may be omitted or revised by using possessives, adjectives, and verbs, as shown below:

Wordy At the *time of registration* students are required *to make* payment *of their library fees.*
Revised At registration students must pay their library fees.
Wordy The producer fired the mother *of the director of the movie.*
Revised The producer fired the movie director's mother.

Including deadwood phrases makes your prose puffy; streamline your sentences to present a simple, direct style.

Avoid Redundancy

Many flabby sentences contain *redundancies* (words that repeat the same idea or whose meanings overlap). Consider the following examples:

In this day and time, people expect to live at least seventy years. ["Day" and "time" present a similar idea.]

He repeated the winning bingo number over again. ["Repeated" means "to say again," so there is no need for "over again."]

The group consensus was that the pizza crust tasted like cardboard. ["Consensus" means "general agreement," so it's unnecessary to add "group."]

Some other common redundancies include:

reverted back   new innovation
reflected back   red in color
retreated back   burned down up
fell down   pair of twins/two twins
climb up   resulting effect (or just "result")
a true fact   final outcome

Carefully Consider your Passive Verbs

When the subject of the sentence performs the action, the verb is *active;* when the subject of the sentence is acted upon, the verb is *passive.* You can often recognize sentences with passive verbs because they contain the word *by,* telling who performed the action.

Passive   The Indians *were considered* uncivilized by the early settlers.
Active   The early settlers *considered* the Indians uncivilized.
Passive   The wedding date *was announced* by the young couple.
Active   The young couple *announced* their wedding date.
Passive   His letter of resignation *was accepted by* the Board of Trustees.
Active   The Board of Trustees *accepted* his letter of resignation.

In addition to being wordy and weak, passive sentences often disguise the performer of the action in question. You might have heard a politician, for example, say something similar to this: "It was decided this year to give all congressmen an increase in salary." The question of *who* decided to raise salaries remains foggy—perhaps purposefully so. But in your own prose, you should strive for clarity and directness; therefore, use active verbs as often as you can except when you wish to stress the person or thing that receives the action, as shown below:

The baby was born September 30, 1980.
The elderly man was struck by a drunk driver.

Special note: Authorities in some professional and technical fields still prefer the passive construction because they wish to put emphasis on the experiment or process rather than on the people performing the action. If the passive voice is preferred in your field, you should abide by that convention when you are writing reports or papers for your professional colleagues.

Avoid Pretentiousness

Another enemy of clear, concise prose is *pretentiousness.* Pompous, inflated language surrounds us, and because it often sounds learned or official, we may be tempted to use it when we want to impress others with our writing. But as George Orwell, author of *1984*, noted, an inflated style is like "a cuttlefish squirting out ink." If you want your prose easily understood, write as clearly and plainly as possible.

To illustrate how confusing pretentious writing can be, here is a copy of a government memo announcing a blackout order, issued in 1942 during World War II:

Such preparations shall be made as will completely obscure all Federal buildings and non-Federal buildings occupied by the Federal government during an air raid for any period of time from visibility by reason of internal or external illumination.

President Franklin Roosevelt intervened and rewrote the order in plain English, clarifying its message and reducing the number of words by half:

Tell them that in buildings where they have to keep the work going to put something across the windows.

By translating the obscure original memo into easily understandable language, Roosevelt demonstrated that a natural prose style can get necessary information to the reader more quickly and efficiently than bureaucratic jargon. (For more advice on ridding your prose of jargon, see pp. 119–121.)

In other—shorter—words, to attract and hold your readers' attention, to communicate clearly and quickly, make your sentences as informative, straightforward, specific, and concise as possible.

Practicing What You've Learned

A. Some of the following sentences are vague, "empty," overpacked, or contorted. Rewrite each one so that it is clear and specific, combining or dividing sentences as necessary.

1. Roger was a pretty neat guy who was important to his company.

2. There's a new detective show on television. It stars Phil Noir and is set in the 1940s.
3. Sarah's room was always a huge disaster.
4. The book is a good one because of all the writer put into it.
5. Some people think capital punishment should be allowed to exist because it acts as a deterrent to people about to commit crimes or who are even considering them, but other people hold the view that they shouldn't have to pay for feeding and housing them for years after the crimes are committed, so they should be executed instead.
6. My junk mail is incredible.
7. I've signed up for a course at my local college. The class is "Cultivating the Mold in Your Refrigerator for Fun and Profit."
8. Reading your horoscope is a fun way to get information about your life, but it's not really the real stuff.
9. I'm not sure but I think that Lois is the author of *The Underachiever's Guide to Very Small Business Opportunities* or is she the writer of *Whine Your Way to Success* because I know she's written several books since she's having an autograph party at the campus bookstore either this afternoon or tomorrow.
10. I can't help but wonder whether or not he isn't unwelcome.

B.   The sentences below contain misplaced words and phrases as well as other faulty constructions. Revise them so that each sentence is clear.

1. If you are accosted in the subway at night, you should learn to escape harm from the police.
2. Desperation is when you try to lose weight through Pyramid Power.
3. Almost dead for five years now, I miss my dog so much.
4. The movie is an example where lots of money was wasted on extravagant stars shot in the dark.
5. The father fed the apple pie to the twins he earlier had dropped in the trash compactor.
6. The reason I stopped the exorcism was because my dandruff wasn't disappearing.
7. We gave our waterbed to friends we didn't want anymore.
8. The story of Rip Van Winkle is one of the dangers endured by those who oversleep.
9. Arthur strained his eyes reading without his glasses really badly.
10. After finishing the last problem, the quiz was over.

C. The sentences below are filled with deadwood, redundancies, and passive constructions. Rewrite each one so that it is concise and direct.

1. In point of fact, the main reason he lost the editing job was primarily because of his careless and sloppy proofreading work.
2. It was revealed today that there are some professors in the Prehistoric History department who are incompetent.
3. My brother, who happens to be a loudmouth, can't drive to work this week due to the fact that he was in a wreck in his car at 2 A.M. Saturday morning.
4. In this modern world of today, we often criticize or disapprove of advertising that is thought to be damaging to women by representing them in an unfair way.
5. When the prosecution tried to introduce the old antique gun, this was objected to by the attorney defending the two twin brothers.
6. What the poet is trying to get across to the reader in the fourth stanza is her feeling of disgust with the telephone company.
7. We very often felt that although we expressed our deepest concerns to our boss, he often just sat there and gave us the real impression that he was taking what we said in a very serious manner although, in our opinion, he did not really and truly care about our concerns.
8. It is a true fact that certainly bears repeating over and over again that learning word processing can help you perform in a more efficient way at work and also can save you lots of time too.
9. Personally, I believe that there are too many people who go to eat out in restaurants who always feel they must continually assert their superior natures by acting in a rude, nasty fashion to the people who are employed to wait on their tables.
10. In order to enhance my opportunities for advancement in the workplace at this point in time, I arrived at the decision to seek the hand of my employer's daughter in the state of matrimony.

Assignment

Write a paragraph of at least five sentences as clearly and concisely as you can. Then rewrite this paragraph, filling it with as many vague words, redundancies, and deadwood constructions as possible. Exchange this rewritten paragraph for a similarly faulty one written by a classmate; give yourselves fifteen minutes to "translate" each other's sentences into effective prose.

DEVELOP A LIVELY STYLE

Good writing demands clarity and conciseness—but that's not all. Good prose must also be lively, forceful, and interesting. It should excite, intrigue, and charm; each line should seduce the reader into the next. Consider, for example, one of the duller textbooks you've read lately. It probably was written clearly, but it may have failed to inform because of its insufferably bland tone; by the time you finished your assignment, most likely your brain was asleep.

You can prevent your readers from succumbing to a similar case of the blahs by developing a vigorous prose style that continually surprises and pleases them. As one writer has pointed out, all subjects— with the possible exceptions of sex and money—are dull until somebody makes them interesting. As you revise your rough drafts, remember: bored readers are not born but made. Therefore, below are some practical suggestions to help you transform ho-hum prose into lively sentences and paragraphs:

Use specific, descriptive verbs. Avoid bland verbs that must be supplemented by modifiers.

Bland His fist *broke* the window *into many little pieces.*
Better His fist *shattered* the window.

Bland Dr. Love *asked* his congregation *about* donating money to his "love mission" *over and over again.*
Better Dr. Love *hounded* his congregation into donating money to his "love mission."

Bland The exhausted runner *walked* up the last hill *very slowly.*
Better The exhausted runner *staggered* up the last hill.

To cut wordiness that weighs down your prose, try to use active verbs instead of nouns and colorless verbs such as "to be," "to have," "to get," "to do," and "to make":

Wordy By sunrise the rebels had *made their way* to the capital city.
Better By sunrise the rebels had *battled* to the capital city.

Wordy At first the players and managers *had an argument* over the money, but finally they *came to an agreement* and *got* the contract dispute settled.

Better   At first the players and managers *argued* over the money, but finally they *agreed* and *settled* the contract dispute.

Wordy   The executives *made the decision* to *have* another meeting on Tuesday.

Better   The executives *decided* to *meet* again on Tuesday.

Use specific, precise modifiers that help the reader see, hear, or feel what you are describing. Adjectives such as "good," "bad," "many," "more," "great," "a lot," "important," and "interesting" are too vague to paint the reader a clear picture. Similarly, the adverbs "very," "really," "too," and "quite" are overused and add little to sentence clarity. The following are examples of weak sentences and their revisions:

Imprecise The potion changed the scientist into a *really old* man.

Better   The potion changed the scientist into a *one hundred-year-old* man.

Imprecise Marcia is a *very interesting* person.

Better   Marcia is *witty, intelligent,* and *talented.*

Imprecise The vegetables tasted *funny.*

Better   The vegetables tasted *like lichen mixed with Krazy Glue.*

(For more advice on using specific, colorful words, see also pp. 116–117 in Chapter 7.)

Emphasize people when possible. Try to focus on persons rather than abstractions whenever you can. Next to our fascinating selves, we most enjoy hearing about other people. Although all the sentences in the first paragraph following are correct, the second one, revised by a class of composition students at Brown University, is clearer and more personal because the jargon has been eliminated and the focus changed from the tuition rules to the students.

Original Tuition regulations currently in effect provide that payment of the annual tuition entitles an undergraduate-degree candidate to full-time enrollment, which is defined as registration for three, four, or five courses per semester. This means that at no time may an undergraduate student's official registration for courses drop below three without a dean's permission for part-time status and that at no time may the official course registration exceed five. (Brown University Course Announcement 1980–81)

Revised If students pay their tuition, they may enroll in three, four, or five courses per semester. Fewer than three or more than five can be taken only with a dean's permission.

Here's a similar example with a bureaucratic focus rather than a personal one:

Original The salary deflations will most seriously impact the secondary educational profession.
Revised High school teachers will suffer the biggest salary reductions.

Obviously, the revised sentence is the more easily understood of the two because the reader knows exactly who will be affected by the pay cuts. In your own prose, wherever appropriate, try to replace vague abstractions such as "society," "culture," "administrative concerns," "programmatic expectations," and so forth, with the human beings you're thinking about. In other words, remember to talk *to* people *about* people.

Vary your sentence style. The only torture worse than listening to someone's nails scraping across a blackboard is being forced to read a paragraph full of identically constructed sentences. To illustrate this point, below are a few sentences composed in the all-too-common subject + predicate pattern:

Soccer is the most popular sport in the world. Soccer exists in almost every country. Soccer players are sometimes more famous than movie stars. Soccer teams compete every few years for the World Soccer Cup. Soccer fans often riot if their team loses. Some fans even commit suicide. Soccer is the only game in the world that makes people so crazy.

Excruciatingly painful, yes? Each of us has a tendency to repeat a particular sentence pattern (though the choppy subject + predicate is by far the most popular); you can often detect your own by reading your prose aloud. To avoid overdosing your readers with the same pattern, vary the length, arrangement, and complexity of your sentences. Of course, this doesn't mean that you should contort your sentences merely for the sake of illustrating variety; just read your rough draft aloud, listening carefully to the rhythm of your prose so you can revise any monotonous passages or disharmonious sounds. (Try, also, to avoid the hiccup syndrome, in which you begin a sentence with the same word that ends the preceding sentence: The first president to install a telephone on his desk was Herbert *Hoover. Hoover* refused to use the telephone booth outside his office.)

Avoid overuse of any one kind of construction in the same sentence. Don't, for example, pile up too many negatives, "who" or "which" clauses, prepositional or infinitive phrases in one sentence.

He *couldn't* tell whether she *didn't* want him to go or *not.*
I gave the money to my brother, *who* returned it to the bank president, *who* said the decision to prosecute was up to the sheriff, *who* was out of town.
I went to the florist *for* my father *for* a dozen roses *for* his date.

Don't change your point of view between or within sentences. If, for example, you begin your essay discussing students as "they," don't switch midway—or mid-sentence—to "we" or "you."

Inconsistent	Students pay tuition, which should entitle *them* to some voice in the university's administration. Therefore, *we* deserve one student on the Board of Regents.
Consistent	Students pay tuition, which should entitle *them* to some voice in the university's administration. Therefore, *they* deserve one student on the Board of Regents.
Inconsistent	*I* like my photography class because *we* learn how to restore *our* old photos and how to take better color portraits of *your* family.
Consistent	*I* like my photography class because *I'm* learning how to restore *my* old photos and how to take better color portraits of *my* family.

Perhaps this is a good place to dispel the myth that the pronoun "I" should never be used in an essay; on the contrary, many of our best essays have been written in the first person. Some of your former teachers may have discouraged the use of "I " for these two reasons: (1) overuse of "I" makes your essay sound like the work of an egomaniac; (2) writing in the first person often results in too many empty phrases such as "I think that" and "I believe that." Nevertheless, if the situation demands a personal point of view, feel free—if you're comfortable doing so—to use the first person, but use it in moderation; make sure that every sentence doesn't begin with "I" plus a verb.

Practicing What You've Learned

A. Replace the underlined words below so that the sentences are clear and vivid. In addition, rephrase any awkward constructions or unnecessarily abstract words you find.

1. After the pilot started acting <u>really crazy,</u> I didn't know the reason why he didn't get taken to the hospital.
2. Professional baseball team management <u>appeared to be rather upset</u> over the testing program for drugs.
3. To watch Jim Bob eat pork chops was <u>most interesting.</u>
4. The teacher <u>said</u> loudly that he <u>did not care for</u> the student's report on common kitchen aphrodisiacs.
5. The workshop on family relationships we're attending is <u>great</u> because you learn to control your parents through blackmail and guilt.
6. The new diet made me feel <u>awful,</u> and it <u>did many horrible things</u> to my body.
7. After reading <u>The Looter's Guide to Riot-Prone Cities,</u> Eddie <u>asked to have</u> a transfer <u>really</u> soon.
8. The wild oats soup was <u>very good,</u> so we drank <u>a lot</u> of it <u>pretty fast.</u>
9. When Alfred <u>hit</u> the ball to the top of the fence of the park, his teammates <u>got excited.</u>
10. My brother is <u>sort of different,</u> but I never thought he'd try to <u>take over</u> my aunt's estate.

B. Fill in the blanks with colorful words. Make the paragraph as interesting, exciting, or humorous as you can. Avoid clichés—make your responses original and creative.

As midnight approached, Janet and Brad _____ toward the

_____ castle to escape the _____ storm. Their

_____ car had _____, _____, and finally

_____ on the road nearby. The night was _____, and

Brad _____ at the shadows with _____ and _____.

As they _____ up the _____ steps to the _____

door, the _____ wind was filled with _____ and

_____ sounds. Janet _____ on the door, and moments

later, it opened to reveal the _____ scientist, clutching a

_____. Brad and Janet _____ at each other and then

_____ (complete this sentence, ending the paragraph and the story).

Assignment

Find a short piece of writing you think is too bland, boring, abstract, or confusing. (Possible sources: your college catalogue, a business contract or letter, your student health insurance policy, or a textbook.) In a well-written paragraph of your own, identify the sample's major problems and offer some specific suggestions for improving the writing. (If time permits, read aloud several of the samples and vote to give one the Most Lifeless Prose Award.)

DEVELOP AN EMPHATIC STYLE

Some words and phrases in your sentences are more important than others and, therefore, need more emphasis. Three ways to vary emphasis are by (1) word order, (2) coordination, and (3) subordination.

Word Order

The arrangement of words in a sentence can determine which ideas receive the most emphasis. To stress a word or phrase, place it at the end of the sentence or at the beginning of the sentence. Accordingly, a word or phrase receives least emphasis when buried in the middle of the sentence. Compare the examples below, in which the word "murder" receives varying degrees of emphasis:

Least emphatic Colonel Mustard knew *murder* was his only solution.
Emphatic *Murder* was Colonel Mustard's only solution.
Emphatic Colonel Mustard had only one solution: *murder.*

Another use of word order to vary emphasis is *inversion*, taking a word out of its natural or usual position in a sentence and inserting it in an unexpected place.

Usual order The *conceited* man congratulates his mother on his birthday.
Inverted order *Conceited* is the man who congratulates his mother on his birthday.

Not all your sentences will contain words that need special emphasis; good writing generally contains a mix of some sentences in natural order and others rearranged for special effects.

Coordination

When you have two closely related ideas and want to stress them equally, coordinate them.[1] In coordination, you join two clauses with a coordinating conjunction (the most common ones are "and," "or," "but," and "so").[2] Use coordination to show a relationship between ideas and to add variety to your sentence structures. Be careful, however, to avoid linking nonrelated ideas, such as the two that appeared in the welfare worker's report quoted earlier in this chapter: "Mrs. Smith hasn't had any clothes for a year and has been visited regularly by the clergy." Study the following examples:

Choppy   The most common girl's name today is Jennifer. The most common boy's name is Michael.

Coordinated The most common girl's name today is Jennifer, *and* the most common boy's name is Michael.

Choppy   Imelda brought home a pair of ruby slippers. Ferdinand made her return them.

Coordinated Imelda brought home a pair of ruby slippers, *but* Ferdinand made her return them.

Sometimes when writers are in a hurry, they join ideas that are clearly related in their own minds, but whose relationship is confusing to the reader:

Confusing My laboratory report isn't finished, and today my sister is leaving for a visit home.

Clear   I'm still working on my laboratory report, so I won't be able to catch a ride home with my sister who's leaving today.

You should also avoid using coordinating conjunctions to string too many ideas together like linked sausages:

Poor   We went inside the famous cave and the guide turned off the lights and we saw the rocks that glowed.

Better After we went inside the famous cave, the guide turned off the lights so we could see the rocks that glowed.

---

[1]To remember that the term "coordination" refers to equally weighted ideas, think of other words with the prefix "co," such as "copilots" or "coauthors."

[2]To remember the coordinating conjunctions think of the word "FANBOY": *for, and, nor, but, or, yet.* Always use a comma and a FANBOY to join two complete sentences.

Subordination

Some sentences contain one main statement and one or more less-emphasized elements; the less important ideas are subordinate to, or are dependent upon, the sentence's main idea.[3] Subordinating conjunctions introducing dependent clauses show a variety of relationships between the clauses and the main part of the sentence. Here are four examples of subordinating conjuctions and their uses:

1. To show time

Without subordination   Superman stopped changing his clothes. He realized the phone booth was made of glass.

With subordination   Superman stopped changing his clothes *when* he realized the phone booth was made of glass.

2. To show cause

Without subordination   John did not pass the army's entrance exam. John did not want to be a soldier.

With subordination   John did not pass the army's entrance exam *because* he did not want to be a soldier.

3. To show condition

Without subordination   Susan ought to study the art of tattooing. She will work with colorful people.

With subordination   *If* Susan studies the art of tattooing, she will work with colorful people.

4. To show place

Without subordination   Bulldozers are smashing the old movie theater. That's the place I first saw Roy Rogers and Dale Evans ride into the sunset.

With subordination   Bulldozers are smashing the old movie theater *where* I first saw Roy Rogers and Dale Evans ride into the sunset.

Subordination is especially useful in ridding your prose of choppy Dick-and-Jane sentences and those "empty sentences" discussed on pp. 83–84. Below are some examples of choppy, weak sentences and their revisions, which contain subordinate clauses:

Choppy   Lew makes bagels on Tuesday. Lines in front of his store are a block long.

---

[3]To remember that the term "subordination" refers to sentences containing dependent elements, think of words such as "a subordinate" (someone who works for someone else) or a post office "substation" (a branch of the post office less important than the main branch).

Better   When Lew makes bagels on Tuesday, lines in front of his store are a block long.

Choppy   I have fond memories of Zilker Park. My husband and I met there.

Better   I have fond memories of Zilker Park because my husband and I met there.

A correctly subordinated sentence is one of the marks of a sophisticated writer, because it presents adequate information in one smooth flow instead of in monotonous drips. Subordination, like coordination, also adds variety to your sentence construction.

Generally, when you subordinate one idea, you emphasize another, so to avoid the tail-wagging-the-dog problem, put your important idea in the main clause. Also, don't let your most important idea become buried under an avalanche of subordinate clauses, as in the sentence that follows:

When he was told by his boss, *who* had always treated him fairly, that he was being fired from a job *that* he had held for twenty years at a factory *where* he enjoyed working *because* the pay was good, Henry felt angry and frustrated.

Practice combining choppy sentences by studying the sentence-combining exercise below. In this exercise a description of a popular movie or book has been chopped into simple sentences and then combined into one complex sentence.

1. *Bananas* (1971)
    The protagonist is a product tester.
    He is bored.
    His boredom is with his everyday routine.
    He goes to a small Latin American country.
    He becomes a dictator.
    He becomes a dictator during a political upheaval.

    A product tester, bored with his everyday routine, goes to a small Latin American country, where he becomes a dictator during a political upheaval.

2. *Friday the 13th* (1980)
    A summer camp reopens.
    It had been closed for twenty years.
    It had been closed because of three murders.
    The camp attracts a killer.
    The killer is vindictive.
    The killer knifes teenagers.
    The teenagers are unsuspecting.

The reopening of a summer camp, closed twenty years earlier after three murders, attracts a vindictive killer who knifes unsuspecting teenagers.

3. *The Color Purple* (1986)
Celie is abused.
She is abused by her father.
Celie gets married.
Her husband is named Mister.
Mister also mistreats her.
Celie is not attractive.
Celie feels inferior.
Mister had a girlfriend.
Her name is Shug.
Celie ultimately learns self-respect.
She learns this from Shug.

After being abused by both her father and her husband Mister, the unattractive Celie feels inferior but ultimately learns self-respect from Shug, Mister's former girlfriend.

Please note that the sentences in the exercises above may be combined effectively in a number of ways. For instance, the description of *Bananas* might be rewritten this way: "Fed up with his boring everyday routine, a product tester becomes a dictator during a political upheaval in a small Latin American country." How might you rewrite the other two sample sentences?

Practicing What You've Learned

A. Revise the sentences below so that the underlined words receive the most emphasis.
1. W. C. Fields once filled a child actor's baby bottle with <u>gin</u> to show his dislike for the little boy.
2. According to recent polls, <u>television</u> is where most Americans get their news.
3. Of all the world's problems, it is <u>hunger</u> that is most urgent.
4. I enjoyed visiting many foreign countries last year, with <u>Greece</u> being my favorite of all of them.
5. The annoying habit of <u>knuckle-cracking</u> is something I can't stand.

B. Rewrite the pairs of choppy sentences below using coordination or subordination.
1. Elbert wanted to win the skateboard championship. He broke his leg the day before the contest.

2. The earthquake shook the city. Louise was practicing primal-scream therapy at the time.

3. Harold couldn't tune in "The Battle of the Butlers of the Rich and Famous." The television was broken.

4. Juanita lost some old friends when she won the lottery. She made lots of new ones.

5. Jim Bob quit drinking beer last month. Our aluminum recycling plant closed a week later.

6. Frances hit her professor with her shoe. He decided to reevaluate her essay.

7. The postman quit because the mailbag was too heavy. He also quit because he could not remember all the zip codes.

8. Most of the guests at the royal reception ordered martinis. The Count preferred a Bloody Mary.

9. Bubba is thirty-five. He still lives with his mother.

10. Nedah has only been skiing a few years. She's already an expert.

C. Combine the simple sentences below into one complex sentence. See if you can guess the name of the books and movies described in the sentences. (Answers appear on p. 107.)

1. A boy runs away from home.
   His companion is a runaway slave.
   He lives on a raft.
   The raft is on the Mississippi River.
   He has many adventures.
   The boy learns many lessons.
   Some lessons are about human kindness.
   Some lessons are about friendship.

2. A young man returns from prison.
   He returns to his family.
   His family lives in the Dust Bowl.
   The family decides to move.
   The family expects to find jobs in California.
   The family finds intolerance.
   They also find dishonest employers.

3. A scientist is obsessed.
   He wants to re-create life.
   He creates a monster.
   The monster rebels against the scientist.
   The monster kills his creator.
   The villagers revolt.
   The villagers storm the castle.

4. A young man falls in love.
   She is a beautiful girl.
   She washed up on a shore.

The shore is in New York.
She is really a mermaid.
He does not know she is a mermaid.
He saw her once before.
He saw her when he was a child.

Assignment

A. Make up your own sentence-combining exercise by finding or writing one-sentence descriptions of popular or recent movies, books, or television episodes. Divide the complex sentences into simple sentences and exchange papers with a classmate. Give yourselves ten minutes to combine sentences and guess the titles or shows.

B. The two paragraphs below are poorly written because of their choppy, wordy, and monotonous sentences. Rewrite each passage so that it is clear, lively, and emphatic.

There is a new invention on the market. It is called a "dieter's conscience." It is a small box to be installed in one's refrigerator. When the door of the refrigerator is opened by you, a tape recorder begins to start. A really loud voice yells, "You eating again? No wonder you're getting fat." Then the very loud voice says, "Close the door; it's getting warm." Then the voice laughs a lot in an insane and crazy fashion. The idea is one that is designed to mock people into a habit of stopping eating.

In this modern world of today, man has come up with another new invention. This invention is called the "Talking Tombstone." It is made by the "Gone-But-Not-Forgotten" Company, which is located in Burbank, California. This company makes a tombstone that has a device in it that makes the tombstone appear to be talking aloud in a realistic fashion when people go close by it. The reason is that the device is really a recording machine that is turned on due to the simple fact of the heat of the bodies of the people who go by. The closer the people get, the louder the sound the tombstone makes. It is this device that individual persons who want to leave messages after death may utilize. A hypochondriac, to cite one example, might leave a recording of a message that says over and over again in a really loud voice, "See, I told you I was sick!" it may be assumed by one and all that this new invention will be a serious aspect of the whole death situation in the foreseeable future.

4. *Splash*
3. *Frankenstein* (or almost any late-night horror movie)
2. *The Grapes of Wrath*
1. *Huckleberry Finn*
Answers to sentence-combining exercise:

Word Logic

The English language contains over a half million words—quite a selection for you as a writer to choose from. But such a wide choice may make you feel like a starving person confronting a six-page, fancy French menu: which choice is best? how do I choose? is the choice so important?

Word choice can make an enormous difference in the quality of your writing for at least one obvious reason: if you substitute an incorrect or vague word for the right one, you take the risk of being totally misunderstood. Ages ago Confucius made the same point: "If language is incorrect, then what is said is not meant. If what is said is not meant, then what ought to be done remains undone." It isn't enough that *you* know what you mean; you must transfer your ideas onto paper in the proper words so that others understand your exact meaning.

To help you avoid possible paralysis from indecision over word choice, this chapter offers some practical suggestions on selecting words that are not only accurate and appropriate but also memorable and persuasive.

SELECTING THE CORRECT WORDS

Accuracy: Confused Words

Unless I get a bank loan soon, I will be forced to lead an <u>immortal</u> life.
Dobermans make good pets if you train them with enough <u>patients.</u>

He dreamed of eating <u>desert</u> after <u>desert</u>.
She had dieted for so long that she had become <u>emancipated</u>.
The young man was completely in <u>ah</u> of the starlette's beauty.

The proceeding sentences share a common problem: each one contains an error in word choice. In each sentence, the underlined word is incorrect, causing the sentence to be nonsensical or silly. To avoid such problems in word choice, make sure you check words for *accuracy*. Use only those words whose precise meaning, usage, and spelling you know; look in your dictionary to double-check any words whose definitions (or spellings) are fuzzy to you. As Mark Twain noted, the difference between the right word and the wrong one is the difference between lightning and the lightning bug.

Here is a list of words that are often confused in writing. Use your dictionary to determine the meanings or usage of any word unfamiliar to you.

affect/effect	lead/led
to/too/two	there/their/they're
its/it's	your/you're
complement/compliment	who's/whose
capitol/capital	stationary/stationery
lay/lie	principal/principle
accept/except	precede/proceed
good/well	cite/sight/site
choose/chose	lose/loose
council/counsel	illusion/allusion
where/wear	than/then

Accuracy: Idiomatic Phrases

Occasionally you may have an essay returned to you with words marked "awkward" or "idiom." In English, as in all languages, we have word groupings that seem governed by no particular logic except the ever-popular "that's-the-way-we-say-it" rule. Many of these idiomatic expressions involve prepositions beginning writers sometimes confuse or misuse. Below are some common idiomatic errors and their corrected forms:

regardless ~~to~~ of	different ~~than~~ ~~to~~ from
insight ~~of~~ into	must ~~of~~ have known
similar ~~with~~ to	superior ~~than~~ to
comply ~~to~~ with	prior ~~than~~ to
~~to~~ in my opinion	contrast ~~against~~ to
aptitude ~~toward~~ for	capable ~~to~~ of
meet ~~to~~ her standards	relate ~~with~~ to

To avoid idiomatic errors, consult your dictionary and read your essay aloud; often your ears will catch mistakes in usage that your eyes have overlooked.[1]

Levels of Language

In addition to choosing the correct word, you should also select words whose status is suited to your purpose. For convenience here, language has been classified into three categories or levels of usage: (1) colloquial, (2) informal, (3) formal.

Colloquial language is the kind of speech you use most often in conversation with your friends, classmates, and family. It may not always be grammatically correct ("it's me"); it may include fragments of speech, contractions, some slang, words identified as nonstandard by the dictionary (such as "yuck" or "lousy"), and shortened or abbreviated words ("grad school," "photos," "T.V."). Colloquial speech is everyday language, and while you may use it in some writing (personal letters, journals, memos, and so forth), you should think carefully about using colloquial language in most college essays or in professional letters, reports, or papers, because such a choice implies a casual relationship between writer and reader.

Informal language is called for in most college and professional assignments. The tone is more formal than in colloquial writing or speech; no slang or nonstandard words are permissible. Informal writing consistently uses correct grammar; fragments are used for special effect or not at all. Authorities disagree on the use of contractions in informal writing: some say avoid them entirely; others say they're permissible; still others advocate using them only to avoid stilted phrases ("let's go," for example, is preferable to "let us go"). Most, if not all, of your essays in English classes will be written in informal language.

Formal language is found in important documents and in serious, often cermonial, speeches. Characteristics include an elevated—but not pretentious—tone, no contractions, and correct grammar. Formal

---

[1]You may not immediately recognize what's wrong with words your teacher has labeled "awk" or "idiom," as these marks often cover many sins. If you're uncertain about an error, don't hesitate to ask your teacher for clarification; after all, if you don't know what's wrong with your sentence, you can't very well avoid making the same mistake again. To illustrate this point, here's a true story: A bright young woman was having trouble with prepositional phrases in her essays, and although her professor repeatedly marked her incorrect expressions with the marginal note "idiom," she never improved. Finally, one day near the end of the term, she approached her teacher in tears and wailed, "Professor Jones, I know I'm not a very good writer, but must you write 'idiot,' 'idiot,' 'idiot' all over my papers?" The moral of this story is simple: it's easy to misunderstand a correction or misread your teacher's writing; since you can't improve until you know what's wrong, always ask when you're in doubt.

writing often uses inverted word order and balanced sentence structure. John F. Kennedy's 1960 Inaugural Address, for example, was written in a formal style ("Ask not what your country can do for you; ask what you can do for your country"). Most people rarely, if ever, need to write formally; if you are called upon to do so, however, be careful to avoid formal diction that sounds pretentious, pompous, or phony.

Tone

Tone is a general word that describes writers' attitudes toward their subject matter and audience. There are as many different kinds of tones as there are emotions. Depending on how the writer feels, an essay may sound humorous, ironic, indignant, or solemn, to name but a few of the possible choices. In addition to presenting a specific attitude, a good writer gains credibility by maintaining a tone that is generally calm, reasonable, and sincere.

While it is impossible to analyze all the various kinds of tones one finds in essays, it is nevertheless beneficial to discuss some of those that repeatedly give students trouble. Listed below are some tones that should be used carefully or avoided altogether:

Invective

Invective is unrestrained anger, usually expressed in the form of violent accusation or denunciation. Let's suppose, for example, you hear a friend argue that "anyone who votes for Joe Smith is a Fascist pig"; if you are considering Smith, you are probably offended by your friend's abusive tone. Raging emotion, after all, does not sway the opinions of intelligient people; they need to hear the facts presented in a calm, clear discussion. Therefore, in you own writing, aim for a reasonable tone. You want your readers to think, "Now here is someone with a good understanding of the situation, who has evaluated it with a calm, analytical mind." Keeping a controlled tone doesn't mean you shouldn't feel strongly about your subject—on the contrary, you certainly should—but you should realize that a hysterical or outraged tone defeats your purpose by causing you to sound irrational and therefore untrustworthy. For this reason, you should probably avoid using profanity in your essays; the shock value of an obscenity may not be worth what you might lose in credibility (and besides, is anyone other than your Aunt Fanny really amazed by profanity these days?). The most effective way to get your point across is to persuade, not offend, your reader.

Sarcasm

In most of your writing you'll discover that a little sarcasm—bitter, derisive remarks—goes a long way. Like invective, too much sarcasm can damage the reasonable tone your essay should present. Instead of saying, "You can recognize the supporters of the new tax law by the points on the tops of their heads," give your readers some reasons why you believe the tax bill is flawed. Sarcasm can be effective, but realize that it often backfires by causing the writer to sound like a childish name-caller rather than a judicious commentator.

Irony

Irony is a figure of speech whereby the writer or speaker says the opposite of what is meant; for the irony to be succcessful, however, the audience must understand the writer's true intent. For example, if you have slopped to school in a rainstorm and your drenched teacher enters the classroom saying, "Ah, nothing like this beautiful sunny weather," you know that your teacher is being ironic. Perhaps one of the most famous cases of irony occurred in 1938, when Sigmund Freud, the famous Viennese psychiatrist, was arrested by the Nazis. After being harassed by the Gestapo, he was released on the condition that he sign a statement swearing he had been treated well by the secret police. Freud signed it, but he added a few words after his signature: "I can heartily recommend the Gestapo to anyone." Looking back, we easily recognize Freud's jab at his captors; the Gestapo, however, apparently overlooked the irony and let him go.

While irony is often an effective device, it can also cause great confusion, especially when it is written rather than spoken. Unless your readers thoroughly understand your position in the first place, they may become confused by what appears to be a sudden contradiction. Irony that is too subtle, too private, or simply out of context merely complicates the issue. Therefore, you must make certain that your reader has no trouble realizing when your tongue is firmly embedded in your check. And unless you are assigned to write an ironic essay (in the same vein, for instance, as Swift's "A Modest Proposal"), don't overuse irony. Like any rhetorical device, its effectiveness is reduced with overkill.

Flippancy or Cuteness

If you sound too flip or bored in your essay ("I hate this assignment, but since it's two A.M., I might as well begin . . ."), your readers will not take you seriously and, consequently, will disregard whatever you have to say. Writers suffering from cuteness will also antagonize their readers. For example, let's assume you're assigned the topic "Which Person Has Done the Most to Arouse the Laboring Class in Twentieth-Century England?" and you begin your essay with a discussion of the man who invented the alarm clock. While that joke might be funny in an appropriate situation, it's not likely to impress your professor, who's looking for serious commentary. How much cuteness is too much is often a matter of taste, but if you have any doubts about the quality of your humor, leave it out. Also, omit personal messages or comic asides to your teacher (such as "Ha, ha, just kidding, teach!" or "I knew you'd love this part"). Humor is often effective, but remember that the point of any essay is to persuade an audience to accept your thesis, not merely to entertain with freestanding jokes. In other words, if you use humor, make sure it is appropriate to your subject matter and that it works to help you make your point.

Sentimentality

Sentimentality is the excessive show of cheap emotions—"cheap" because they are not deeply felt but evoked by clichés and stock, tear-jerking situations. In the nineteenth century, for example, a typical melodrama played on the sentimentality of the audience by presenting a black-hatted, cold-hearted, mustache-twirling villain tying a golden-haired, pure-hearted "Little Nell" to the railroad tracks after driving her ancient, sickly mother out into a snowdrift. Today, politicians (among others) often appeal to our sentimentality by conjuring up vague images they feel will move us emotionally rather than rationally to take their side: "My friends," says Senator Stereotype, "this fine nation of ours was founded by men like myself, dedicated to the principles of family, flag, and freedom. Vote for me, and let's get back to those precious basics that make life in America so grand." Such gush is hardly convincing; good writers and speakers use logic and reason to persuade their audience. For example, don't allow yourself to become too carried away with emotion as did this student: "My dog, Cuddles, is the sweetest, cutest, most precious little puppy dog in the whole wide world, and she will always be my best friend." In addition to sending the reader into sugar shock, this passage fails to present any sound reasons why anyone should appreciate Cuddles. In other words, be sincere in your writing, but don't lose so much control of your emotions that you become mushy or maudlin.

Preachiness

Even if you are so convinced of the rightness of your position that a burning bush couldn't change your mind, try not to sound smug about it. No one likes to be lectured by someone perched atop the mountain of morality. Instead of preaching, adopt a tone that says, "I believe my position is correct, and I am glad to have this opportunity to explain why." Then give your reasons and meet objections in a positive but not holier-than-thou manner.

Pomposity

The "voice" of your essay should sound as natural as possible; don't strain to sound scholarly, scientific, or sophisticated. If you write "My summer sojourn through the western states of this grand country was immensely pleasurable" instead of "My vacation last summer in the Rockies was fun," you sound merely phony, not dignified and learned. Select only words you know and can use easily. Never write anything you wouldn't say in an ordinary conversation. (For more information on correcting pretentious writing, see p. 93 and pp. 119–121.)

> To achieve the appropriate tone, be as sincere, forthright, and reasonable as you can. Let the tone of your essay establish a basis of mutual respect between you and your reader.

Connotation and Denotation

A word's *denotation* refers to its literal meaning, the meaning defined by the dictionary; a word's *connotation* refers to the emotional associations surrounding its meaning. For example, "home" and "residence" both may be defined as the place where one lives, but "home" carries connotations of warmth, security, and family that "residence" lacks. Similarly, "old" and "antique" have identical denotative meanings, but "antique" has the more positive connotation because it suggests something that also has value. Reporters and journalists do the same job, but the latter name somehow seems to indicate someone more sophisticated and professional. Because many words with similar denotative meanings do carry different connotations, good writers must be careful with their word choice. *Select only words whose connotations fit your purpose.* If, for example, you want to describe your grandmother in a positive way as someone who stands up for herself, you might refer to her as "assertive" or "feisty"; if you want to present her negatively, you might call her "aggressive" or "pushy."

In addition to selecting words with the appropriate connotations for your purpose, be careful to avoid offending your audience with particular connotations. For instance, if you were trying to persuade a group of politically conservative doctors to accept your stand on Medicare, you would not want to refer to your opposition as "right-wingers" or "reactionaries," extremist terms that have negative connotations. Remember, you want to inform and persuade your audience, not antagonize them.

You should also be alert to the use of words with emotionally charged connotations, especially in advertising and propaganda of various kinds. Car manufacturers, for example, often use names of swift, bold, or graceful animals (Jaguar, Cougar, Impala) to sway prospective buyers; cosmetic manufacturers in recent years have taken advantage of the trend toward lighter makeup by associating words such as "nature," "natural," "organic," and "healthy glow" with their products. Politicians, too, are heavy users of connotation; they often drop in emotionally positive, but practically meaningless, words and phrases such as "defender of the American Way" and "friend of the common man" to describe themselves, while describing their opponents with such negative, emotionally charged labels as "radical" and "elitist." Of course, intelligent readers, like intelligent voters and consumers, want more than emotion-laden words; they want facts and logical argument. Therefore, as a good writer, you should use connotation as only one of many persuasive devices to enhance your presentation of evidence; never depend solely on an emotional appeal to convince your audience that your position—or thesis—is correct.

Practicing What You've Learned

A. Some of the underlined words below are used incorrectly; some are correct. Substitute the accurate word wherever necessary.

1. The finances of the chicken ranch are in <u>fowl</u> shape because the hens are <u>lying</u> down on the job.
2. The professor, <u>whose</u> famous for his <u>photogenic</u> memory, graciously <u>excepted</u> a large <u>amount</u> of <u>complements</u>.
3. <u>Its</u> <u>to</u> bad you don't like <u>they're</u> new Popsicle sculpture since <u>their</u> giving it <u>to</u> you for Christmas.
4. Vacations of <u>to</u> weeks with <u>to</u> friends are always <u>to</u> short, and while <u>you're</u> <u>to</u> tired <u>to</u> return <u>to</u> work, <u>your</u> <u>to</u> broke not <u>to</u>.
5. Sara June felt she deserved an "A" in math, <u>irregardless</u> of her 59 average in the <u>coarse</u>.
6. "I am impressed by the <u>continuity</u> of his physical presence"— Howard Cosell
7. Did the high school <u>principal</u> <u>loose</u> <u>you're</u> heavy <u>medal</u> record and <u>it's</u> album jacket <u>too?</u>
8. The new city <u>counsel</u> parade ordinance will <u>effect</u> everyone in the <u>capitol</u> city <u>except</u> members of the Lawn Chair Marching Band.
9. My opinion of the new <u>cite</u> for Imelda's Shoe 'n Shop Store is different <u>than</u> <u>theirs</u>.
10. <u>You're</u> looking very <u>well</u> tonight, I must say, though you may be an optical <u>allusion</u>.

B. The sentences below contain words and phrases that interfere with the sincere, reasonable tone good writers try to create. Rewrite each sentence replacing sarcasm, sentimentality, cuteness, invective, and pretentiousness with more appropriate language.

1. The last dying rays of day were quickly ebbing in the West as if to signal the feline to begin its lonely vigil.
2. Only a jerk would support the President's Mideast peace plan.
3. I was desirous of acquiring knowledge about members of our lower income brackets.

4. If the bill to legalize marijuana is passed, we can safely assume that the whole country will soon be going to pot (heh, heh!).
5. I just love to look at those teensie little white mice with their cute, itty-bitty red eyes.

C. In each group of words listed below, identify the words with the most pleasing and most negative connotations.
1. teacher/instructor/educator/professor/lecturer
2. slender/slim/skinny/thin/slight/anorexic
3. famous/notorious/well-known/infamous
4. wealthy/opulent/rich/affluent/privileged
5. dull/drab/quiet/boring/colorless

D. Replace the underlined words in the sentences below with words arousing more positive feelings:
1. The <u>stench</u> from Jean's kitchen meant dinner was ready and was about to be served.
2. My neighbor was a <u>fat</u> <u>spinster lady</u>.
3. The coach had <u>rigid</u> rules for all his players.
4. His <u>obsession</u> with his yard pleased the city's beautification committee.
5. The <u>slick</u> car salesman made a <u>pitch</u> to the <u>old geezer</u> who walked in the door.
6. Textbook writers admit to having a few <u>bizarre</u> habits.
7. Carol was a <u>mediocre</u> student.
8. His <u>odd</u> clothes made Mary think he was a <u>bum</u>.
9. The High Priest explained his tribe's <u>superstitions</u>.
10. Many of the Board members were amazed to see how Algernon <u>dominated</u> the meeting.

SELECTING THE BEST WORDS

In addition to selecting the correct word and appropriate tone, good writers also choose words that firmly implant their ideas in the minds of their readers. The best prose not only makes cogent points but also states these points memorably. To help you select the best words to express your ideas, the following is a list of do's and don't's covering the most common diction (word choice) problems in students' writing today:

Do make your words as precise as possible. Always choose vigorous, active verbs and colorful, specific nouns and modifiers. "The big tree was hit by lightning," for example, is not as informative or interesting as "Lightning splintered the neighbors' thirty-foot oak." *Don't* use words whose meanings are unclear:

VAGUE VERBS

Unclear She is *involved in* a lawsuit. [How?]
Clear She is suing her dentist for filling the wrong tooth.

Unclear Tom can *relate to* Jennifer. [What's the relationship?]
Clear Tom understands Jennifer's family problems.

Unclear He won't *deal* with his ex-wife. [In what way?]
Clear He refuses to speak to his ex-wife.

Unclear Clyde *participated* in an off-Broadway play. [How?]
Clear Clyde held the cue cards for the actors.

VAGUE NOUNS

Unclear The burglar took several valuable *things* from our house.[2] [What items?]
Clear The burglar took a *color T.V., a stereo, and a microwave oven* from our house.

Unclear When I have my car serviced, there is always *trouble*. [What kind?]
Clear When I have my car serviced, *the mechanics always find additional repairs and never have the car ready when it is promised.*

Unclear When I have *problems*, I always call my friends for advice. [What problems?]
Clear *If my girlfriend breaks up with me, my roof needs repairing, or my heart needs surgery*, I always call my friends for advice.

Unclear I like to have *fun* while I'm on vacation. [What sort of activities?]
Clear I like to *eat in fancy restaurants, fly stunt kites, and walk along the beach* when I'm on vacation.

VAGUE MODIFIERS

Unclear His *terrible* explanation left me *very* confused. [Why "terrible"? How confused?]
Clear His disorganized explanation left me too confused to begin the project.

Unclear The boxer hit the punching bag *really* hard. [How hard?]
Clear The boxer hit the punching bag so hard it split open.

---

[2]One specific piece of advice: banish the word "thing" from your writing. In nine out of ten cases, it is a lazy substitute for some other word. Unless you mean "an inanimate object," replace "thing" with the specific word it stands for.

Unclear	When I had the flu, I was *extremely* sick. [How sick?]
Clear	When I had the flu, I had a fever of 103° and a throat so sore I had to miss work.
Unclear	*Casablanca* is a *good* movie *with something for everyone.* [Why "good" and for everyone?]
Clear	*Casablanca* is a witty, sentimental movie that successfully combines an adventure story and a romance.

Do make your word choices as fresh and original as possible. Instead of saying, "My hometown is very quiet," you might say, "My hometown's definition of an orgy is a light burning after midnight." In other words, if you can make your readers admire and remember your prose, you have a better chance of persuading them to accept your ideas.

Conversely, to avoid ho-hum prose, *don't* fill your sentences with clichés and platitudes—overworked phrases that cause your writing to sound lifeless and trite. Although we use clichés in everyday conversation, good writers avoid them in writing because (1) they are often vague or imprecise (just how pretty is "pretty as a picture?"), (2) they are used so frequently that they rob your prose style of personality and uniqueness ("it was raining cats and dogs"—does that phrase help your reader "see" the particular rainstorm you're trying to describe?).

Novice writers often include trite expressions because they do not recognize them as clichés; therefore, below is a partial list (there are literally thousands more) of phrases to avoid. Instead of using cliché, try substituting an original phrase to describe what you see or feel. Never try to disguise a cliché by putting it in quotation marks—a baboon in dark glasses and a wig is still a baboon.

busy as a bee	hit below the belt
cross that bridge when I come to it	found a silver lining
	smell a rat
Happy as a lark	hot as fire
jump to a conclusion	cold as ice
blind as a bat	mad as a wet hen
squeal like a stuck pig	quick as a wink
got what he deserved	in a nutshell
to be left in the cold	better late than never
poor as a church mouse	fate worse than death
acted like a rat	few and far between
painted the town red	true blue
didn't sleep a wink	the Grim Reaper
all work and no play	in hot water
eat, drink, and be merry	all hell broke loose
sweat of one's brow	blessing in disguise

crack of dawn	needle in a haystack
a crying shame	bed of roses
white as a sheet	soft as silk
depths of despair	hard as nails
dead of night	white as snow
shadow of a doubt	almightly dollar
hear a pin drop	naked truth
nip in the bud	blessed event
clinging vine	it stands to reason
budding genius	after all is said and done
first and foremost	to make a long story short

It would be impossible, of course, to memorize all the clichés and trite expressions in our language, but do check your prose for recognizable overworked phrases so that your words will not be predictable and, consequently, dull. If you aren't sure if a phrase is a cliché—but you've heard it used frequently—your prose will probably be stronger if you substitute an original phrase for the suspected one.

Don't use trendy expressions or slang in your essays. Slang generally consists of commonly used words made up by special groups to communicate among themselves. Slang has many origins, from sports to space travel; for example, surfing gave us the expression "to wipe out" (to fail), the military lent "snafu" (from the first letters of "situation normal—all fouled up"), the astronauts provided "A-OK" (all systems working).

While slang often gives our speech color and vigor, it is unacceptable in many writing assignments for several reasons. First, slang is often part of a private language understood only by members of a particular professional, social, or age group. Secondly, slang often presents a vague picture or one that changes meanings from person to person or from context to context. More than likely, each person has a unique definition for a particular slang expression, and while these definitions may overlap, they are not precisely the same. Consequently, your reader could interpret your words one way while you mean them in another, a dilemma that might result in total miscommunication. Too often beginning writers rely on vague, popular clichés ("His behavior really grossed me out") instead of thinking of specific words to express specific ideas. Moreover, slang becomes dated quickly, and almost nothing sounds worse than yesterday's "in" expressions. (In his movie *Annie Hall*, Woody Allen pointed out the silliness of some of our psychological slang; when he was told to "mellow out," he replied, "When I get mellow, I ripen and then I rot.") Try to write so that your prose will be as fresh and pleasing ten years from now as today. Don't allow slang to give your writing a flippant tone that detracts from a serious discussion. Therefore, to communicate clearly with your reader, avoid including slang in your essays. Putting slang in quotation marks isn't the solution—omit the slang and use precise words instead.

   Do select simple, direct words your readers can easily understand. *Don't* use pompous or pseudosophisticated language in place of plain speech. Wherever possible, avoid *jargon*—that is, words and phrases that are unnecessarily technical, pretentious, or abstract.

   Technical jargon—terms specific to one area of study or specialization—should be omitted or clearly defined in essays directed to a general audience because such language is often inaccessible to anyone outside the writer's particular field. By now most of us are familiar with bureaucratese, journalese, and psychobabble, in addition to gobbledygook from business, politics, advertising, and education. If, for example, you worry that "a self-actualized person such as yourself cannot transcend either your hostile environment or your passive-aggressive behavior to make a commitment to a viable lifestyle and meaningful interpersonal relationships," then you are indulging in psychological or sociological jargon; if you "review existing mechanisms of consumer input, thruput, and output via the consumer communications channel module," you are speaking business jargon. While most professions do have their own terms, you should limit your use of specialized language to writing aimed solely at your professional colleagues; always try to avoid technical jargon in prose directed at a general audience.

   Today the term "jargon" also refers to prose containing an abundance of abstract, pretentious, multisyllable words. The use of this kind of jargon often betrays a writer's attempt to sound sophisticated and intellectual; actually, it only confuses meaning and delays communication. Here, for instance, is an excerpt of incomprehensible jargon from a college president who obviously prefers twenty-five-cent words to simple, straightforward nickel ones: "We will divert the force of this fiscal stress into leverage energy and pry important budgetary considerations and control out of our fiscal and administrative procedures." Or look at the thirty-eight-word definition of "exit" written by an Occupational Safety and Health Administration bureaucrat: "That portion of a means of egress which is separated from all spaces of the building or structure by construction or equipment as required in this subpart to provide a protected way of travel to the exit discharge." Such language is not only pretentious and confusing but almost comic in its wordiness.

   Jargon is so pervasive these days that even some English teachers are succumbing to its use. A group of high school teachers, for instance, was asked to indicate a preference for one of the following sentences:

   His expression of ideas that are in disagreement with those of others will often result in his rejection by them and his isolation from the life around him.

   If he expresses ideas that others disagree with, he will often be rejected by them and isolated from the life around him.

Surprisingly, only nineteen percent chose the more direct second sentence. The others saw the wordy, pompous first statement as "mature" and "educated," revealing that some teachers themselves may be both the victims and perpetrators of doublespeak.

To avoid such verbal litter in your own writing, try to follow these four rules:

1. Always select the plainest, most direct words you know.

Jargon I want to interface with the author because I discovered an error on the page that terminates the volume.

Revised I want to talk to the author because I found an error on the last page of the book.

2. Replace nominalizations (nouns that are made from verbs and adjectives, usually by adding endings such as *-tion, -ism, -ness*, or *-al*) with simpler verbs and nouns.

Jargon The departmental head has come to the recognition that the utilization of verbose verbalization renders informational content inaccessible.

Revised The department head recognizes that wordiness confuses meaning.

3. Avoid adding *-ize* or *-wise* to verbs and adverbs.

Jargon *Weatherwise*, it looked like a good day to *finalize* her report on wind tunnels.

Revised The day's clear weather would help her finish her report on wind tunnels.

4. Drop out meaningless tack-on words such as "factor," "aspect," and "situation."

Jargon The convenience factor of the neighborhood grocery store is one aspect of its success.

Revised The convenience of the neighborhood grocery store contributes to its success.

Remember that good writing is clear and direct, never wordy, cloudy, or ostentatious. (For more hints on developing a clear style, see pp. 83–93.)

Do call things by their proper names. Don't sugarcoat your terms by substituting euphemisms—words that sound nice or pretty applied to subjects some people find distasteful. For example, you've probably heard someone say, "she passed away" instead of "she died," or "he was under the influence of alcohol" instead of "he was drunk," or "she was a lady of the night" instead of "she was a prostitute." Often euphemisms are used to soften names of jobs: "sanitary engineer" for garbage collector, "field representative" for salesperson, "information processor" for typist, and so forth.

Some euphemisms are dated and now seem plain silly; in Victorian times, for example, the word "leg" was considered unmentionable in polite company, so people spoke of "piano limbs" and asked for the "first joint" of a chicken rather than the drumstick. The phrases "white meat" and "dark meat" were euphemisms some people used to avoid asking for a piece of chicken breast or thigh.

Today, euphemisms still abound. Though our generation is perhaps more direct about sex and death, many current euphemisms gloss over unpleasant or unpopular business, military, and political practices. When he was president of Uganda, for example, Idi Amin called his feared and despised secret police "the State Research Unit"; our own Central Intelligence Agency once called its assassination teams "Health Alteration Committees" and reportedly conducted brainwashing experiments under the cover of an organization known as the "Society for the Investigation of Human Ecology." A 1984 handbook for Nicaraguan rebels written and published by the CIA offered helpful advice about "neutralization" of government officials. Euphemisms also thrive in other government agencies. A former budget director gave us "revenue enhancements" instead of new taxes, and a Secretary of Health, Education, and Welfare once tried to camouflage cuts in social services by calling them "advance downward adjustments." In the same vein we learn that government programs no longer simply fail; they are "rendered inoperative." And in some jails a difficult prisoner, who once would have been sent to solitary confinement, is now placed in the "meditation room" or in the "adjustment center." In some hospitals, sick people do not die—they experience "negative patient care outcome." The military, too, has added its share of euphemisms to the language; these range from the comic transformation of the lowly shovel into a "combat emplacement evacuator" to the deadly serious use of the words "liberation" and "pacification" to mean the invasion and destruction of other countries.

Because euphemisms can be used unscrupulously to manipulate people by sugarcoating the truth, you should always avoid them in your own prose and be suspicious of them in the writing of others. As Aldous Huxley, author of *Brave New World*, noted, "An education for freedom is, among other things, an education in the proper uses of language."

In addition to weakening the credibility of one's ideas, euphemisms can make prose unnecessarily abstract, wordy, pretentious, or even silly. For a clear and natural prose style, use terms that are straightforward and simple. In other words, call a spade a spade, not "an implement for use in horticultural environments."

Avoid sexist language. Most people will agree that language helps shape thought. Consequently, writers should avoid using any language that promotes demeaning stereotypes. Sexist language, in particular, often subtly suggests that women are less rational, intelligent, or capable of handling certain tasks or jobs. In order to make your writing as accurate and unbiased as possible, here are a half-dozen simple suggestions for ways to write nonsexist prose:

1. Try using plural nouns to eliminate the need for the singular pronouns "he" and "she":

Original Today's *doctor* knows *he* must carry extra malpractice insurance.

Revision Today's *doctors* know *they* must carry extra malpractice insurance.

2. Try substituting nonsexist occupational titles for those ending in "man" or "woman":

Original The *fireman* and the *saleslady* watched the *policeman* arrest the *mailman*.

Revision The *firefighter* and the *sales clerk* watched the *police officer* arrest the *mail carrier*.

3. Don't contribute to stereotyping by assigning particular roles solely to men or women:

Original *Mothers* concerned about the possibility of Reyes Syndrome should avoid giving their sick children aspirin.

Revision *Parents* concerned about the possibility of Reyes Syndrome should avoid giving their sick children aspirin.

4. Try substituting nonsexist words such as "people," "persons," "one," "voters," "workers," "students," etc., for "man" or "woman":

Original Any *man* who wants to become a corporation executive before thirty should buy this book.

Revision *Anyone* who wants to become a corporation executive before thirty should buy this book.

5. Don't use inappropriate diminutives:

Original In the annual office picture, the photographer asked the men to stand behind the *girls*.

Revision In the annual office picture, the photographer asked the men to stand behind the *women*.

6. Be consistent in your treatment of men's and women's names, marital status, professional titles, and physical appearances:

Original   Neither Melville, *the inspired novelist,* nor Miss
Dickinson, *the plain spinster poetess of Amherst,* gained
fame or fortune in their lifetimes.
Revision   Neither Melville, the *novelist,* nor Dickinson, the *poet,*
gained fame or fortune in their lifetimes.

Revising your writing to eliminate sexist references does not mean
turning clear phrases into awkward or confusing jumbles of "he/she
told him/her that the car was his/hers." By consistently following the
suggestions above, you should be able to make your prose both clear
and inoffensive to all members of your audience.

***Do enliven your writing with figurative language, when
appropriate.*** Figurative language produces pictures or images in a
reader's mind, often by comparing something unfamiliar to something
familiar. The two most common figurative devices are the simile and
the metaphor. A *simile* is a comparison between two people, places,
feelings, or things, using the word "like" or "as"; a more forceful comparison, omitting the word "like " or "as," is a *metaphor.* Below are two
examples:

Simile   George eats his meals like a hog.
Metaphor   George is a hog at mealtime.

In both sentences George, whose eating habits are unfamiliar to the
reader, is likened to a hog, whose sloppy manners are generally well
known. By comparing George to a hog, the writer gives the reader a
clear picture of George at the table. Figurative language cannot only
help you present your ideas in clear, concrete, economical ways, but
can also make your prose more memorable—especially if the image or
picture you present is a fresh, arresting one. Below are some examples
of striking images designed to catch the reader's attention and to clarify
the writer's point:

- An hour away from her is like a month in the country.
- The atmosphere of the meeting room was as tense as a World
  Series game tied up in the ninth inning.
- If love makes the world go round, jealousy is the monkey
  wrench thrown into the gears.
- The banker looked at my loan application like an English
  teacher looks at a misspelled word.
- Dreams are the mind's rewriting of reality.
- The factory squatted on the bank of the river like a huge black
  toad.

Figurative language can spice up your prose, but like any spice, it
can be misused, thus spoiling your soup. Therefore, *don't* overuse figurative language; not every point needs a metaphor or simile for clarity

or emphasis. Too many images are confusing. Moreover, *don't* use stale images. (Clichés—discussed on pp. 118–119 —are often tired metaphors or similes: snake in the grass, hot as fire, quiet as a mouse, etc.) If you can't catch your readers' attention with a fresh picture, don't bore them with a stale one.

And finally, don't mix images—this too often results in a confusing or unintentionally comic scene. For example, a former mayor of Denver once responded to a question about city fiscal requirements this way: "I think the proper approach is to go through this Garden of Gethsemane that we're in now, give birth to a budget that will come out of it, and then start putting our ducks in order with an appeal and the backup we would need to get something done at the state level." Or take ex-president Gerald Ford's description of the difficulties involved in building his presidential library: "Two years ago, we were literally back on our own goal line and we had a long row to hoe. Now we are on the doorstep of success." Perhaps a newspaper columnist wins the prize for confusion with this triple-decker: "The Assemblymen also were miffed at their Senate counterparts because they have refused to bite the bullet that now seems to have grown to the size of a millstone to the Assemblymen whose necks are on the line."

In summary, use figurative language sparingly and consistently to present a vivid picture to your reader.

Do vary your word choice so that your prose does not sound wordy, repetitious, or monotonous. Consider the following sentence:

According to child psychologists, depriving a child of artistic stimulation in the earliest stages of childhood can cause the child brain damage.

Reworded, the sentence below eliminates the tiresome, unnecessary repetition of the word "child":

According to child psychologists, depriving infants of artistic stimulation can cause brain damage.

By omitting or changing repeated words, you can add variety and crispness to your prose. Of course, don't ever change your words or sentence structure to achieve variety at the expense of clarity or precision; at all times your goal is making your prose clear to your readers.

Do remember that wordiness is a major problem for all writers, even the professionals. State your thoughts directly and specifically in as few words as are necessary to communicate your meaning clearly. In addition to the advice given here on avoiding wordy, vague jargon, euphemisms, clichés, and so forth, you should review the sections on simplicity and conciseness in Chapter 6.

> The most important key to effective word choice is *revision*. As you write your first draft, don't fret about selecting the best words to communicate your ideas; in later drafts one of your main tasks will be replacing the inaccurate or imprecise words with better ones (Dorothy Parker, famous for her witty essays, once lamented, "I can't write five words but that I change seven"). All good writers rewrite, so revise your prose to make each word count.

Practicing What You've Learned

A. Underline the vague nouns, verbs, and modifiers in the sentences below. Then rewrite each one so that the sentence says something that is clear and specific.

   1. The experiment had very bad results.

   2. The speaker came up with some odd items.

   3. The house was big, old, and ugly.

   4. The man was a nice guy with a good personality.

   5. I felt that the whole ordeal was quite an experience.

   6. The machine we got was missing a few things.

   7. The woman was really something special.

   8. The classroom material wasn't interesting.

   9. The child made a lot of very loud noises.

   10. The cost of the unusual meal was amazing.

B. Rewrite the following sentences, eliminating all the clichés, sexist language, and euphemisms you find.

   1. When my mother didn't return from the little girl's room, we decided she was as slow as molasses.

   2. According to former-president Jimmy Carter, the aborted rescue of the hostages in Iran was an incomplete success.

   3. On election day, all of us over the ripe old age of eighteen should exercise our most sacred democratic privilege.

   4. After all is said and done, the range technicians and the agricultural producers will still be the new disadvantaged class.

   5. Each officer in the Armed Forces realizes that someday he may be called upon to use the peacekeepers to depopulate an emerging nation.

6. Although he once regarded her as sweet and innocent, he realized then and there that she was really a wolf in sheep's clothing.

7. Any good cook will be green with envy when she tastes her neighbor's apple pie.

8. The City Councilman was stewing in his juices when he learned that his son had been arrested for fooling around with the ballot box.

9. After the policemen detained the rebels, some of the newspapermen who had been watching the riot experienced unlawful deprivation of life.

10. The successful Congressman knows when to say, "That information is classified for reasons of national security."

C. Rewrite the following sentences, replacing the jargon, slang, and vague language with clear, precise words and phrases.

1. To maintain a state of high-level wellness, one should use a wooden interdental stimulator at least once a day.

2. All of us could relate to Mabel's essay on the significant educational factors involved in the revenue enhancement tax-base erosion control program.

3. A new tranquility bag has been placed in our family's recreational eco-unit for habitability improvement.

4. Jim and Ida no longer had a meaningful relationship, so she decided to share some of her feelings with him in an attempt to get them back into a better space.

5. The employee was outplaced for a lack of interpersonal skills and for failing to optimize productivity.

6. The students at their pupil stations were told to impact the sugar and flour and then to utilize the oven in order to produce one dozen chocolate chip cookie units.

7. The magnitude, the complexity, and the nature of the job should relate to the level of detail, the time, and the effort expended in document implementation and evaluation.

8. My institute of higher learning announced today that its academic evaluation program had been delayed and in all probability indefinitely postponed due to circumstances relating to financial insolvency.

9. The objective inherent in the functioning of this committee is the establishment of a viable base from which it can consider the initially motivating factors of its conception.

10. "We were not micromanaging Grenada intelligencewise until about that time frame," said Admiral Wesley L. McDonald, when asked what was happening on the island just prior to the United States' 1983 rescue mission.

Assignment

Write two of the following paragraphs and then exchange them with those written by a classmate. Translate faulty prose into crisp, clear sentences.

- a paragraph of clichés and vague language arguing the value of having a particular major in college
- a paragraph of jargon and euphemisms by a politician explaining why he/she accepted money from an undercover agent
- a paragraph of vague language and clichés persuading your banker to advance you funds to invest in a get-rich-quick scheme
- a paragraph of slang, clichés, and sexist language advising your friends on their approaching marriage
- a paragraph of jargon and vague language praising a product you've invented and are trying to market

THE BASICS OF THE SHORT ESSAY: PART ONE SUMMARY

Here are ten rules to keep in mind while you are writing the rough drafts of your essay:

1. Be confident that you have something important and interesting to say.
2. Identify your particular audience and become determined to communicate effectively with them.
3. Use prewriting techniques to help you focus on one main idea that will become the thesis of your essay.
4. Organize your essay's points logically, in a persuasive and coherent order.
5. Develop each of your ideas with enough specific details.
6. Cut out any irrelevant material that disrupts the smooth flow from idea to idea.
7. Compose sentences that are clear, concise, and informative.
8. Select accurate, vivid words.
9. Revise your prose.
10. Revise your prose.

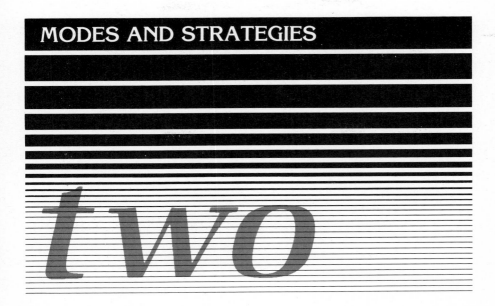

MODES AND STRATEGIES

two

PART TWO

Communication may be divided into four types (or "modes" as they are often called): exposition, argumentation, description, and narration. While each one will be explained in greater detail in this section of the text, the four modes may be defined briefly as follows:

exposition	the writer intends to explain or inform
argumentation	the writer intends to convince or persuade
description	the writer intends to create in words a picture of a person, place, object, or feeling
narration	the writer intends to tell a story or recount an event

While we commonly refer to exposition, argumentation, description, and narration as the basic types of prose, in reality it is difficult to find any one mode in a pure form. In fact, almost all essays are combinations of two or more modes; it would be virtually impossible, for instance, to write a story—narration—without including description or to argue without also giving some information. Nevertheless, by determining a writer's *main* purpose, we can usually identify an essay or prose piece as primarily exposition, argumentation, description, or narration. In other words, an article may include a brief description of a new mousetrap, but if the writer's main intention is to explain how the trap works, then we may designate the essay as exposition. In most cases, the primary mode of any essay will be readily apparent to the reader.

In Part Two of this text, you will study each of the four modes in detail and learn some of the patterns of development, called *strategies,* that will enable you to write the kind of prose most frequently demanded in college and professional work. Mastering the most common prose patterns in their simplest forms now will help you successfully assess and organize any kind of complex writing assignment you may face in the future.

8

Exposition

Exposition refers to prose whose primary purpose is giving information. Some familiar examples of expository writing include encyclopedias, dictionaries, news magazines, and textbooks. In addition, much of your own college work may be classified as exposition: book reports, political analyses, lesson plans, laboratory and business reports, and most essay exams, to cite only a few of the possibilities.

But while all expository writing does present information, a good expository essay is more than a collection of facts, figures, and details. First, each essay should contain a thesis statement announcing the writer's purpose and position. Then the essay should be organized so that the body paragraphs explain and support that thesis. In an expository essay the writer says, in effect, here are the facts *as I see them;* therefore, the writer's main purpose is not only to inform the readers but also to convince them that this essay explains the subject matter in the clearest, most truthful way.

THE STRATEGIES OF EXPOSITION

There are a variety of ways to organize an expository essay, depending upon your purpose. The most common strategies, or patterns, of organization include development by *example, process analysis, comparison and contrast, definition, classification,* and *casual analysis.* However, an essay is rarely developed completely by a single strategy (an essay developed by comparison and contrast, for instance, may also contain examples; a classification essay may contain definitions, and so forth); therefore, as in the case of the four modes, we identify the kind of expository essay by its *primary* strategy of development. To help you understand every expository strategy thoroughly before going on to the next, each is presented here separately. Each discussion section follows a similar pattern, which includes the definition of the strategy, some familiar examples, tips on developing your essay, warnings about common problems, a list of essay topics, a revision worksheet, and two sample essays—one written by a student and the other by a professional writer.

STRATEGY ONE: DEVELOPMENT BY EXAMPLE

Perhaps you've heard a friend complain lately about a roommate. "Tina is an inconsiderate boor, impossible to live with," she cries. Your natural response might be to question your friend's rather broad accusation: "What makes her so terrible? What does she do that's so bad?" Your friend might then respond with specific examples of Tina's insensitivity: she never washes her dishes, she ties up the telephone for hours, and she plays her stereo until three every morning. By citing several examples, your friend clarifies and supports her general criticism of Tina, thus persuading you to accept her point of view.

Examples in an essay work precisely the same way as in the hypothetical story above: they *support, clarify, interest,* and *persuade.*

In your writing assignments, you might want to assert that dorm food is cruel and inhuman punishment, that recycling is a profitable hobby, or that the cost of housing is rising dramatically. But without some carefully chosen examples to show the truth of your statements, these remain unsupported generalities or mere opinions. Your task, then, is to provide enough specific examples to support your general statements, to make them both clear and convincing. Below is a statement offering the reader only hazy generalities:

Our locally supported T.V. channel presents a variety of excellent educational shows. The shows are informative on lots of different subjects for both children and adults. The information they offer makes channel 19 well worth the public funds that support it.

Rewritten below, the same paragraph explains its point clearly through the use of specific examples:

Our locally supported T.V. channel presents a variety of excellent educational shows. For example, young children can learn their alphabet and numbers from *Sesame Street;* imaginative older children can be encouraged to create by watching *Kids' Writes,* a show on which four hosts read and act out stories written and sent in by youngsters from eight to fourteen. Adults may enjoy learning about antiques and collectibles from a program called *The Collector;* each week the show features an in-depth look at buying, selling, trading, and displaying collectible items, from Depression glass to teddy bears to Shaker furniture. Those folks wishing to become handy around the home can use information on repairs from plumbing to wiring on *This Old House*, while the nonmusical can learn the difference between skat singing and arias on such programs as *Jazz!* and *Opera Today.* And the money-minded can profit from the tips dropped by stockbrokers who appear on *Wall Street Week.* The information offered makes these and other educational shows on channel 19 well worth the public funds that support the station.

Although the preceding example is based on real shows, you may also use personal experiences, hypothetical situations, anecdotes, research material, facts, testimony, or any combination thereof, to explain or support the points in your essays.

You may also find that in some cases, one long, detailed example (called an *extended example*) is more useful than several brief examples. If you were writing a paragraph urging the traffic department to install a stop sign at a particularly dangerous corner, you probably should cite numerous examples of accidents there. On the other hand, if you were praising a certain kind of local architecture, you might select one representative house and discuss it in detail. In the paragraph below, for instance, the writer might have supported his main point by citing a number of cases in which lives had been saved by Citizens' Band radios; he chose instead to offer one detailed example, in the form of a personal experience:

Although some people think of a Citizens' Band radio as an expensive toy or merely a gadget to outwit the local highway patrol, a C.B. radio can be, and frequently is, a life-saving device. Last year, for example, I used my C.B. to summon help for my seriously ill grandfather, who might have died had the radio not been working. We had gone out into the country to see a rarely visited relative; late that night, coming back, we took the wrong ranch road and became completely lost. About that time, my grandfather began to gasp and complain of terrible pain in his left arm and chest. I quickly recognized the symptoms of a heart attack and sprang to my car's radio. Within moments I had raised several nearby ranchers, who figured out where we were from the description I gave of the landmarks around us. Help arrived shortly thereafter, and my grandfather was taken to the nearest hospital, where he recovered. Thanks to the C.B. radio, a tragedy was averted.

The story of the grandfather's rescue illustrates the writer's claim that C.B. radios can save lives; without such an example, the writer's statement would be only an unsupported generalization.

In addition to making general statements specific and thus more convincing, good examples can explain and clarify unfamiliar, abstract, or difficult concepts for the reader. For instance, Newton's law of gravity might be more easily understood once it is explained through the simple, familiar example of an apple falling from a tree.

Moreover, clear examples can add to your prose vivid details that hold the reader's attention while you explain your points. A general statement decrying animal abuse, for instance, may be more effective accompanied by several examples detailing the brutal treatment of one particular laboratory's research animals.

The use of good examples is not, however, limited only to essays primarily developed by example. In actuality, you will probably use examples in every essay you write. You couldn't, for instance, write an essay classifying kinds of popular movies without including examples to help identify your categories. Similarly, you couldn't write essays defining the characteristics of a good teacher or a comparison between two kinds of cars without ample use of specific examples. To illustrate the importance of examples in all patterns of essay development, here are two excerpts from student essays reprinted in other parts of this text. The first excerpt comes from an essay classifying the Indian eras at Mesa Verde National Park, (pp. 186–188). In his discussion of a particular time period, the writer uses a dwelling called Balcony House as an example to illustrate his claims about the Indians' new skills in building construction.

The third period lasted until A.D. 1300 and saw the innovation of pueblos, or groups of dwellings, instead of single-family units. Nearly eight hundred dwellings show the large number of people who inhabited the complex, tunneled houses, shops, storage rooms, courtyards, and community centers whose masonry walls, often elaborately decorated, were three and four stories high. At the spacious Balcony House pueblo, for example, an adobe court lies beneath another vaulted roof; on three sides stand two-story houses with balconies that lead from one room to the next. In back of the court is a spring, and along the front side is a low wall that kept the children from falling down the seven-hundred-foot cliff to the canyon floor below. Balcony House also contains two *kivas*, circular subterranean ceremonial chambers that show the importance of fellowship and religion to the Indians of this era.

Another student uses a personal example to help her support a point in her essay that contrasts a local co-op to a big chain grocery store (pp. 163–165). By using her friend's experience as an example, the writer shows the reader how a co-op may assist local producers in the community:

Direct selling offers two advantages for producers: they get a better price for their wares than by selling them through a middleman, and at the same time they establish an independent reputation for their business, which can be immensely valuable to their success later on. In Fort Collins, for example, Luna tofu (bean curd) stands out as an excellent illustration of this kind of mutual support. Several years ago my friend Carol Jones began making tofu in small batches to sell to the co-op as a way to earn a part-time income as well as to contribute to the co-op. Her enterprise has now grown so well that last year her husband quit his job to go into business with her full time. She currently sells to distributors and independent stores from here to Denver; even Lane Grocer, who earlier would not consider selling her tofu even on a trial basis, is now thinking about changing its policy.

Learning to support, explain, or clarify your assertions by clear, thoughtful examples will help you develop virtually every piece of writing you are assigned, both in school and on the job. Development by example is the most widely used of all the expository strategies and by far the most important.

Developing Your Essay

An essay developed by example is one of the easiest to organize. In most cases, your first paragraph will present your thesis; each body paragraph will contain a topic sentence and as many effectively arranged examples as necessary to explain or support each major point; your last paragraph will conclude your essay in some appropriate way. Although the general organization is fairly simple, you should double-check the examples in your rough draft by asking these questions:

Are all my examples relevant? Each specific example should support, clarify, or explain the general statement it illustrates; each example should provide the reader with additional insight into the subject under discussion. Keep the purpose of your paragraphs in mind: don't wander off into an analysis of the causes of crime if you are only supposed to show examples of it in your neighborhood.

Are my examples well chosen? To persuade your reader to accept your opinion, you should select those examples that are the strongest and most convincing. Let's say you were writing a research paper exposing a government agency's history of wastefulness. To illustrate your claim, you would pick out those cases that most obviously show gross or ridiculous expenditures, rather than asking your readers to consider some unnecessary but minor expenses. In other words, when you have a number of examples, analyze them and then select the best ones to support your point.

Are there enough examples to make each point clear and persuasive? Put yourself in your reader's place: would you be convinced with three brief examples? Five? One extended example? Two? Use your own judgment, but be careful to support or explain your major points adequately. It's better to risk overexplaining than to leave your reader confused or unconvinced.

Problems to Avoid

The most common weakness in essays developed by example is a lack of specific detail. Too often novice writers present a sufficient number of relevant, well-chosen examples, but the illustrations themselves are too general, vague, or brief to be helpful. Examples should be clear, specific, and adequately detailed so that the reader receives the full persuasive impact of each one. For instance, in an essay claiming that college football has become too violent, don't merely say: "Too many players got hurt last year." Such a statement only hints; it lacks enough development to be fully effective. Go into more detail by giving the readers examples of jammed fingers, wrenched backs, bruised legs, broken kneecaps, and busted dreams. Present these examples in specific, vivid language; once your readers begin to "see" that field covered with blood and broken bodies, you'll have less trouble convincing them that your point of view is accurate.

The second biggest problem in example essays is the lack of coherence. The reader should never sense an interruption in the flow of thought from one example to the next in paragraphs containing more than one example. Each body paragraph of this kind should be more than a topic sentence and a choppy list of examples. You should first arrange the examples in an order that best explains the major point presented by your topic sentence; then carefully check to make sure each example is smoothly connected in thought to the statements preceding and following it. You can avoid a listing effect by using transition devices where necessary to ensure easy movement from example to example and from point to point. A few common transition words often found in essays of example include "for instance," "for example," "to illustrate," "in particular," and "in addition." (For a list of other transition words and additional help on writing coherent paragraphs, review pp. 50–55.)

Essay Topics

Use the statements below to lead you to your essay topic. Be sure to narrow these suggestions as you focus your thesis.

1. Heroes today are merely media creations rather than truly admirable people.
2. First impressions are often the best/worst means of judging people.
3. Failure is a better teacher than success.

4. My fear of flying (or whatever) prevents me from living a normal life.
5. The willingness to undertake adventure is a necessary part of a happy life.
6. Doing good deeds can backfire.
7. Complaining can produce unforeseen results.
8. Travel can be the best medicine.
9. Consumers are often at the mercy of unscrupulous companies.
10. Visits to the doctor/dentist/vet often prove more traumatic than the illness.
11. Failure to keep my mouth shut (or some other bad habit) gets me into trouble.
12. Success involves sacrifice.
13. Modern technology often produces more inconvenience than convenience.
14. Job hunting today is a difficult process.
15. Science fiction writers often accurately predict the future.
16. My hometown was a terrible/wonderful place to grow up.
17. Many required courses are/are not relevant to a student's education.
18. My high school did/did not adequately prepare me for college.
19. The most popular attitude among students today is "I'm apathetic, and I don't care."
20. Fad diets can have harmful results.

Sample Student Essay

Study the use of specific examples in the brief student essay that follows. See if you can identify the transition devices that help move the reader from point to point and from example to example.

RIVER RAFTING TEACHES WORTHWHILE LESSONS

Introduction: A description

Thesis

Essay map

Sun-warmed water slaps you in the face, the blazing sun beats down on your shoulders, and canyon walls speed by as you race down rolling waves of water. No experience can equal that of river rafting. Along with being fun and exciting, rafting has many educational advantages as well, especially for those involved in school-sponsored rafting trips. River trips teach students how to prevent some of the environmental destruction that concerns the park officials and, in addition, river trips also teach students to work together in a way few other experiences can.

Topic sentence one:
Trip teaches respect
for environment

The most important lesson a rafting trip teaches students is respect for the environment. When students are exposed to the outdoors, they can better learn to appreciate its beauty and feel the need to preserve it. For example, I went on a rafting trip three summers ago with the biology department at my high school. Our trip lasted seven days down the Green River through the isolated Desolation Canyon in Utah. After the first day of rafting, I found myself surrounded by steep canyon walls and saw virtually no evidence of human life. The starkly beautiful, unspoiled atmosphere soon became a major influence on us during the trip.

Two examples of
respect:
1. cleaning up trash
2. foregoing suds
   in river

By the second day I saw classmates, whom I had previously seen fill an entire room with candy wrappers and empty soda cans, voluntarily inspecting our campsite for trash. And when twenty-four high school students sacrifice washing their hair for the sake of a sudless and thus healthier river, some new, better attitudes about the environment have definitely been established.

Topic sentence two:
The trip teaches
cooperation

In addition to the respect for nature a rafting trip encourages, it also teaches the importance of group cooperation. Since school-associated trips put students in command of the raft, the students find that in order to stay in control each member must be reliable, able to do his or her own part, and alert to the actions of others. These skills are quickly learned when students see the consequences of noncooperation. Usually this occurs the first day, when the left side of the raft paddles in one direction, and the right the other way, and half the crew ends up seasick from going in circles. An even better illustration is another experience I had on my river trip. Because an upcoming rapid was usually not too rough, our instructor said a few of us

Two examples of
noncooperation:
1. difficulties in
   paddling raft
2. a near accident

could jump out and swim in it. Instead of deciding as a group who should go, though, five eager swimmers bailed out. This left me, an angry instructor, and another student to steer the raft. As it turned out, the rapid was fairly rough, and we soon found ourselves heading straight for a huge hole (a hole is formed from swirling funnel-like currents and can pull a raft under). The combined effort of the three of us was not enough to get the raft completely clear of the hole, and the raft tipped up vertically on its side, spilling us into the river. Luckily, no one was hurt, and the raft did not topple over, but the near loss of our food rations for the next five days, not to mention the raft itself, was enough to make us all more willing to work as a group in the future.

Conclusion:
Importance of lessons
Despite the obvious benefits rafting offers, the number of river permits issued to school groups continues to decline because of financial cutbacks. It is a shame that those in charge of these cutbacks do not realize that in addition to having fun and learning about themselves, students are learning valuable lessons through rafting trips—lessons that may help preserve the rivers for future rafters.

Professional Essay

SO WHAT'S SO BAD ABOUT BEING SO-SO?

Lisa Wilson Strick

Lisa Wilson Strick is a freelance writer who publishes in a variety of women's magazines, frequently on the subjects of family and education. This essay first appeared in *Woman's Day* in 1984.

THE OTHER AFTERNOON I was playing the piano when my seven-year-old walked in. He stopped and listened awhile, then said: "Gee, Mom, you don't play that thing very well, do you?" 1

No, I don't. I am a piano lesson dropout. The fine points of fingering totally escape me. I play everything at half-speed, with many errant notes. My performance would make any serious music student wince, but I don't care. I've enjoyed playing the piano badly for years. 2

I also enjoy singing badly and drawing badly. (I used to enjoy sewing badly, but I've been doing that so long that I finally got pretty good at it.) I'm not ashamed of my incompetence in these areas. I do one or two other things well and that should be enough for anybody. But it gets boring doing the same things over and over. Every now and then it's fun to try something new. 3

Unfortunately, doing things badly has gone out of style. It used to be a mark of class if a lady or a gentleman sang a little, painted a little, played the violin a little. You didn't have to be *good* at it; the point was to be fortunate enough to have the leisure time for such pursuits. But in today's competitive world we have to be "experts"—even in our hobbies. You can't tone up your body by pulling on your sneakers and slogging around the block a couple of times anymore. Why? Because you'll be laughed off the street by the "serious" runners—the ones who log twenty-plus miles a week in their headbands, sixty-dollar running suits and fancy shoes. The shoes are really a big deal. If you say you're thinking about taking up almost any sport, the first thing the aficionados will ask is what you plan to do about shoes. Leather or canvas? What type of soles? Which brand? This is not the time to mention that the gym shoes you wore in high school are still in pretty good shape. As far as sports enthusiasts are concerned, if you don't have the latest shoes you are hopelessly committed to mediocrity. 4

The runners aren't nearly so snobbish as the dance freaks, however. In case   5
you didn't know, "going dancing" no longer means putting on a pretty dress and
doing a few turns around the ballroom with your favorite man on Saturday night.
"Dancing" means squeezing into tights and a leotard and leg warmers, then sweat-
ing through six hours of warm-ups and five hours of ballet and four hours of jazz
classes. Every week. Never tell anyone that you "like to dance" unless this is the
sort of activity you enjoy. (At least the costume isn't so costly, as dancers seem to
be cultivating a riches-to-rags look lately.)

We used to do these things for fun or simply to relax. Now the competition   6
you face in your hobbies is likely to be worse than anything you run into on the
job. "Oh, you've taken up knitting," a friend recently said to me. "Let me show
you the adorable cable-knit, popcorn-stitched cardigan with twelve tiny reindeer
prancing across the yoke that I made for my daughter. I dyed the yarn myself."
Now why did she have to go and do that? I was getting a kick out of watching my
yellow stockinette muffler grow a couple of inches a week up till then. And all I
wanted was something to keep my hands busy while I watched television anyway.

Have you noticed what this is doing to our children? "We don't want that dodo   7
on our soccer team," I overheard a ten-year-old sneer the other day. "He doesn't
know a goal kick from a head shot." As it happens, the boy was talking about my
son, who did not—like some of his friends—start soccer instruction at age three
(along with preschool diving, creative writing and Suzuki clarinet). I'm sorry, Son, I
guess I blew it. In *my* day when we played softball on the corner lot, we expected
to give a little instruction to the younger kids who didn't know how. It didn't matter
if they were terrible; we weren't out to slaughter the other team. Sometimes we
didn't even keep score. To us, sports were just a way of having a *good time.* Of
course we didn't have some of the nifty things kids have today—such as matching
uniforms and professional coaches. All we had was a bunch of kids of various ages
who enjoyed each other's company.

I don't think kids have as much fun as they used to. Competition keeps getting   8
in the way. The daughter of a neighbor is a nervous wreck worrying about getting
into the *best* gymnastics school. "I was a late starter," she told me, "and I only get
to practice five or six hours a week, so my technique may not be up to their standards." The child is nine. She doesn't want to *be* a gymnast when she grows up;
she wants to be a nurse. I asked what she likes to do for fun in her free time. She
seemed to think it was an odd question. "Well, I don't actually *have* a lot of free
time," she said. "I mean homework and gymnastics and flute lessons kind of eat it
all up. I have flute lessons three times a week now, so I have a good shot at getting
into the all-state orchestra."

Ambition, drive and the desire to excel are all admirable within limits, but I   9
don't know where the limits are anymore. I know a woman who has always wanted
to learn a foreign language. For years she has complained that she hasn't the time
to study one. I've pointed out that an evening course in French or Italian would
take only a couple of hours a week, but she keeps putting it off. I suspect that what
she hasn't got the time for is to become completely fluent within the year—and
that any lesser level of accomplishment would embarrass her. Instead she spends

her evenings watching reruns on television and tidying up her closets—occupations at which no particular expertise is expected.

I know others who are avoiding activities they might enjoy because they lack   10
the time or the energy to tackle them "seriously." It strikes me as so silly. We are talking about *recreation*. I have nothing against self-improvement. But when I hear a teenager muttering "practice makes perfect" as he grimly makes his four-hundred-and-twenty-seventh try at hooking the basketball into the net left-handed, I wonder it some of us aren't improving ourselves right into the loony bin.

I think it's time we put a stop to all this. For sanity's sake, each of us should   11
vow to take up something new this week—and to make sure we never master it completely. Sing along with grand opera. Make peculiar-looking objects out of clay. I can tell you from experience that fallen soufflés still taste pretty good. The point is to enjoy being a beginner again; to rediscover the joy of creative fooling around. If you find it difficult, ask any two-year-old to teach you. Two-year-olds have a gift for tackling the impossible with zest; repeated failure hardly discourages them at all.

As for me, I'm getting a little out of shape so I'm looking into tennis. A lot of   12
people I know enjoy it, and it doesn't look too hard. Given a couple of lessons I should be stumbling gracelessly around the court and playing badly in no time at all.

Questions on Content, Structure, and Style

1. Why does Strick begin her essay with the comment from her son and the list of activities she does badly?
2. What is Strick's thesis? Is it specifically stated or clearly implied?
3. What examples does Strick offer to illustrate her belief that we no longer take up hobbies for fun? Are there enough well-chosen examples to make her position clear?
4. What is the effect, according to Strick, of too much competition on kids? In what ways does she show this effect?
5. What does Strick gain by using dialogue in some of her examples?
6. Why does Strick include the example of the woman who wants to learn a foreign language?
7. Does Strick use enough details in her examples to make them clear, vivid, and persuasive? Point out some of her details to support your answer.
8. What solution to the problem does Strick offer? How does she clarify her suggestion?
9. Characterize the tone of Strick's essay. Is it appropriate for her purpose and for her intended audience? Why/why not?
10. Evaluate Strick's conclusion. Does it effectively wrap up the essay?

Vocabulary

errant (2)	excel (9)
incompetence (3)	fluent (9)
aficionados (4)	zest (11)
mediocrity (4)	

A Revision Worksheet for Your Example Essay

As you write your rough drafts, consult Chapter 5 for guidance through the revision process. In addition, here are a few questions to ask yourself as you revise your example essay:

1. Is the essay's thesis clear to the reader?
2. Do the topic sentences support the thesis?
3. Do the examples in each paragraph effectively illustrate the claim of the topic sentence?
4. Are there enough well-chosen examples to make each point clear and convincing?
5. Is each example developed in enough specific detail? Where could more details be added?
6. If a paragraph contains multiple examples, are they arranged in the most effective order, with smooth transition from one to another?
7. If a paragraph contains an extended example, does the action flow logically and with coherence?

After you've revised your essay extensively, you might exchange rough drafts with a classmate and answer these questions for each other, making specific suggestions for improvement wherever appropriate.

STRATEGY TWO: DEVELOPMENT BY PROCESS ANALYSIS

Process analysis identifies and explains what steps must be taken to complete an operation or procedure. There are two kinds of process analysis essays: directional and informative.

A *directional process* tells the reader how to do or make something; in other words, it gives directions. You are more familiar with directional process than you might think; when you open a telephone book, for example, you see the pages in the front explaining how to make a long-distance call. When you tell friends how to find your house, you're asking them to follow a directional process. The most widely read books in American libraries fall into the how-to-do-it (or how-to-fix-it) category: how to wire a house, how to repair a car, how to play winning poker, how to become a millionaire overnight, and so forth. And almost every home contains at least one cookbook full of recipes providing step-by-step directions for preparing various dishes. (Even Part One of this text is, in detailed fashion, a directional process telling how to write a short essay, with steps beginning with the selection of a topic and concluding with advice on revision.)

An *informative process* tells the reader how something is or was made or done, or how something works. Informative process differs from directional process in that it is not designed primarily to tell people how to do it; instead, it describes the steps by which someone other than the reader does or makes something (or how something was made or done in the past). For example, an informative process essay might describe how a television show is produced, how scientists discovered polio vaccine, how you chose your major in college, how the Huns sacked Rome, or how an engine propels a tank. In other words, this type of essay gives information on processes that are not intended to be—or cannot be—duplicated by the individual reader.

Developing Your Essay

Of all the expository essays, students usually agree that the process paper is the easiest to organize, mainly because it is presented in simple, chronological steps. To prepare a well-written process essay, however, you should remember the following advice:

Select an appropriate subject. First, make sure you know your subject thoroughly; one fuzzy step could wreck your entire process. Second, choose a process that is simple and short enough to describe in detail. In a 500–800 word essay, for instance, it's better to describe how to fold a paper boat for a child's toy than to try telling how to construct a life-size replica of Noah's Ark. On the other hand, don't choose a process so simple-minded, mundane, or mechanical that it insults your readers' intelligence. (Ten years ago at a major state university it was popular to assign a process essay on "How To Sharpen a Pencil"; with the assignment of such stirring, creative topics, it's a wonder that English department produced any majors at all that year.)

Describe any necessary equipment and define special terms. In some process essays, you will need to indicate what equipment, ingredients, or tools are required. Such information is often provided in a paragraph following the thesis, before the process itself is described; in other cases, explanation of proper equipment is presented as the need arises in each step of the process. As the writer, you must decide which method is best for your subject. The same is true for any terms that need defining. Don't lose your reader by using terms only you, the specialist, can comprehend. Always remember that you're trying to tell people about a process they don't understand.

State your steps in a logical, chronological order. Obviously, if someone wanted to know how to bake bread, you wouldn't begin with "Put the prepared dough in the oven." Start at the beginning and carefully follow through, step by step, until the process is completed. Don't omit any steps or directions, no matter how seemingly insignificant. Without complete instructions, for example, the would-be baker might end up with a gob of dough rather than a loaf of bread—simply because the directions didn't say to preheat the oven.

Explain each step clearly, sufficiently, and accurately. If you've ever tried to assemble a child's toy or a piece of furniture, you probably already know how frustrating—and infuriating—it is to work from vague, inadequate directions. Save your readers from tears and tantrums by describing each step in your process as clearly as possible. Use enough specific details to distinguish one step from another. As the readers finish each step, they should know how the subject matter is supposed to look, feel, smell, taste, or sound at that stage of the process. You might also explain why each step is necessary ("Cutting back the young avocado stem is necessary to prevent a spindly plant." "Senator Snort then had to win over the chairman of the Arms Committee to be sure his bill would go to the Senate floor for a vote"). In some cases, especially in directional processes, it's helpful to give warnings ("When you begin tightrope walking, the condition of your shoes is critical; be careful the soles are not slick") or descriptions of errors and how to rectify them ("If you pass a white church, you've gone a block too far; turn right at the church and circle back on Candle Lane." "If the sauce appears gray and thick, add one teaspoon more of cornstarch until the gravy is white and bubbly").

Organize your steps effectively. If you have a few big steps in your process, you probably will devote a paragraph to each one. On the other hand, if you have several small steps, you should organize them into a few manageable units. For example, in an essay on "How to Prepare Fresh Fish" the list of small steps on the left has been grouped into three larger units, each of which becomes a body paragraph:

1. scaling	I. Cleaning
2. beheading	A. scaling
3. gutting	B. beheading
4. washing	C. gutting
5. seasoning	II. Cooking
6. breading	A. washing
7. frying	B. seasoning

8. draining	C. breading
9. portioning	D. frying
10. garnishing	III. Serving
	A. draining
	B. portioning
	C. garnishing

In addition, don't forget to use enough transition devices between steps to avoid the effect of a mechanical list. Some frequently used linking words in process essays include the following:

next	first, second, third, etc.
then	at this point
now	following
to begin	when
finally	at last
before	afterward

Vary your transition words sufficiently so that your steps are not linked by a monotonous repetition of "and then" or "next."

Problems to Avoid

Don't forget to include a thesis. You already know, of course, that every essay needs a thesis, but the advice bears repeating here because for some reason some writers often omit the statement in their process essays. Your thesis might be (a) your reason for presenting this process—why you feel it's important or necessary for the readers to know ("Because rescue squads often arrive too late, every adult should know how to give artificial respiration to accident victims") or (b) an assertion about the nature of the process itself ("Needlepoint is a simple, restful, fun hobby for both men and women"). Here are some other subjects and sample theses:

- Donating blood is not the painful process one might suspect.
- The raid on Pearl Harbor wasn't altogether unexpected.
- Returning to school as an older-than-average student isn't as difficult as it may look.
- Sponsoring a five-mile run can be a fun way for your club or student organization to raise money for local charities.
- Challenging a speeding ticket is a time-consuming, energy-draining, but financially rewarding endeavor.
- The series of public protests that led to the return of the traditional Coca-Cola was an unparalleled success in the history of American consumerism.

Presenting a thesis and referring to it in each step gives your essay unity and coherence, as well as ensuring against a monotonous list of steps.

Pay special attention to your conclusion. Don't allow your essay to grind to an abrupt halt after the final step. You might conclude the essay by telling the significance of the completed process or by explaining other uses it may have. Or, if it is appropriate, finish your essay with an amusing story or comment. However you conclude, leave the reader with a feeling of satisfaction, with a sense of having completed an interesting procedure. (For more information on writing good conclusions, see pp. 68–70.)

Essay Topics

Below are suggested topics for both directional and informative process essays. Some of the topics may also be used in humorous essays such as "How to Flunk a Test," "How to Remain a Bench Warmer," or "How to Say Nothing in Eight-Hundred Words."

1. how to stop smoking (or break some other habit)
2. how to select a college course or major
3. how to begin a collection or hobby
4. how to buy a computer
5. how to save money
6. how to meet the person of your dreams
7. how something in nature works or was formed
8. how a company sells a product
9. how a piece of equipment or a machine works
10. how to cure a cold or hangover
11. how to lose or gain weight
12. how you arrived at a major decision
13. how to select a car (new or used), house, apartment, roommate, spouse
14. how to vacation on five dollars a day
15. how a famous invention occurred
16. how to get rid of roaches or other pests (human or otherwise)
17. how to succeed or fail in a job interview
18. how to repair some small item
19. how to plan the perfect party, wedding, funeral, birthday, etc.
20. how a historial event occurred

Sample Student Essay

The essay below is a directional process telling readers how to put on a successful garage sale. To make the instructions clear and enjoyable, the writer adopted a chronological order and used many specific examples, details, and warnings.

CATCHING GARAGE SALE FEVER

Introduction: A series of questions to hook the reader

Ever need some easy money fast? To repay those incredible overdue library fines you ran up writing your last research paper? Or to raise money for that much-needed vacation to old Mexico you put on credit cards last Spring Break? Or maybe you feel you simply have to clear out some junk before the piles block the remaining sunlight from your windows? Whether the problem is cash flow or trash flow, you can solve it easily by holding what is fast becoming an All-American sport: the weekend garage sale.

Thesis

As a veteran of some half-dozen successful ventures, I can testify that garage sales are the easiest way to make quick money, with a minimum of physical labor and the maximum of fun.

Step One: Taking inventory

Most garage sale "experts" start getting ready at least two weeks before the sale by taking inventory. Look through your closets and junk drawers to see if you actually have enough items to make a sale worthwhile. If all you have is a mass of miscellaneous small items, think about waiting or joining a friend's sale, because you do need at least a couple of larger items (furniture is always a big seller) to draw customers initially. Also, consider whether the season is appropriate for your items; sun dresses and shorts, for example, sell better in the spring and summer; coats and boots in the fall. As you collect your items, don't underestimate the "saleability" of some of your junk—the hideous purple china bulldog Aunt Clara gave you for Christmas five years ago may be perfect for someone's Ugly Mutt Collection.

Step Two: Deciding when and where

As you sort through your junk closets, begin thinking about the time and place of your sale. First, decide if you want a one- or two-day sale. If you opt for only one day, Saturdays are generally best because most people are free that day. Plan to start early—by 8 A.M. if possible—because the experienced buyers get up and get going so they can hit more sales that way. Unless you have nothing else to do that day, plan to end your sale by mid-afternoon; most people have run out of buying energy (or money) by 3 P.M. Deciding on the location of your sale depends, of course, on your housing situation, but you still might need to make some choices. For instance, do you want to put your items out in a driveway, a backyard, or actually in the garage (weather might affect this decision)? Or perhaps a side yard gets more passers-by? Wherever you decide, be sure that there are plenty of places for customers to park close by without blocking your neighbors' driveways.

Step Three: Advertising the sale

Unless you live in a very small town or on a very busy street, you'll probably want to place an inexpensive ad in the "garage sale" column of your local newspaper that is scheduled to run a day or two before, and the day of, your sale. Your ad should tell the times and place of the sale (give brief directions or mention landmarks if the location is hard to find) as well as a brief list of some of your items. Few people will turn out for "household goods" alone; some popular items include bookcases, antiques, books, fans, jewelry, toys, baby equipment, and name-brand clothes. One other piece of advice about the ad copy: it

A warning

should include the phrase "no early sales" unless you want to be awakened at 6:30 A.M., as I was one Saturday, by a bunch of semi-pro garage sale buyers milling restlessly around in your yard, looking like zombies out of a George Romero horror movie. In addition to your newspaper ad, you may also wish to put up posters in places frequented by lots of people; laundromats and grocery stores often have bulletin boards for such announcements. You can also put up signs on nearby well-traveled streets, but one warn-

Another warning

ing: in some towns it's illegal to post anything on utility poles or traffic signs, so be sure to check your local ordinances first.

Step Four: Pricing the merchandise

Tagging your items with their prices is the least fun, and it can take a day or a week depending on how many items you have and how much time each day you can devote to the project. You can buy sheets of little white stickers or use pieces of masking tape to stick on the prices, but if you want to save time, consider grouping some items and selling them all for the same price—all shirts, for example, are 50¢. Be realistic about your prices; the hand-crafted rug from Greece may have been expensive and important to you, but to others, it's a worn doormat. Some experts suggest pricing your articles at about one-fourth their original value, unless you have special reasons not to (an antique or popular collectors' item, for instance, may be more valuable now than when you bought it). Remember that you can always come down on your prices if someone is interested in a particular item.

Step Five: Setting up
your sale

A note on equipment

By the day before your sale you should have all your items clean and tagged. One of the beauties of a garage sale is that there's very little equipment to collect. You'll need tables, benches, or boards supported by bricks to display your goods; a rope tied from side to side of your garage can double as a clothes rack. Try to spread out your merchandise rather than dumping articles in deep boxes; no customer wants to feel like a baglady rummaging through a trash barrel. Most importantly, you'll need a chair and a table to hold some sort of money box, preferably one with a lock. The afternoon before the sale, take a trip to the bank if you need to, to make sure you have enough one-dollar bills and coins to make plenty of change. The evening before the sale, set up your items on your display benches in the garage or indoors near the site of your sale so that you can quickly set things out in the morning. Get a good night's sleep so you can get up to open on time: the early bird does get the sales in this business.

Step Six: Running the
sale

The sale itself is, of course, the real fun. Half the enjoyment is haggling with the customers, so be prepared to joke and visit with the shoppers. Watching the different kinds of people who show up is also a kick—you can get a cross-section from college students on a tight budget to harried mothers toting four kids to real eccentrics in fancy cars who will argue about the price of a 75¢ item (if you're a creative writer, don't forget to take notes for your next novel!). If the action slows in the afternoon, you can resort to a half-price or two-for-one sale by posting a large sign to that effect; many shoppers can't resist a sale at a sale!

Step Seven: Closing
up

By late afternoon you should be richer and junk-free, at least to some extent. If you do have items left after the half-price sale, decide whether you want to box them up for the next sale or drop them by a charitable organization such as Goodwill (some organizations will even pick up your donations; others have convenient drop boxes). After you've taken your articles inside, don't forget to take down any signs you've posted in the neighborhood; old withered garage sale signs fluttering in the breeze are an eyesore. Last, sit down and count your profits, so you can go out in the evening to celebrate a successful business venture.

Conclusion: A
summary of the
benefits and a
humorous warning

The money you make is, of course, the biggest incentive for having one or two sales a year. But the combination of money, clean closets, and memories of the characters you meet can be irresistible. Garage sales can rapidly get in your blood; once you hold a successful one, you're tempted to have another as soon as the junk starts to mount up. And having sales somehow leads to attending them too, as it becomes fun to see what other folks are selling at bargain prices. So be forewarned: you too can be transformed into a garage sale junkie, complete with a now-popular car bumper sticker that proudly proclaims to the world: "Caution! I brake for garage sales"!

Professional Essay

TO BID THE WORLD FAREWELL
Jessica Mitford

Jessica Mitford has written many articles and books, including *Daughters* and *Rebels, The Trial of Doctor Spock,* and *Kind and Unusual Punishment,* a critical study of the American penal system. This essay is an excerpt from her best-selling book *The American Way of Death.*

EMBALMING is indeed a most extraordinary procedure, and one must wonder at   1
the docility of Americans who each year pay hundreds of millions of dollars for its perpetuation, blissfully ignorant of what it is all about, what is done, how it is done. Not one in ten thousand has any idea of what actually takes place. Books on the subject are extremely hard to come by. They are not to be found in most libraries or bookshops.

In an era when huge television audiences watch surgical operations in the com-   2
fort of their living rooms, when, thanks to the animated cartoon, the geography of the digestive system has become familiar territory even to the nursery school set, and in land where the satisfaction of curiosity about almost all matters is a national pastime, the secrecy surrounding embalming can, surely, hardly be attributed to the inherent gruesomeness of the subject. Custom in this regard has within this century suffered a complete reversal. In the early days of American embalming, when it was performed in the home of the deceased, it was almost mandatory for some relative to stay by the embalmer's side and witness the procedure. Today, family members who might wish to be in attendance would certainly be dissuaded by the funeral director. All others, except apprentices, are excluded by law from the preparation room.

A close look at what does actually take place may explain in large measure   3
the undertaker's intractable reticence concerning a procedure that has become his major *raison d'être.* Is it possible he fears that public information about embalming might lead patrons to wonder if they really want this service? If the funeral men are loath to discuss the subject outside the trade, the reader may, understandably,

---

be equally loath to go on reading at this point. For those who have the stomach for it, let us part the formaldehyde curtain. . . .

The body is first laid out in the undertaker's morgue—or rather, Mr. Jones is 4
reposing in the preparation room—to be readied to bid the world farewell.

The preparation room in any of the better funeral establishments has the tiled 5
and sterile look of a surgery, and indeed the embalmer-restorative artist who does his chores there is beginning to adopt the term "dermasurgeon" (appropriately corrupted by some mortician-writers as "demisurgeon") to describe his calling. His equipment, consisting of scalpels, scissors, augers, forceps, clamps, needles, pumps, tubes, bowls and basins, is crudely imitative of the surgeon's as is his technique, acquired in a nine- or twelve-month post-high-school course in an embalming school. He is supplied by an advanced chemical industry with a bewildering array of fluids, sprays, pastes, oils, powders, creams, to fix or soften tissue, shrink or distend it as needed, dry it here, restore the moisture there. There are cosmetics, waxes and paints to fill and cover features, even plaster of Paris to replace entire limbs. There are ingenious aids to prop and stabilize the cadaver: a Vari-Pose Head Rest, the Edwards Arm and Hand Positioner, the Repose Block (to support the shoulders during the embalming), and the Throop Foot Positioner, which resembles an old-fashioned stocks.

Mr. John H. Eckels, president of the Eckels College of Mortuary Science, thus 6
describes the first part of the embalming procedure: "In the hands of a skilled practitioner, this work may be done in a comparatively short time and without mutilating the body other than by slight incision—so slight that it scarcely would cause serious inconvenience if made upon a living person. It is necessary to remove the blood, and doing this not only helps in the disinfecting, but removes the principal cause of disfigurement due to discoloration."

Another textbook discusses the all-important time element: "The earlier this is 7
done, the better, for every hour that elapses between death and embalming will add to the problems and complications encountered. . . ." Just how soon should one get going on the embalming? The author tells us, "On the basis of such scanty information made available to this profession through its rudimentary and haphazard system of technical research, we must conclude that the best results are to be obtained if the subject is embalmed before life is completely extinct—that is, before cellular death has occurred. In the average case, this would mean within an hour after somatic death." For those who feel that there is something a little rudimentary, not to say haphazard, about this advice, a comforting thought is offered by another writer. Speaking of fears entertained in early days of premature burial, he points out. "One of the effects of embalming by chemical injection, however, has been to dispel fears of live burial." How true; once the blood is removed, chances of live burial are indeed remote.

To return to Mr. Jones, the blood is drained out through the veins and replaced 8
by embalming fluid pumped in through the arteries. As noted in *The Principles and Practices of Embalming*, "every operator has a favorite injection and drainage point—a fact which becomes a handicap only if he fails or refuses to forsake his favorites when conditions demand it." Typical favorites are the carotid artery, femoral artery, jugular vein, subclavian vein. There are various choices of embalming

fluid. If Flextone is used, it will produce a "mild flexible rigidity. The skin retains a velvety softness, the tissues are rubbery and pliable. Ideal for women and children." It may be blended with B. and G. Products Company's Lyf-Lyk tint, which is guaranteed to reproduce "nature's own skin texture . . . the velvety appearance of living tissue." Suntone comes in three separate tints: Suntan; Special Cosmetic Tint, a pink shade "especially indicated for young female subjects"; and Regular Cosmetic Tint, moderately pink.

About three to six gallons of a dyed and perfumed solution of formaldehyde,   9
glycerin, borax, phenol, alcohol and water is soon circulating through Mr. Jones, whose mouth has been sewn together with a "needle directed upward between the upper lip and gum and brought out through the left nostril," with the corners raised slightly "for a more pleasant expression." If he should be bucktoothed, his teeth are cleaned with Bon Ami and coated with colorless nail polish. His eyes, meanwhile, are closed with flesh-tinted eye caps and eye cement.

The next step is to have at Mr. Jones with a thing called a trocar. This is a   10
long, hollow needle attached to a tube. It is jabbed into the abdomen, poked around the entrails and chest cavity, the contents of which are pumped out and replaced with "cavity fluid." This done, and the hole in the abdomen sewn up, Mr. Jones' face is heavily creamed (to protect the skin from burns which may be caused by leakage of the chemicals), and he is covered with a sheet and left unmolested for a while. But not for long—there is more, much more, in store for him. He has been embalmed, but not yet restored, and the best time to start the restorative work is eight to ten hours after embalming, when the tissues have become firm and dry.

The object of all this attention to the corpse, it must be remembered, is to make   11
it presentable for viewing in an attitude of healthy repose. "Our customs require the presentation of our dead in the semblance of normality . . . unmarred by the ravages of illness, disease or mutilation," syas Mr. J. Sheridan Mayer in his *Restorative* Art. This is rather a large order since few people die in the full bloom of health, unravaged by illness and unmarked by some disfigurement. The funeral industry is equal to the challenge: "In some cases the gruesome appearance of a mutilated or disease-ridden subject may be quite discouraging. The task of restoration may seem impossible and shake the confidence of the embalmer. This is the time for intestinal fortitude and determination. Once the formative work is begun and affected tissues are cleaned or removed, all doubts of success vanish. It is surprising and gratifying to discover the results which may be obtained."

The embalmer, having allowed an appropriate interval to elapse, returns to the   12
attack, but now he brings into play the skill and equipment of sculptor and cosmetician. Is a hand missing? Casting one in plaster of Paris is a simple matter. "For replacement purposes, only a cast of the back of the hand is necessary; this is within the ability of the average operator and is quite adequate." If a lip or two, a nose or an ear should be missing, the embalmer has at hand a variety of restorative waxes with which to model replacements. Pores and skin texture are simulated by stippling with a little brush, and over this cosmetics are laid on. Head off? Decapitation cases are rather routinely handled. Ragged edges are trimmed, and head joined to torso with a series of splints, wires and sutures. It is a good idea to have a little something at the neck—a scarf or high collar—when time for viewing

comes. Swollen mouth? Cut out tissue as needed from inside the lips. If too much is removed, the surface contour can easily be restored by padding with cotton. Swollen necks and cheeks are reduced by removing tissue through vertical incisions made down each side of the neck. "When the deceased is casketed, the pillow will hide the suture incisions . . . as an extra precaution against leakage, the suture may be painted with liquid sealer."

The opposite condition is more likely to present itself—that of emaciation. His hypodermic syringe now loaded with massage cream, the embalmer seeks out and fills the hollowed and sunken areas by injection. In this procedure the backs of the hands and fingers and the under-chin area should not be neglected. **13**

Positioning the lips is a problem that recurrently challenges the ingenuity of the embalmer. Closed too tightly, they tend to give a stern, even disapproving expression. Ideally, embalmers feel, the lips should give the impression of being ever so slightly parted, the upper lip protruding slightly for a more youthful appearance. This takes some engineering, however, as the lips tend to drift apart. Lip drift can sometimes be remedied by pushing one or two straight pins through the inner margin of the lower lip and then inserting them between the two front teeth. If Mr. Jones happens to have no teeth, the pins can just as easily be anchored in his Armstrong Face Former and Denture Replacer. Another method to maintain lip closure is to dislocate the lower jaw, which is then held in its new position by a wire run through holes which have been drilled through the upper and lower jaws at the midline. As the French are fond of saying, *il faut souffrir pour être belle.*[1] **14**

If Mr. Jones has died of jaundice, the embalming fluid will very likely turn him green. Does this deter the embalmer? Not if he has intestinal fortitude. Masking pastes and cosmetics are heavily laid on, burial garments and casket interiors are color-correlated with particular care, and Jones is displayed beneath rose-colored lights. Friends will say, "How *well* he looks." Death by carbon monoxide, on the other hand, can be rather a good thing from the embalmer's viewpoint: "One advantage is the fact that this type of discoloration is an exaggerated form of a natural pink coloration." This is nice because the healthy glow is already present and needs but little attention. **15**

The patching and filling completed, Mr. Jones is now shaved, washed and dressed. Cream-based cosmetic, available in pink, flesh, suntan, brunette and blond, is applied to his fands and face, his hair is shampooed and combed (and, in the case of Mrs. Jones, set), his hands manicured. For the horny-handed son of toil special care must be taken; cream should be applied to remove ingrained grime, and the nails cleaned. "If he were not in the habit of having them manicured in life, trimming and shaping is advised for better appearance—never questioned by kin." **16**

Jones is now ready for casketing (this is the present participle of the verb "to casket"). In this operation his right shoulder should be depressed slightly "to turn the body a bit to the right and soften the appearance of lying flat on the back." Positioning the hands is a matter of importance, and special rubber positioning blocks may be used. The hands should be cupped slightly for a more lifelike, relaxed appearance. Proper placement of the body requires a delicate sense of bal- **17**

---

[1]"One must suffer in order to be beautiful."

ance. it should lie as high as possible in the casket, yet not so high that the lid, when lowered, will hit the nose. On the other hand, we are cautioned, placing the body too low "creates the impression that the body is in a box."

Jones is next wheeled into the appointed slumber room where a few last   18
touches may be added—his favorite pipe placed in his hand or, if he was a great reader, a book propped into position. (In the case of little Master Jones a Teddy bear may be clutched.) Here he will hold open house for a few days, visiting hours 10 A.M. to 9 P.M.

Questions on Content, Structure, and Style

1. By studying the first three paragraphs, summarize both Mitford's reason for explaining the embalming process and her attitude toward undertakers who wish to keep their patrons uninformed about this procedure.
2. Identify this process as either directional or informative.
3. Does this process flow smoothly from step to step? Identify the transition devices connecting the paragraphs.
4. Does Mitford use enough specific details to help you visualize each step as it occurs? Point out examples of details that create vivid descriptions by appealing to your sense of sight, smell, or touch.
5. How does the technique of using the hypothetical "Mr. Jones" make the explanation of the process more effective? Why didn't Mitford simply refer to "the corpse" or "a body" throughout her essay?
6. What is Mitford's general attitude toward this procedure? The overall tone of the essay? Study Mitford's choice of words and then identify the tone in each of the following passages:

   "The next step is to have at Mr. Jones with a thing called a trocar." $(10)^2$

   "The embalmer, having allowed an appropriate interval to elapse, returns to the attack. . . ." (12)

   "Friends will say, 'How *well* he looks.'" (15)

   "On the other hand, we are cautioned, placing the body too low 'creates the impression that the body is in a box.'" (17)

   "Here he will hold open house for a few days, visiting hours 10 A.M. to 9 P.M." (18)

   What other words and passages reveal Mitford's attitude and tone?

7. Why does Mitford repeatedly quote various undertakers and textbooks on the embalming and restorative process ("'needle directed upward between the upper lip and gum and brought out through the left nostril'")? Why is the quote in

---

²Numbers in parentheses following questions and vocabulary terms refer to paragraphs in the essay.

paragraph 7 that begins, "'On the basis of such scanty information made available to this profession through its rudimentary and haphazard system of technical research'" particularly effective in emphasizing Mitford's attitude toward the funeral industry?

8. What does Mitford gain by quoting euphemisms used by the funeral business, such as "dermasurgeon," "Repose Block," and "slumber room"? What are the connotations of the words "poked," "jabbed," and "left unmolested" in paragraph 10? What effect is Mitford trying to produce with the series of questions (such as "Head off?") in paragraph 12?

9. Evaluate Mitford's last sentence. Does it successfully sum up the author's attitude and conclude the essay?

10. By supplying information about the embalming process, did Mitford change your attitude toward this procedure or toward the funeral industry? Should we subject our dead to this process? Are there advantages Mitford fails to mention? How would you prepare an essay to defend your position?

Vocabulary

docility (1)
perpetuation (1)
inherent (2)
mandatory (2)
intractable (3)
reticence (3)
raison d'être (3)
ingenious (5)
cadaver (5)

somatic (7)
rudimentary (7)
dispel (7)
pliable (8)
semblance (11)
ravages (11)
stippling (12)
emaciation (13)

A Revision Worksheet for Your Process Essay

As you write your rough drafts, consult Chapter 5 for guidance through the revision process. In addition, here are a few questions to ask yourself as you revise your process essay:

1. Is the essay's purpose clear to the reader?
2. Has the need for any special equipment been noted and explained adequately? Are all terms unfamiliar to the reader defined clearly?
3. Does the essay include all the steps (and warnings, if appropriate) necessary to understanding the process?
4. Is each step described in enough detail to make it understandable to all readers? Where could more detail be effectively added?

5. Are all the steps in the process presented in an easy-to-follow chronological order, with smooth transitions between steps or stages?
6. Have any series of small steps been organized into paragraphs describing a logical stage in the process?
7. Does the essay have a pleasing conclusion?

After you've revised your essay extensively, you might exchange rough drafts with a classmate and answer these questions for each other, making specific suggestions for improvement wherever appropriate.

STRATEGY THREE: DEVELOPMENT BY COMPARISON AND CONTRAST

Every day you exercise the mental process of comparison and contrast. When you get up in the morning, for instance, you may compare two choices of clothing—a short-sleeved shirt versus a long-sleeved one— and then make your decision after hearing the weather forecast. Or you may compare and choose between Sugar-Coated Plastic Pops and Organic Mullet Kernels for breakfast, between the health advantages of walking to campus and the speed afforded by your car or bicycle. Once on campus, preparing to register, you may first compare both professors and courses; similarly, you probably compared the school you attend now to others before you made your choice. In short, you frequently use the process of comparison and contrast to come to a decision or make a judgment about two or more objects, persons, ideas, or feelings.

When you write a comparison or contrast essay, your judgment about the two elements[3] in question becomes your thesis statement; the body of the paper then shows why you arrived at that judgment. For example, if your thesis states that Mom's Kum-On-Back Hamburger Haven is preferable to McPhony's Mystery Burger Stand, your body paragraphs might contrast the two restaurants in terms of food, service, and atmosphere, revealing the superiority of Mom's on all three counts.

Developing Your Essay

There are two principal patterns of organization for comparison and contrast essays. For most short papers you should choose one of the patterns and stick with it throughout the essay. Later, if you are assigned a longer essay, you may want to mix the patterns for variety

---

[3]It is, of course, possible to compare or contrast more than two elements. But until you feel confident about the organizational patterns for this kind of essay, you should probably stay with the simpler format.

as many professional writers do, but do so only if you can maintain clarity and logical organization.

Pattern One: Point by Point

This method of organization calls for body paragraphs that compare and contrast the two subjects first on point one, then on point two, then point three, and so on. Study the example outlined below:

Thesis: Mom's Hamburger Haven is a much better restaurant than McPhony's because of its superior food, service, and atmosphere.
Point 1: Food
    A. Mom's
    B. McPhony's
Point 2: Service
    A. Mom's
    B. McPhony's
Point 3: Atmosphere
    A. Mom's
    B. McPhony's
Conclusion

If you select this pattern of organization, you must make a smooth transition from subject "A" to subject "B" in each discussion to avoid a choppy seesaw effect. Be consistent: present the same subject first in each discussion of a major point; above, for instance, Mom's is always introduced before McPhony's.

Pattern Two: The Block

This method of organization presents body paragraphs in which the writer first discusses subject "A" on points one, two, three, etc., then discusses subject "B" on the same points. The model below illustrates this block pattern:

Thesis: Mom's Hamburger Haven is a better restaurant than McPhony's because of its superior food, service, and atmosphere.
    A. Mom's
        1. Food
        2. Service
        3. Atmosphere
    B. McPhony's
        1. Food
        2. Service
        3. Atmosphere
Conclusion

If you use the block pattern, you should discuss the three points—food, service, atmosphere—in the same order for each subject. In addition, you must include in your discussion of subject "B" specific references to the points you made earlier about subject "A" (see outline). In other words, because your statements about Mom's superior food may be several pages away by the time your comments on McPhony's food appear, the readers may not remember precisely what you said. Gently, unobtrusively, remind them with a specific reference to the earlier discussion. For instance, you might begin your paragraph on McPhony's service like this: "Unlike the friendly, attentive help at Mom's, service at McPhony's features grouchy persons who wait on you as if they consider your presence an intrusion on their privacy." The discussion of atmosphere might begin, "McPhony's atmosphere is as cold, sterile, and plastic as its decor, in contrast to the warm, homey feeling that pervades Mom's." Without such connecting phrases, what should be one unified essay will look more like two distinct mini-essays, forcing readers to do the job of comparing or contrasting for you.

Problems to Avoid

The single most serious error is the "so-what" thesis. Writers of comparison and/or contrast essays often wish to convince their readers that something—a restaurant, a teacher, a product—is better (or worse) than something else: "Mom's Haven is a better place to eat than McPhony's." But not all comparison/contrast essays must assert the absolute superiority or inferiority of their subjects. Sometimes writers simply want to point out the similarities and/or differences in two or more people, places, objects, and that's fine, too—*as long as the writer avoids the "so-what" thesis problem.* Too often novice writers will present thesis statements such as "My youngest sister and I are very different" or "Having a blended family with two stepbrothers and stepsisters has its advantages and disadvantages." To such theses, the readers can only respond, "So what? Who cares?" There are many similarities and differences (or advantages and disadvantages) between countless numbers of things—but why should your readers care about those described in your essay? Comparing or contrasting for no apparent reason is a waste of the readers' valuable time; instead, find a purpose that will draw in your audience. You may indeed wish to write an essay contrasting the pros and cons of your blended family, but do it in a way that has a universal appeal or application; for instance, you might revise your thesis to say something like "Although a blended family often does experience petty jealousies and juvenile bickering, the benefits of having stepsiblings as live-in friends far outweigh the problems," and then use your family to show the advantages and disadvantages. In this way, your readers realize they will learn something about the blended family, a common phenomenon today, as well as learning some information about you and your particular family. Another way to avoid the "so-what" problem is to direct your thesis to a particular audience. For instance, you might say that "While Stella's Sweatateria and the Fitness Fanatics Gym are similar in their low student membership prices and excellent instructors, Stella's is the place to go for those seeking a variety of exercise classes rather than hardcore bodybuilding machines." Or your thesis may wish to show a particular relationship between two subjects. Instead of writing "There are many similarities between the movie *Riot of the Killer Snails* and Mary Sheeley's novel *Salt on the Sidewalk*," write "The many similarities in character and plot—the monster, the scientist, and vegetable garden scene—clearly suggest that the movie director was greatly influenced by—if not actually guilty of stealing—parts of Mary Sheeley's novel." In other words, tell your readers your point and then use comparison and/or contrast to support that idea; don't just compare or contrast items in a vacuum. Ask yourself, "What is the significant point I want my readers to learn or understand from reading this comparison/contrast essay?"

Describe your subjects clearly and distinctly. To comprehend a difference or a similarity between two things, the reader must first be able to "see" them as you do. Consequently, you should use as many vivid examples and details as possible to describe both your subjects. Beware a tendency to overelaborate on one subject and then grossly skimp on the other, an especially easy trap to fall into in an essay that asserts "X" is preferable to "Y." By giving each side a reasonable treatment, you will do a better job of convincing your reader that you know both sides and have made a valid judgment.

Avoid a choppy essay. Whether you organize your essay by the point-by-point method or the block pattern, you need to use enough transition devices to ensure a smooth flow from one subject to another and from one point to the next. Without transitions, your essay may assume the distracting movement of a Ping-Pong game, as you switch back and forth between discussions of your two subjects. Listed below are some appropriate words to link your points:

COMPARISON	CONTRAST
also	however
similarly	on the contrary

COMPARISON	CONTRAST
too	on the other hand
both	in contrast
like	although
not only . . . but also	unlike
have in common	though
share the same	instead of
in the same manner	but

(For a review of other transition devices, see pp. 52–55.)

Essay Topics

Following are some topics that may be compared and contrasted. Remember to narrow your subject, formulate a thesis that presents a clear point, and follow one of the two organizational patterns discussed on pp. 159–160.

1. an expectation and its reality
2. a first impression and a later point of view
3. two views on a current controversial issue (campus, local, national, or international)
4. two conflicting theories you are studying in another college course
5. a memory of a person or place and a more recent encounter with that person or place
6. coverage of the same story by two newspapers or magazines (the *National Enquirer* and the *Dallas Morning News*, for example, or *Time* and *Newsweek*)
7. a hero today and yesterday
8. two commercials for a similar product
9. two pieces of technology you've owned or operated
10. a public or private myth and its reality
11. two solutions to a problem in your professional field
12. one of today's popular entertainments and one from an earlier era (board or card games, for instance)
13. two places you've lived
14. two politicians or public figures from today or from the past
15. two books or a book and its movie or a movie and its sequel
16. two jobs or employers
17. two places that are special for you
18. an opinion you held before coming to college that has changed now that you are in college
19. two sports or athletes or pieces of sports equipment

20. the perfect parent/friend/roommate/spouse and your real
     parent/friend/roommate/spouse

Sample Student Essay

Note that this writer takes a definite stand—that local food co-ops are
superior to chain stores—and then contrasts two local stores, Lane Grocer and the Fort Collins Co-op, to prove her thesis. She selected the
point-by-point pattern to organize her essay, contrasting prices, atmosphere, and benefits to local producers. See if you can identify her transition devices as well as some of her uses of detail that make the essay
more interesting and convincing.

BRINGING BACK THE JOY OF MARKET DAY

Thesis

Essay map

Point one: Prices

Examples of Lane
Grocer's prices
contrasted to
examples of co-op
prices (in next
paragraph)

Now that the old family-run corner grocery is almost
extinct, many people are banding together to form their
own neighborhood stores as food cooperatives. Locally
owned by their members, food co-ops such as the one here
in Fort Collins are welcome alternatives to the impersonal
chain-store markets such as Lane Grocer. In exchange for
volunteering a few hours each month, co-op members share
savings and a friendly experience while they shop; local producers gain loyal, local support from the members as well
as better prices for their goods in return for providing the
freshest, purest food possible.

Perhaps the most crucial distinction between the two
kinds of stores is that while supermarkets are set up to generate profit for their corporations, co-ops are nonprofit
groups whose main purpose is to provide their members
and the community with good, inexpensive food and basic
household needs. At first glance, supermarkets such as
Lane Grocer may appear to be cheaper because they offer
so many specials, which they emphasize heavily through
ads and in store promotions. These special deals, known as
"loss-leaders" in the retail industry, are more than made up
for by the extremely high markups on other products. For
example, around Thanksgiving Lane Grocer might have a
sale on flour and shortening and then set up the displays
with utmost care so that as customers reach for the flour
they will be drawn to colorful bottles of pie spices, fancy
jars of mincemeat, or maybe an inviting bin of fresh-roasted
holiday nuts, all of which may be marked up 100% or
more—way above what is being lost on the flour and
shortening.

The Fort Collins Co-op rarely bothers with such pricing gimmicks; instead, it tries to have a consistent markup— just enough to meet overhead expenses. The flour at the co-op may cost an extra few cents, but that same fancy spice bottle that costs over $1.00 from the supermarket display can be refilled at the co-op for less than 25¢. The nuts, considered by regular groceries as a seasonal "gourmet" item, are sold at the co-op for about two-thirds the price. Great savings like these are achieved by buying in bulk and having customers bag their own groceries. Recycled containers are used as much as possible, cutting down substantially on overhead. Buying in bulk may seem awkward at first, but the extra time spent bagging and weighing their own food results in welcome savings for co-op members.

Point two: Atmosphere

Description of Lane Grocer's atmosphere contrasted to description of the co-op's atmosphere

Once people have gotten accustomed to bringing their own containers and taking part in the work at the co-ops, they often find that it's actually more fun to shop in the friendly, relaxed atmosphere of the co-ops. At Lane Grocer, for example, I often find shopping a battle of tangled metal carts wielded by bored customers who are frequently trying to manage one or more cranky children. The long aisles harshly lit by rows of cold fluorescent lights and the bland commercial music don't make the chore of shopping any easier either. On the other hand, the Fort Collins Co-op may not be as expertly planned, but at least the chaos is carried on in a friendly way. Parents especially appreciate that they can safely let their children loose while they shop because in the small, open-spaced co-op even toddlers don't become lost as they do in the aisles of towering supermarket shelves. Moreover, most members are willing to look after the children of other members if necessary. And while they shop, members can choose to listen to the FM radio or simply to enjoy each other's company in relative quiet.

Point three: Benefits to local producers

As well as benefiting member consumers, co-ops also help small local producers by providing a direct market for their goods. Large chain stores may require minimum wholesale quantities far beyond the capacity of an individual producer, and mass markets like Lane Grocer often feel they are "too big" to negotiate with small local producers. But because of their small, independent nature co-ops welcome the chance to buy direct from the grower or producer. Direct selling offers two advantages for producers: they get a better price for their wares than by selling them through a middleman, and at the same time they establish an independent reputation for their business, which can be

No benefits at Lane Grocer contrasted to two benefits at the co-op

immensely valuable to their success later on. In Fort Collins, for example, Luna tofu (bean curd) stands out as an excellent illustration of this kind of mutual support. Several years ago my friend Carol Jones began making tofu in small batches to sell to the co-op as a way to earn a part-time income as well as to contribute to the co-op. Her enterprise has now grown so well that last year her husband quit his job to go into business with her full time. She currently sells to distributors and independent stores from here to Denver; even Lane Grocer, who earlier would not consider selling her tofu even on a trial basis, is now thinking about changing its policy.

Conclusion:
Summarizing the
advantages of co-ops
over chain stores

Of course, not all co-ops are like the one here in Fort Collins, but that is one of their best features. Each one reflects the personalities of its members, unlike the supermarket chain stores that vary only slightly. Most important, though, while each has a distinctive character, co-ops share common goals of providing members with high-quality, low-cost food in a friendly, cooperative spirit.

Professional Essay

PRUFROCK[4] BEFORE THE TELEVISION SET

Michael J. Arlen

Michael J. Arlen is a television critic and staff writer for *The New Yorker* magazine. He won the Screen Directors' Guild for television criticism in 1968 and the National Book Award for contemporary affairs in 1976. Arlen is also the author of seven books, including *Living-Room War* (1969), *Passage to Ararat* (1975), and *The Camera Age* (1981). This selection was taken from one of Arlen's *New Yorker* columns.

A few days ago, while seated snugly in an airplane seat on my way back to New York from Chicago, with a drink in front of me, and last week's copy of *Sports Illustrated* on my lap, and the soothing hum of the engines washing over my ears (and with the memory of the taxi ride and traffic jam and ticket-counter chaos already receding), it occurred to me that there was a rather striking similarity   1

---

[4]Prufrock is the protagonist of a well-known poem by T. S. Eliot, "The Love Song of J. Alfred Prufrock." In the poem Prufrock is presented as a passive man who wonders if he should take actions to control his life ("Do I dare/Disturb the universe?").

between what I was experiencing then, flying in a modern airliner, and what I've felt often happens as I watch television. To begin with, both are largely passive experiences; or, they have been made into passive experiences. But this passivity is, itself, interesting and complicated, for not only does it involve obvious conditions of quietude and inaction, as well as the illusion of privacy; it also implies, and sometimes makes explicit, a quite formal undertaking of nonaggressive behavior on the part of the passenger or viewer. In fact, there is something to be said for the notion that much of the "pleasure" involved with riding in a commercial airliner, or in watching an evening's television schedule, has to do as much with this subjective state of nonaggression (in contrast with the aggressions of the "outside world") as it has with the supposedly greater and more evident pleasure of the trip or the actual programs.

Consider, for example, the airplane journey. In many ways, levels of ordinary comfort for passengers have been, if anything, decreasing since the days of the old Pan American "Yankee Clipper." Even so, there is undoubted pleasure to be had in a routine jetliner trip of reasonable length (and admittedly one without crying babies or furious grandparents on one's lap). As an extreme example of this, I mention the experience of a friend who, being harried to exhaustion by a project in New York, determined suddenly to fly to California for a few days by the sea. As soon as he was airborne on the way out, he began to relax. Five hours later in California, however, as soon as he was on the ground, dealing with baggage and car rentals and freeways and finally his motel-by-the-sea, he began again to unravel. The same evening, he drove back to the airport, took a return flight to New York, and after five more hours of airplane massage, was in a suitable condition for resuming work.

People still talk of the romance of travel, and perhaps it is still romance for fashionable visitors to Ethiopian ruins, or even for cruise-ship passengers. Indeed, travel was once an active and difficult undertaking, with the pleasure therein consisting in actively engaging in the difficulties and surmounting them—though even surmounting them wasn't always all that important. The important thing was to participate, to experience. But in much travel nowadays, it seems to me, the key element is nonparticipation. Not only is aggressive behavior discouraged or proscribed but nonaggressive behavior is formally encouraged as the norm. Thus, the pleasure of much of modern travel lies in the restful illusion that nonaggressive behavior is "being oneself."

On an airplane, for instance, the passenger lumpishly settles into his narrow seat, usually dishevelled in mind or spirit from the hurly-burly of the outside world, sometimes still quivering from the hazards of actually getting to the airplane. The stewardess has already relieved him of his coat and briefcase, his downtown symbols. Sometimes, wifelike, she will have given him an initial, token reward for having reached her: a cup of coffee, a ginger ale, a Bloody Mary. Prufrock has arrived home. Prufrock need do nothing more, except buckle himself to his seat, and follow modest instructions "for his own safety," and act unaggressively. In fact, for doing so, he will be rewarded: by great speed and forward motion (i.e., by progress), by the benign smiles of the stewardess, by the loan of a magazine, by the outright gift of an airline magazine ("You's to keep"), by drinks, by the hospitality of a meal, even by the appurtenances of an overnight guest—a pillow and blanket. A shower of benefits is rained upon the passenger by the authorities of the airplane (including periodic descriptions of the unseen ground being traversed, delivered over loud-speaker by the unseen captain), who ask in return only that the passenger do noth-ing, stay quiet, keep still. Bathroom privileges are given, but can easily be revoked. Primary addictive substances, such as cigarettes, are permitted more rapidly and easily than secondary substances, such as alcohol, which might cause disquiet or might "spill." When all the right conditions are met, modest walking about is allowed, but since there is usually no place to walk to, it is a privilege rarely accepted. Even when the seat-belt sign has been turned off, so the captain has announced, one would do well to keep buckled.

In short, passivity reigns in the modern airliner. And when aggression reap-   5
pears, it is sternly chastised. For example, after the plane has landed but before it has arrived at the gate, several passengers—doubtless summoned again to aggres-sive behavior by the imminence of the outside world—will leap to their feet and begin reaching for coats and bags like children who have been held too long in school. At this point, the formerly benign stewardess becomes severe and quickly reprimands the aggressive passengers. If these passengers do not abandon their aggressive behavior and return to the passivity of their seats, she says, they will be deprived of the one thing they still lack: further forward motion. Thereupon, the misbehaving passengers feign nonaggressive behavior until the second the plane has docked at the gate and they have been released from passivity. Immediately, aggression returns and now all the passengers push past each other down the air-port corridors and once again start fighting over baggage, taxis, buses, or parking space.

The experience of watching most commercial television seems to involve a   6
similar voyage and a similar stylized passivity. Here, of course, the seat belts are figurative rather than actual, though I notice that there are a variety of "TV lounge chairs" now on the market, whose chief function seems to be safely to enclose the viewer during his nightly journey. Also, it is an interesting (if taste-numbing) coin-cidence that the TV dinner and the standard airline meal are made the same way, with the same technology and the same results. With television, the forward motion is through time, not space; but the effect is somewhat the same, since in the mod-ern world final destinations rarely exist. The end of each day's program schedule, as with O'Hare Airport, is as much a beginning as a terminus.

Rewards for good behavior flow ceaselessly throughout the evening, according   7
to a set routine. In return for sitting still in front of his television set, the viewer is rewarded not only by the vague, general, forward-seeming flow of the entertainment but, more specifically, by periodic "messages" from the authority of the television station which promise him two levels of benefits. On the higher, symbolic level, there is the romantic promise of an upward alteration or enhancement of his life, by the acquisition of a new car, or a new deodorant, or a new kind of floor tile. This is deeply moving but it is remote, as is the promise of romance in travel. On a more immediate level, then, the viewer is rewarded by a trip to the bathroom or another bottle of beer from the refrigerator: these are stand-ins for the larger, dreamlike rewards.

Aggressive behavior is not actively prohibited, but it is discouraged. There are   8 almost no viewer phone-in programs, as on radio. Live audiences are few. Real audience participation is almost nonexistent, save for the inflated hysteria of a few game shows. Indeed, even some of the new game shows have become quite stylized and remote, with earnest, sedate couples trying to guess the authorship of "Hamlet" in the company of a lonely host and much electronic paraphernalia. On what are described as comedy or drama or adventure programs, there remains scarcely any nourishment of the viewer's active participation, in the form of emotionally involving stories. Thus, a middling detective series such as "Baretta" becomes oddly noticeable, as if it contained a certain gritty substance that somehow spoke to the still-awake part of the viewer's mind—that part persistently untouched by the noisiest bang-bang of cop-show revolvers or even by the sight of artillery explosions in foreign lands. In recent years, many news programs have taken steps toward greater informality and a semblance of involvement on the part of the newscasters. But the involvement of these newsmen has been mostly with each other. The audience continues voyaging, buckled into its Barcaloungers, attending no longer to the voice of a single, solemn captain but to the equally distant, cheery chitchat of two or three of them.

What is strange about this new passivity, regarding both travel and broadcast-   9
ing, is that not so long ago the reverse was considered normal. That is, flying was once a highly participatory activity—as was automobile driving, as was broadcasting. Thirty-five years ago, the driver of an ordinary car was intimately involved with the event of driving, by means of direct access to his steering wheel, brakes, transmission, and the outside environment. In the same period, a listener to Edward R. Murrow's broadcasts from London was directly involved with the event of broadcasting as well as the events of the Second World War that Murrow was describing. Since then, however, the automobile driver has given up his direct involvement in favor of power controls, automatic transmission, and sealed-in passenger interiors, while the television audience has largely given up its involvement with drama and news in favor of undemanding, mechanical entertainment and uninvolving news. Nowadays, only aggressive people insist on direct, or participatory, driving, by means of sports cars; at least, they are owned by people who are willing to appear aggressive. And only an aggressive minority, perhaps of a different cultural nature, appears to prefer participatory television, such as the music and serious drama programs that now and then are shown on public television.

The question remains: Have we somehow demanded this period of passivity   10
for ourselves (one in which we may, so to speak, draw a breath in order to reach the summit of this peculiar century), or has it been foisted upon us by the onrush of technical systems? Certainly it's true that technical systems assert a logic of their own, as well as clearly seeming to "prefer" a passivity on the part of their components, whether semiconductors or passengers or viewers. At the same time, if fear of flying evoked the seat belt and the stewardess, then fear of another kind has surely evoked our present uninvolving programs, news and entertainment both. Is it fear of communication, of "too much"? Or fear of ourselves? Are we the people meekly buckled in by seat belts or the people rushing pell-mell down the airport corridors and fighting over taxis? Or is there any difference?

At least, nowadays when one has something to think about one can usually   11 find the time and space for it, either by flying to Chicago or by turning on the television set.

Questions on Content, Structure, and Style

1. What is Arlen's thesis and where is it stated?
2. In his discussion of the airplane journey and television viewing, does Arlen primarily compare the two activities or contrast them? Does he use the point-by-point method or the block method to present his discussion?
3. How does Arlen use examples in paragraph 4 to illustrate his point that "passivity reigns in the modern airliner"? How does paragraph 5 also support this point?
4. How does Arlen smoothly make the transition from his discussion of airplane trips to television watching?
5. What are some of the similarities Arlen sees between airplane rides and television viewing?
6. Does Arlen provide enough points of comparison between his two subjects, and are all his examples persuasive? Select two or three of his examples and tell why you agree or disagree with Arlen's claims.
7. For what reason does Arlen criticize television in paragraph 8? What supporting evidence does he provide? Do you agree with his assessment of television shows and news broadcasts? Why/why not?
8. In paragraph 9 Arden contrasts air travel and television broadcasting to what subjects? What is his purpose in such a contrast?
9. Why does Arlen ask a series of questions in paragraph 10? Are they an appropriate way to lead into the conclusion of this essay? Does the concluding sentence effectively wrap up Arlen's essay?
10. Write a brief evaluation of Arlen's essay. Did he persuade you to accept his thesis? Why/why not? Which of his points were stronger or weaker than others, in your opinion?

Vocabulary

To understand this essay completely, you should know the meaning of the following words:

passivity (1)	chastised (5)
explicit (1)	imminence (5)
harried (2)	reprimands (5)
dishevelled (4)	feign (5)
benign (4)	semblance (8)
appurtenances (4)	foisted (10)

A Revision Worksheet for Your Comparison or Contrast Essay

As you write your rough drafts, consult Chapter 5 for guidance through the revision process. In addition, here are a few questions to ask yourself as you revise your comparison/contrast essay:

1. Does the essay contain a thesis that makes a significant point instead of a "so-what?" thesis?
2. Is the material organized into the best pattern for the subject matter?
3. If the essay is developed by the point-by-point pattern, are there enough transition words used to avoid the see-saw effect?
4. If the essay is developed by the block pattern, are there enough transition devices and references connecting the two subjects to avoid the split-essay problem?
5. Are the points of comparison/contrast presented in a logical, consistent order that the reader can follow easily?
6. Are both subjects given a reasonably balanced treatment?
7. Are both subjects developed in enough specific detail so that the reader clearly understands the comparison or contrast? Where might more detail be added?

After you've revised your essay extensively, you might exchange rough drafts with a classmate and answer these questions for each other, making specific suggestions for improvement wherever appropriate.

STRATEGY FOUR: DEVELOPMENT BY DEFINITION

Frequently in conversation we must stop to ask, "What do you mean by that?" because in some cases our failure to comprehend just one particular term may lead to total misunderstanding. Suppose, for example, in a discussion with a friend, you refer to a new law as a piece of "liberal legislation"; if you and your friend do not share the same definition of "liberal," your remark may be completely misinterpreted. Take another example: you tell your parents that the Punk era is over; if they don't know what Punk is, they miss the point entirely. In other words, definition of terms or ideas is often essential to meaningful communication.

Sometimes a dictionary definition or a one- or two-sentence explanation is all a term needs (Hemingway, for example, once defined courage as "grace under pressure").[5] Occasionally, however, you will find it

---

[5]Even graffiti employs definition. One bathroom wall favorite: "Death is Nature's way of telling you to slow down." Another, obviously written by an English major: "A double negative is a no-no."

necessary to provide an *extended definition*—that is, a longer, more detailed explanation that thoroughly defines the subject. Essays of extended definitions are quite common; think, for instance, of the articles you've seen lately on "mercy killing" that try to define death, or the arguments on abortion that define "life" in a variety of ways. Other recent essays have grappled with such complex concepts as the liberated woman/man, pornography, discrimination, and "reverse" discrimination. The controversial verdict in the trial of John Hinckley, accused of the attempted assassination of President Ronald Reagan in 1981, produced many articles and editorials debating the meaning of criminal "insanity." And the 1985 New York subway incident in which Bernard Goetz shot several young men who had accosted him caused much debate over the notion of "self-defense."

Why Do We Define?

Essays of extended definition are usually written for one or more of the following reasons:

1. to provide an interpretation of a vague, controversial, or misunderstood term (such as "obscenity," "welfare," or "euthanasia")
2. to explain an abstract term or concept (such as "heroic," "success," or "jealousy")
3. to define a new or unusual term, often found in slang, dialect, or the jargon of a particular field of study or industry (such as "nerdy," "objective correlative," or "floppy discs")
4. to offer an objective definition of an unfamiliar term for use by a particular audience ("electron microscope," "food processor," or "soft contact lenses")
5. to entertain by presenting the interesting history, uses, effects, etc., of a common word or expression ("phobia," "rock and roll," or "science fiction")

Developing Your Essay

Here are four suggestions to help you prepare your essay of extended definition:

Know your purpose. Sometimes we need to define a term as clearly and objectively as possible; as a laboratory assistant, for instance, you might need to explain a technical measuring instrument to a group of new students. At other times, however, we may wish to persuade as well as inform our readers. People's interpretations of words, especially abstract or controversial terms, can, and often do, differ greatly depending on their point of view. After all, one person's "protest march" can be another person's street riot. Consequently, before you begin writing, decide on your purpose. If your readers need objective information only, make your definition as unbiased as you can; if your goal is to convince them that your point of view is the right or best one, you may adopt a variety of persuasive techniques as well as subjective language. For example, readers of a paper on the new 24-hour emergency-care offices springing up around the country entitled "Doc in the Box" should quickly realize that they are not getting an objective treatment.

Give your readers a reason to read.   One way to introduce your subject is to explain the previous use, misuse, or misunderstanding of the term; then present your new or different interpretation of the term or concept. An introduction and thesis defining a slang word, for instance, might state: "Despite the visions of cornbread dressing and cranberries it conjures up for most Americans, the word 'turkey' does not always refer to the Thanksgiving bird. Today, 'turkey' is also a common slang expression designed primarily to tease or even insult someone." Or take this introduction and thesis aimed at a word the writer feels is unclear to many readers: "When the credits roll at the end of a movie, much of the audience may be perplexed to see the job of 'best boy' listed. No, the 'best boy' doesn't stand up with the groom at a wedding of children— he (or she) is, in fact, the key electrician's first assistant, who helps rig the lights for the movie's director of photography."

Keep your audience in mind to anticipate and avoid problems of clarity.   Because you are trying to present a new or improved definition, you must strive above all for clarity. Ask yourself, "Who is my intended audience? What terms or parts of my definition are strange to them?" You don't help your audience, for example, by defining one campus slang expression in terms of other bits of unfamiliar slang. If, in other words, you defined "space cadet" as an "air head," you're probably confusing your readers more than you are informing them. If your assignment doesn't specify a specific audience, you may find it useful to imagine one. You might pretend, for instance, that you're defining a campus or slang expression to your parents or that you're explaining an ambiguous term to a foreign visitor. After all, your definition is effective only if your explanation is clear not just to you but to those unfamiliar with the term or concept under discussion.

Use as many strategies as necessary to clarify your definition.   Depending on your subject, you may use any number of the following methods in your essay to define your term:

1. state some examples
2. describe the parts

3. compare and contrast to similar terms
4. explain an operation or process
5. give some familiar synonyms
6. define by negation (i.e., tell what the term doesn't mean)
7. present the history
8. discuss causes or effects

To illustrate some of the methods suggested above, let's suppose you wanted to write an extended definition of modern country music. You might choose one or more of these methods:

- describe the parts: music, lyrics, and typical subject matter
- compare or contrast to other kinds of music, such as bluegrass and western swing
- give some examples of famous country songs
- trace its historical development from traditional country music to its present state

In the paper on country music or in any definition essay, you should, of course, use only those methods that will best define your term. Never include methods purely for the sake of exhibiting a variety of techniques. You, the writer, must decide which method or methods work best, which should receive the most emphasis, and in which order the chosen methods of definition should appear.

Problems to Avoid

Here is a list of "don'ts" for the writer of extended definition essays:

Don't present an incomplete definition. An inadequate definition is often the result of choosing a subject too broad or complex for your essay. You probably can't, for instance, do a good job of defining "twentieth-century modern art" in all its varieties in a short essay; you might, however, acquaint your reader with some specific school of modern art, such as impressionism, cubism, expressionism, surrealism, or pop. Therefore, narrow your subject to a manageable size and then define it as thoroughly as possible.

Don't introduce your essay with a quotation from Webster's. In fact, try to avoid long, direct quotes from dictionaries or encyclopedias altogether. If you must include a lengthy standard definition of the term, put the dictionary's definition in your own words. Dictionary definitions are generally so dull and overused that they often drive composition teachers to seek more interesting jobs, such as measuring spaghetti in a pasta factory. Don't bore your audience to death; it's a terrible way to go.

Don't define vaguely or by using generalities. As always, use specific, vivid details to explain your subject. If, for example, you define a Shaker chair as "something with four legs," you have also described a dog, cat, horse, and cow, none of which are remotely akin to your subject. Consequently, you must select details that will make your subject distinct from any other. Including concrete examples is frequently useful in any essay but especially so when you are defining an abstract term such as "pride," "faith," or "prejudice." To make your definition both interesting and clear, always add as many precise details as possible. (For a review of using specific, colorful language, see pp. 96–98 and 116–118.)

Don't offer circular definitions. To identify a poet as "one who writes poetry" or the American Dream as "the dream most Americans hold dear" is about as helpful as a doctor telling a patient, "Your illness is primarily a lack of good health." Explain your subject; don't just rename it.

Essay Topics

Below are several suggestions for terms whose meanings are often unclear. Narrow any topic that seems too broad for your assignment, and decide before writing whether your definition will be objective or subjective. (Student writers, by the way, often note that abstract concepts are harder to define than the more concrete subjects, so proceed at your own risk, and remember to use plenty of specific detail in your essay.)

1. any current slang, campus, or local expression
2. a term from your field of study
3. conceit or hypocrisy
4. success or failure
5. a good/bad teacher, clerk, coach, friend, parent, date or spouse
6. heroism or cowardice
7. Army brat (or some other stereotype)
8. any kind of music, painting, architecture, or dance
9. a feminist or a chauvinist pig/sow
10. any current fad or style
11. a rebel or conformist
12. power
13. a good/bad restaurant, store, movie theater, nightspot, class
14. class or *panache*
15. sex appeal
16. a freshman
17. a political group or movement
18. a term from a hobby

19. a medical term or illness
20. a term from a sport

Sample Student Essay

A student studying to become a veterinarian wrote the following essay based on her class notes, to illustrate her understanding of an important term in her field, equine encephalomyelitis. Note that she uses a variety of methods to explain the disease.

EQUINE ENCEPHALOMYELITIS: A POTENTIAL KILLER

Introduction: The importance of understanding the term and a general definition (including origin of the term)

Because of its potential as an epidemic killer, equine encephalomyelitis, sleeping sickness in horses caused by a virus, must be understood by both veterinarians and horse owners. Carried by two types of mosquitoes, the *Culex tarsallis* and the *Culiseta melanura,* encephalomyelitis attacks the horse through the bloodstream, affecting the spinal column and the brain. The word "encephalomyelitis" comes from the Greek "encephalos" or brain, and the Greek word for marrow, since the disease attacks the core of the spinal column and inflames the brain.

Description of the types of the disease

Three types of encephalomyelitis have been pinpointed in the United States: two discovered in North America, the eastern in Kentucky and the western in Texas, and one South American strain discovered in Venezuela. According to Dr. Frank Kuder, Professor of Animal Science at DSU, the Venezuelan strain was first diagnosed in that country in 1936 but didn't appear in the U.S., in Texas, until 1971; especially virulent, it has a mortality rate of 80–90% and may attack humans. The other two types have caused the deaths of nearly a million horses in this country since 1930; eastern sleeping sickness has a mortality rate of more than 90%, while the western type isn't as bad—50% or less.

Effects of the disease

Once an animal has been infected, usually by mosquitoes, the disease follows a definite sequence: the virus travels through the bloodstream to the brain, where it attacks the cells; the brain's blood vessels are engorged with blood and the animal becomes very excitable; body temperature rises, and then lethargy sets in. The animal may wander aimlessly, crashing into things, and become increasingly sleepy, even resting its head on nearby objects. Grinding of teeth, inability to swallow, paralysis of the lips, blindness, and unconsciousness precede death. If affected animals don't recover—and the mortality rates cited above show that few do—death occurs in about four days.

<table>
<tr><td>Treatment of the diseased horse</td><td>Medically, treatment of a horse with the disease is nearly impossible, and often the animal is put to death to minimize suffering. There are steps to take to make the horse more comfortable, though, if treatment is attempted. It should be put into a dark place away from other animals and protected from excitement and noise. Cold packs should be placed on the skull, and a sedative should be given, along with easily swallowed, easily digested foods. With the nearly inevitable death comes the problem of disposal of the carcass; experts say it should be burned to avoid contamination of other animals and migratory birds.</td></tr>
<tr><td>Conclusion: How to avoid the disease</td><td>Horses of any age can be effectively protected from all three strains of this disease by proper annual vaccination with chick-embryo vaccines. For all areas, especially where blood-sucking insects are prevalent year round, it is best to vaccinate in late winter or very early spring. Since the insect larvae abound in marshy areas and stagnant waters, it is crucial when animals are raised in such areas to use screened stables and insect repellents, and pasture the horses in the daytime when such insects are less numerous. With such preventive measures, horse owners and veterinarians working together can halt the spread of one of the world's most serious equine diseases.</td></tr>
</table>

Professional Essay

GOBBLEDYGOOK

Stuart Chase

Stuart Chase, a long-time consultant to various government agencies, has written many books, including *Democracy Under Pressure* and *The Tyranny of Words.* This essay is an excerpt from *Power of Words.*

—

SAID FRANKLIN ROOSEVELT, in one of his early presidential speeches: "I see one-third of a nation ill-housed, ill-clad, ill-nourished." Translated into standard bureaucratic prose his statement would read:

It is evident that a substantial number of persons within the Continental boundaries of the United States have inadequate financial resources with which to purchase the products of agricultural communities and industrial establishments. It would appear that for a considerable segment of the population, possibly as much as 33.3333* percent of the total,

---

*Not carried beyond four places. [Chase's note]

there are inadequate housing facilities, and an equally significant proportion is deprived of the proper types of clothing and nutriment.

This rousing satire on gobbledygook—or talk among the bureaucrats—is   2
adapted from a report* prepared by the Federal Security Agency in an attempt to break out of the verbal squirrel cage. "Gobbledygook" was coined by an exasperated Congressman, Maury Maverick of Texas, and means using two, or three, or ten words in the place of one, or using a five-syllable word where a single syllable would suffice. Maverick was censuring the forbidding prose of executive departments in Washington, but the term has now spread to windy and pretentious language in general.

"Gobbledygook" itself is a good example of the way a language grows. There   3
was no word for the event before Maverick's invention; one had to say: "You know, that terrible, involved, polysyllabic language those government people use down in Washington." Now one word takes the place of a dozen.

A British member of Parliament, A. P. Herbert, also exasperated with bureau-   4
cratic jargon, translated Nelson's** immortal phrase, "England expects every man to do his duty":

England anticipates that, as regards the current emergency, personnel will face up to the issues, and exercise appropriately the functions allocated to their respective occupational groups.

A New Zealand official made the following report after surveying a plot of   5
ground for an athletic field:†

It is obvious from the difference in elevation with relation to the short depth of the property that the contour is such as to preclude any reasonable development potential for active recreation.

Seems the plot was too steep.

An office manager sent this memo to his chief: 6

Verbal contact with Mr. Blank regarding the attached notification of promotion has elicited the attached representation intimating that he prefers to decline the assignment.

Seems Mr. Blank didn't want the job.

A doctor testified at an English trial that one of the parties was suffering from "circumorbital haematoma."

---

*This and succeeding quotations from F.S.A. report by special permission of the author, Milton Hall. [Chase's note]
**Horatio Nelson (1758–1805), English naval hero, victor over the French at Trafalgar.
†This item and the next two are from the piece on gobbledygook by W. E. Farbstein, *New York Times,* March 29, 1953. [Chase's note]

Seems the party had a black eye.

In August 1952 the U.S. Department of Agriculture put out a pamphlet entitled: "Cultural and Pathogenic Variability in Single-Condial and Hyphaltip Isolates of Hemlin-Thosporium Turcicum Pass."

Seems it was about corn leaf disease.

On reaching the top of the Finsteraarhorn in 1845, M. Dollfus-Ausset, when he   7
got his breath, exclaimed:

The soul communes in the infinite with those icy peaks which seem to have their roots in the bowels of eternity.

Seems he enjoyed the view.

A government department announced: 8

Voucherable expenditures necessary to provide adequate dental treatment required as adjunct to medical treatment being rendered a pay patient in in-patient status may be incurred as required at the expense of the Public Health Service.

Seems you can charge your dentist bill to the Public Health Service. Or can you? . . .

Reducing the Gobble

As government and business offices grow larger, the need for doing something   9
about gobbledygook increases. Fortunately, the biggest office in the world is working hard to reduce it. The Federal Security Agency in Washington,* with nearly 100
million clients on its books, began analyzing its communication lines some years
ago, with gratifying results. Surveys find trouble in three main areas: correspondence with clients about their social security problems, office memos, official
reports.

Clarity and brevity, as well as common humanity, are urgently needed in this   1(
vast establishment which deals with disability, old age, and unemployment. The
surveys found instead many cases of long-windedness, foggy meanings, clichés,
and singsong phrases, and gross neglect of the reader's point of view. Rather than
talking to a real person, the writer was talking to himself. "We often write like a
man walking on stilts."

Here is a typical case of long-windedness: 1

Gobbledygook as found: "We are wondering if sufficient time has passed so that you
are in position to indicate whether favorable action may now be taken on our
recommendation for the reclassification of Mrs. Blank, junior clerk-stenographer, CAF 2, to
assistant clerk-stenographer, CAF 3?"

---

*Now the Department of Health, Education, and Welfare. [Chase's note]

Suggested improvement: "Have you yet been able to act on our recommendation to reclassify Mrs. Blank?"

Another case:

Although the Central Efficiency Rating Committee recognizes that there are many desirable changes that could be made in the present efficiency rating system in order to make it more realistic and more workable than it now is, this committee is of the opinion that no further change should be made in the present system during the current year. Because of conditions prevailing throughout the country and the resultant turnover in personnel, and difficulty in administering the Federal programs, further mechanical improvement in the present rating system would require staff retraining and other administrative expense which would seem best withheld until the official termination of hostilities, and until restoration of regular operations.

The F.S.A. invites us to squeeze the gobbledygook out of this statement. Here is my attempt: 12

The Central Efficiency Rating Committee recognizes that desirable changes could be made in the present system. We believe, however, that no change should be attempted until the war is over.

This cuts the statement from 111 to 30 words, about one-quarter of the origi-   13
nal, but perhaps the reader can do still better. What of importance have I left out?
Sometimes in a book which I am reading for information—not for literary plea-   14
sure—I run a pencil through the surplus words. Often I can cut a section to half its length with an improvement in clarity. Magazines like *The Reader's Digest* have reduced this process to an art. Are long-windedness and obscurity a cultural lag from the days when writing was reserved for priests and cloistered scholars? The more words and the deeper the mystery, the greater their prestige and the firmer the hold on their jobs. And the better the candidate's chance today to have his doctoral thesis accepted.
The F.S.A. surveys found that a great deal of writing was obscure although   15
not necessarily prolix. Here is a letter sent to more than 100,000 inquirers, a classic example of murky prose. To clarify it, one needs to *add* words, not cut them:

In order to be fully insured, an individual must have earned $50 or more in covered employment for as many quarters of the coverage as half the calendar quarters elapsing between 1936 and the quarter in which he reaches age 65 or dies, whichever first occurs.

Probably no one without the technical jargon of the office could translate this; nevertheless, it was sent out to drive clients mad for seven years. One poor fellow wrote back: "I am no longer in covered employment. I have an outside job now."
Many words and phrases in officialese seem to come out automatically, as if   16
from lower centers of the brain. In this standardized prose people never *get jobs,* they "secure employment"; *before* and *after* become "prior to" and "subsequent

to"; one does not *do,* one "performs"; nobody *knows* a thing, he is "fully cogni-
zant"; one never *says,* he "indicates." A great favorite at present is "implement."

Some charming boners occur in this talking-in-one's-sleep. For instance: 17

The problem of extending coverage to all employees, regardless of size, is not as
simple as surface appearances indicate.

Though the proportions of all males and females in ages 16–45 are essentially the
same . . .

Dairy cattle, usually and commonly embraced in dairying . . .

In its manual to employees, the F.S.A. suggests the following: 18

Instead of	*Use*
give consideration to	consider
make inquiry regarding	inquire
is of the opinion	believes
comes into conflict with	conflicts
information which is of a confidential nature	confidential information

Professional or office gobbledygook often arises from using the passive rather   19
than the active voice. Instead of looking you in the eye, as it were, and writing "This
act requires . . ." the office worker looks out of the window and writes: "It is
required by this statute that . . ." When the bureau chief says, "We expect Congress
to cut your budget," the message is only too clear; but usually he says, "It is
expected that the departmental budget estimates will be reduced by Congress."

Gobbled: "All letters prepared for the signature of the Administrator will be single
spaced."

Ungobbled: "Single space all letters for the Administrator." (Thus cutting 13 words to
7.)

Only People Can Read

The F.S.A. surveys pick up the point . . . that human communication involves   2
a listener as well as a speaker. Only people can read, though a lot of writing seems
to be addressed to beings in outer space. To whom are you talking? The sender of
the officialese message often forgets the chap on the other end of the line.

A woman with two small children wrote the F.S.A. asking what she should do   2
about payments, as her husband had lost his memory. "If he never gets able to
work," she said, "and stays in an institution would I be able to draw any benefits?
. . . I don't know how I am going to live and raise my children since he is disable to
work. Please give me some information. . . ."

To this human appeal, she received a shattering blast of gobbledygook, begin-   2
ning, "State unemployment compensation laws do not provide any benefits for sick
or disabled individuals . . . in order to qualify an individual must have a certain
number of quarters of coverage . . ." et cetera, et cetera. Certainly if the writer had
been thinking about the poor woman he would not have dragged in unessential

material about old-age insurance. If he had pictured a mother without means to care for her children, he would have told her where she might get help—from the local office which handles aid to dependent children, for instance.

Gobbledygook of this kind would largely evaporate if we thought of our mes- 23 sages as two way—in the above case, if we pictured ourselves talking on the door-step of a shabby house to a woman with two children tugging at her skirts, who in her distress does not know which way to turn.

Results of the Survey

The F.S.A. survey showed that office documents could be cut 20 to 50 per- 24 cent, with an improvement in clarity and a great saving to taxpapers in paper and payrolls.

A handbook was prepared and distributed to key officials.* They read it, 25 thought about it, and presently began calling section meetings to discuss gobble-dygook. More booklets were ordered, and the local output of documents began to improve. A Correspondence Review Section was established as a kind of laboratory to test murky messages. A supervisor could send up samples for analysis and sug-gestions. The handbook is now used for training new members; and many employ-ees keep it on their desks along with the dictionary. Outside the Bureau some 25,000 copies have been sold (at 20 cents each) to individuals, governments, busi-ness firms, all over the world. It is now used officially in the Veterans Administration and in the Department of Agriculture.

The handbook makes clear the enormous amount of gobbledygook which auto- 26 matically spreads in any large office, together with ways and means to keep it under control. I would guess that at least half of all the words circulating around the bureaus of the world are "irrelevant, incompetent, and immaterial"—to use a favorite legalism; or are just plain "unnecessary"—to ungobble it.

My favorite story of removing the gobble from gobbledygook concerns the 27 Bureau of Standards at Washington. I have told it before but perhaps the reader will forgive the repetition. A New York plumber wrote the Bureau that he had found hydrochloric acid fine for cleaning drains, and was it harmless? Washington replied: "The efficacy of hydrochloric acid is indisputable, but the chlorine residue is incom-patible with metallic permanence."

The plumber wrote back that he was mighty glad the Bureau agreed with him. 28 The Bureau replied with a note of alarm: "We cannot assume responsibility for the production of toxic and noxious residues with hydrochloric acid, and suggest that you use an alternate procedure." The plumber was happy to learn that the Bureau still agreed with him.

Whereupon Washington exploded: "Don't use hydrochloric acid; it eats hell out 29 of the pipes!"

Questions on Content, Structure, and Style

1. As explained by Chase, what is gobbledygook? What are its main characteristics?

---

*By Milton Hall. [Chase's note]

2. What is Chase's attitude toward gobbledygook?

3. Where did the term originate and why?

4. To define his term, Chase relies primarily upon what means of development? Cite evidence to support your answer. Does he successfully explain his definition?

5. What, according to the F.S.A. surveys, is one of the main reasons people produce gobbledygook? What should people think about before they write?

6. Does all gobbledygook come from government bureaucrats? What are some other common sources?

7. What are some of the specific ways Chase and the F.S.A. suggest to clear up murky prose?

8. In paragraph 2, Chase refers to the F.S.A.'s "attempt to break out of the verbal squirrel cage." What does this phrase mean? Is it effective?

9. How does the conclusion successfully summarize Chase's thesis?

10. Can you find or think of other examples of gobbledygook? Do you think that gobbledygook is under control—or is it spreading? What evidence can you cite to support your opinion?

Vocabulary

To understand this essay completely, you should know the meanings of the following words:

ill-clad (1)	exasperated (2)
satire (2)	censuring (2)
polysyllabic (3)	prolix (15)
jargon (4)	cognizant (16)
cloistered (14)	implement (16)

A Revision Worksheet for Your Extended Definition Essay

As you write your rough drafts, consult Chapter 5 for guidance through the revision process. In addition, here are a few questions to ask yourself as you revise your extended definition essay:

1. Is the subject narrowed to manageable size, and is the purpose of the definition clear to the readers?

2. If the definition is objective, is the language as neutral as possible?

3. If the definition is subjective, is the point of view obvious to the readers?

4. Are all the words and parts of the definition itself clear to the essay's particular audience?

5. Are there enough explanatory methods (examples, descriptions, history, causes, effects, etc.) used to make the definition clear and convincing?
6. Have the various methods been organized and ordered in an effective way?
7. Does the essay contain enough specific details to make the definition clear and distinct rather than vague or circular? Where could additional details be added?

After you've revised your essay extensively, you might exchange rough drafts with a classmate and answer these questions for each other, making specific suggestions for improvement wherever appropriate.

STRATEGY FIVE: DEVELOPMENT BY CLASSIFICATION

We classify knowledge to make it easier to comprehend. Without some sort of imposed system of order, a body of information would be only a jumble of facts and figures. For example, at some point you've probably turned to the classified ads in the newspaper; if the ads were not classified into categories such as "houses to rent," "cars for sale," and "help wanted," you would have to search through countless ads to find the service or item you needed. Classification, then, means approaching a subject by separating it into groups, types, or categories.

Classification occurs everywhere around you. As a student, you may be classified as a freshman, sophomore, junior, or senior; you may also be classified by your major. If you vote, you may be categorized as a Democrat, Republican, Socialist, or whatever; if you attend religious services, you may be classified as Baptist, Methodist, Catholic, Jewish, and so on. The car you drive may be classified as luxury, family size, compact, or economy; the movies you see have already been typed as "G," "PG," "R," or "X." Professionals classify almost every kind of knowledge: ornithologists classify birds; etymologists classify words by origins; botanists classify plants; zoologists classify animals, and so on. The list of classification examples is practically endless.

Developing Your Essay

A classification paper is generally easy to develop. Each class or category is identified and described in a major part of the body of the essay. Frequently, one body paragraph will be devoted to each category. Here are three additional rules for classification essays:

Select one principle of classification and stick to it. If you are classifying students by major, for instance, don't suddenly switch to classification by college: French, economics, psychology, *arts and sciences,* math, and chemistry. A similar error occurs in this classification of dogs by breeds because it includes a physical characteristic: spaniels, terriers, *long-haired*, hounds, and retrievers. Decide on what basis of division you will classify your subject and then be consistent throughout your essay.

State the purpose of your classification. Don't just announce, "There are three kinds of 'X.'" Instead, tell the readers why it's important they know about this classification or why this particular classification is meaningful. Here are some sample theses for classification essays:

By recognizing the three kinds of poisonous snakes in this area, campers and backpackers may be able to take the proper medical steps if they are bitten.

Knowing the four types of spinning reels will enable novice fishermen to purchase the equipment best suited to their needs.

While karate has become a popular form of exercise as well as of self-defense, few people actually know what the six levels of achievement—or "belts" as they are called—really stand for.

Don't just classify for the sake of classifying; organize your material for a particular reason and then explain to your reader what that reason is.

Account for all the parts in your classification. Don't, for instance, claim to classify all the evergreen trees native to your hometown and then leave out one or more species. For a short essay, narrow your ruling principle rather than omit categories. You couldn't, for instance, classify all the architectural styles in America in a short paper, but you could discuss the *major* styles on your campus. In the same manner, the enormous task of classifying all types of mental illness could be narrowed to the most common forms of schizophrenia. However you narrow your topic, remember that in a formal classification, all the parts must be accounted for.

Like most rules, the one above has an exception. If your instructor permits, you can also write a satirical or humorous classification. In this sort of essay, you make up your own categories as well as your thesis. One writer, for example, recently wrote about the kinds of moviegoers who spoil the show for everyone else, such as "the babbling idiot," "the laughing hyena," and "the wandering dawdler." Another female student described blind dates to avoid, including "Mr. Neanderthal," "Timothy Timid," "Red, the Raging Rebel," and "Frat-Rat Freddie," among others. Still another student classified the various kinds of people who frequent the school library at two A.M. In this kind of informal essay, the thesis rule still holds true: though you start by making a humorous or satirical point about your subject, your classification must be more than mere silliness. Effective humor should ultimately make good sense, not nonsense.

Problems to Avoid

Avoid underdeveloped categories. A classification is not a mechanical list; each category should contain enough specific details to make it clearly recognizable and interesting. To present each category, you may draw upon the methods of development you already know, such as example, comparison and contrast, and definition.

Avoid indistinct categories. Each category should be a separate unit; there should be no overlap among categories. For example, in a classification of shirts by fabric, the inclusion of flannel with silk, nylon, and cotton is an overlap because flannel is a kind of cotton. Similarly, in a classification of soft drinks by flavor, to include sugar-free with cola, root beer, orange, grape, etc., is misleading because sugar-free drinks come in many different flavors. In other words, make each category unique.

Avoid too few or too many categories. A classification essay should have at least three categories, avoiding the either-or dichotomy. On the other hand, too many categories give a short essay the appearance of a list rather than a discussion. Whatever the number, don't forget to use transition devices for an easy movement from category to category.

Essay Topics

Narrow your subject by selecting an appropriate principle of classification. Some of the suggestions are intended for humorous essays.

1. kinds of plants, insects, or animals
2. teachers
3. T.V. game shows
4. doctors or dentists
5. methods of advertising for a particular product, such as cigarettes or perfume
6. bad dates
7. fast-food restaurants
8. approaches to studying a subject
9. roommates
10. salesclerks/waiters/waitresses
11. sports fans or amateur athletes

12. hitchhikers or bikers
13. people who accost you on campus
14. ways of accomplishing a task (such as three ways to conduct an experiment, four ways to introduce a bill into Congress, etc.)
15. people who play video games or board games
16. kinds of tools or equipment for a particular task in your field of study
17. theories explaining "X" (the disappearance of the dinosaurs, for example)
18. diets or exercise programs
19. reasons people jog (or participate in some other activity)
20. vegetarians or breathatarians

Sample Student Essay

In the essay below, the student writer divided the Mesa Verde Indian Era into three time periods that correspond to changes in the people's domestic skills, crafts, housing, etc. Note the writer's use of description and examples to help the reader see the advances from one time period to another.

THE INDIAN ERA AT MESA VERDE

Introduction: Establishing a reason for knowing the classification

Visiting Mesa Verde National Park is a trip back in time to two-and-a-half centuries before Columbus. The Park, located in southwestern Colorado, is the setting of a silent stone city, ten ruins built into protective seven-hundred-foot cliffs that housed hundreds of Indians from the pre-Columbian era to the end of the thirteenth century. If you visit the Park, you'll enjoy its architecture and history more if you know a little about the various people who lived there. The Indian Era may be divided into three time periods that show growing sophistication in such activities as crafts, hunting, trade, and housing: Basket Maker (A.D. 1–450), Modified Basket Maker (A.D. 450–750), and Pueblo (A.D. 750–1300).*

Principle of classification of the Indian Era

Time period one: The beginnings

The earliest Mesa Verdeans, the Basket Makers, whose forefathers had been nomads, sought shelter from the dry plains in the cliff caves and became farmers. During growing seasons they climbed up toe-holds cut in the cliffs and grew beans and squash on the green mesa above. Settling down also meant more time for crafts. They didn't make pottery yet but instead wove intricate baskets that held

*Last summer I worked at Mesa Verde as a guide for the Parks Service; the information in this paper is based on the tour I gave three times a week to hundreds of visitors to the Park. [Student writer's note]

water. Instead of depending on raw meats and vegetables, they could now cook food in these baskets by dropping heated rocks into the water. Because the Basket Makers hadn't invented the bow and arrow yet, they had to rely on the inaccurate spear, which meant little fresh meat and few animal skins. Consequently, they wore little clothing but liked bone, seed, and stone ornaments.

Time period two: Advances in skills, trade, and housing

The second period, A.D. 450–750, saw the invention of pottery, the bow and arrow, and houses. Pottery was apparently learned from other tribes. From crude clay baked in the sun, the Indians advanced to clay mixed with straw and sand and baked in kilns. Paints were concocted from plants and minerals, and the Indians produced a variety of beautifully decorated mugs, bowls, jars, pitchers, and canteens. Such pots meant that water could be stored for longer periods, and perhaps a water supply encouraged more trade with neighboring tribes. These Mesa Verdeans also acquired the bow and arrow, a weapon that improved their hunting skills, and enlarged their wardrobes to include animal skins and feather blankets. Their individual living quarters, called pithouses, consisted of twenty-foot-wide holes in the ground with log, grasses, and earthen framework over them.

Time period three: More advances in community living, trade, and skills

The third period lasted until A.D. 1300 and saw the innovation of pueblos, or groups of dwellings, instead of single-family units. Nearly eight hundred dwellings show the large number of people who inhabited the complex, tunneled houses, shops, storage rooms, courtyards, and community centers whose masonry walls, often elaborately decorated, were three and four stories high. At the spacious Balcony House pueblo, for example, an adobe court lies beneath another vaulted roof: on three sides stand two-story houses with balconies that lead from one room to the next. In back of the court is a spring, and along the front side is a low wall that kept the children from falling down the seven-hundred-foot cliff to the canyon floor below. Balcony House also contains two *kivas,* circular subterranean ceremonial chambers that show the importance of fellowship and religion to the Indians of this era. During this period the Indians were still farmers and potters, but cotton cloth and other non-native products found at the ruins suggest a healthy trade with the south. But despite the trade goods, sophisticated pottery, and such innovations in clothing as the "disposable" juniper-bark diapers of babies, life was still primitive; the Indians had no system of writing, no wheel, and no metal.

Conclusion: Decline
of the Indian Era

Near the end of the thirteenth century, the cliff dwellings became ghost towns. Archaelogists don't know for certain why the Indians left their elaborate homes, but they
speculate that a drought that lasted some twenty years
may have driven them south into New Mexico and Arizona,
where strikingly similar crafts and tools have been found.
Regardless of their reason for leaving, the Indians left an
amazing architectural and cultural legacy. Learning about
the people who lived in Mesa Verde centuries ago provides
an even deeper appreciation of the cliff palaces that awe
thousands of National Park visitors every year.

Professional Essay

FOUR HANG-UPS
William Zinsser

William Zinsser is a critic, editor, writer, and teacher of writing at Yale University. His
books include *The Lunacy Boom* (1970), *On Writing Well* (1976), and *Writing with
a Word Processor* (1983), from which this selection was taken.

I FOUND myself thinking about some of the psychological blocks that people   1
would bring to their first encounters with a word processor. Different blocks would
be brought by different people, but all of them would be injurious and would have
to be confronted and cleared away.

The hardest thing for me to think about was the idea of getting along without   2
paper. The idea is alien to everything we know in our bones. People have been
writing on paper, or papyrus, for four or five thousand years—long enough, anyway, to get into the habit. Paper is where we transact most of the routine business
of life: letters, postcards, notes, lists, memos, bills, checks, receipts, notices,
reminders to ourselves. Writing something on paper is one of the basic comforts.
Even those of us who keep messy desks know that if we just burrow long enough
in the piles of stuff we'll find the scrap of paper we're looking for—the one we
didn't throw away because we knew that someday we might need it. The nightmare
is to lose the crucial nugget of information: the recipe torn from a magazine, the
name of the perfect little country inn, the phone number of a plumber who will
come on Saturday.

Writers are unusually afraid of loss. The act of writing is so hard that just to   3
get anything on paper is a small victory. A few terrible sentences are better than
no sentences at all; they may at least contain a thought worth saving, a phrase that
can be reshaped. The important thing is that these fragments exist somewhere in

---

the physical world. The paper that they're written on can be held, stared at, marked up, put aside and reexamined later. Ten or twenty pages can be spread out on the floor and rearranged with scissors and paste. Scissors and paste are honorable writers' tools. So is the floor.

I could hardly imagine throwing all this away—not only the paper itself, but the security blanket. With my new word processor I would type my words and see them materialize on a screen. At that moment the words would, I suppose, exist. But would they *really* exist? Not in any sense that I had ever thought of words before. They would be mere shadows of light. If I pressed the wrong key, couldn't they just vanish into thin air? (No air is thinner than the air into which a writer starting out on a word processor thinks his words will vanish.) Or even if I pressed the right key and stored my words correctly overnight on a disk, would I be able to call them back in the morning? Would I ever see them again? The chances of my never seeing them again struck me as high. I didn't trust what I couldn't hold. Paper was the one reality in writing.   4

That was my first block. I wondered how I would get past it—and if I would.   5

The second block was what I'll call the humanist hang-up. This is the snobbery   6
of liberal-arts types who don't understand science or technology and don't want to. It's a group that I belong to myself, so I know its biases and phobias. Our unifying belief is that science has somehow been the cause of everything that has messed up the world and made it so complex and impersonal. If it would just go away. If we could just be left to our exquisitely sensitive appreciation of art and music and literature, of history and philosophy and the classics—the really civilized fields.

Perhaps we aren't snobs so much as we are cowards. We're afraid of how   7
stupid we feel in the presence of science, and so we take refuge in feeling superior. We have never had an aptitude for math or chemistry or engineering, and we are fearful that we won't understand what we read and hear every day about quantum physics, or solid state electronics, or gene splicing, or quasars and quarks.[1] These are mysteries too arcane for us dummies to fathom. Better not to try.

But what really makes us dummies is that we give up so easily. I often think   8
of the pleasure I've lost by shying away from fields that I thought would be too hard to grasp. Only in recent years have I started to glimpse the elegance of the physical and mathematical world by reading the work of scientists who also were writers—men and women like Rachel Carson, Lewis Thomas, Margaret Mead, René Dubos, Jeremy Bernstein and Loren Eiseley. They seem to me to be the true humanists. I envy them their gift for seeing the world whole and not in isolated parts.

Most of us who are afraid of science are also uncomfortable with machines.   9
As a boy I was never taught to tinker and to fix things, and as a man I have lived in a society of servicemen who will repair what has gone wrong. When a piece of machinery breaks, my instinct has always been to hit it, or to yank at it—to force it, somehow, to lurch back into action. It's the blind instinct of a man who regards machines as his enemy. Only later does it occur to me that the broken gadget was

---

[1]Quasars are starlike objects that often emit radio frequency and radiation; quarks are subatomic particles that have electronic charges one-third to two-thirds that of the electron.

built to operate by a series of logical steps and that I might locate the problem by tracing those steps. Even then the idea that I might be able to fix it is almost inconceivable, and when I occasionally succeed I tend to think it was mostly luck.

It's not that I disapprove of technology. On the contrary, I'm grateful for its   10
blessings. I love to drive a car, though I have only a vague notion of what is under the hood or how the combustion engine works. I love to fly in a plane, though I'm fuzzy about the law of aerodynamics that holds such an immense object up in the sky. Surely it defies that other law (which I also hope nobody asks me to explain)— the law of gravity. I'm a fan of the electric light, but my knowledge of the ohm is limited to crossword puzzles—and that goes for the erg and the ampere and the watt.[2]

The point is that it's not necessary to understand the wonders of technology   11
in order to enjoy them, and this should be as true of computers as it is of cars. Yet there is no end of grumbling about them. "I don't want to have anything to do with computers," I keep hearing people say. I used to say it myself, and part of me still continued to think it.

That was obviously a hang-up.   12

The third block is the exact opposite of the one I have just described. It belongs   13
to all the people who are not liberal-arts types—people whose bent is for science and technology and commerce and industry. Their block is that they don't think they have to bother to learn how to write clear English. At the IBM showroom I had seen enough of the word processor to suspect that it could greatly help people to clean up their sentences by focusing their mind on the act of writing and revising. But over the years I had also seen enough writing by America's technical and business people to feel that they are almost beyond salvation.

Here is a typical example of how corporate America conducts its daily business   14
in memos:

> Product usability objective setting should be a direct outgrowth of the initial
> opportunity definition of your program, plus the specific usability oriented information
> gathered during priority setting and the requirements definition activity.

It's little short of criminal to inflict such a memo on a group of employees or   15
colleagues. How much energy do Americans expend every day trying to figure out what people in authority are trying to say? How many good ideas are lost in the murk of Memoville? How many official explanations totally fail to explain? Consider how the airlines tell their passengers—in a notice stapled to every ticket—what to expect if a flight is overbooked:

OVERBOOKING OF FLIGHTS

> If there are not enough volunteers the airline will deny boarding to other persons in
> accordance with its particular boarding priority.

[2]An ohm is a unit of electrical resistance; an erg is a centimeter-gram-second unit of energy; an ampere is a unit of electrical current in the meter-kilogram-second system.

This kind of writing is endemic to American life. Much of what is disseminated by businesses, banks, insurance companies, manufacturers, technical firms, government agencies, educational systems and health institutions—both internally and to the public—is as hard to decipher as an ancient rune,[3] and a great deal of it makes no sense at all. This is because the people who are doing the writing don't stop to think that this is in fact what they are doing. Writing is something that "writers" do.

But writers are only a fraction of the population. The rest of the citizens are in some other line of work, and vast numbers of them write something during the day that gets foisted on other people. Yet very few people realize how badly they write and how badly this hurts them and their career and their company. People are judged on the basis of who they appear to be in their writing, and if what they write is pompous or fuzzy or disorganized they will be perceived as all those things. Bad writing makes bright people look dumb.

How did we get into this fix? It's the humanist hang-up in reverse. People who never had a knack for words usually hated English when they were in school and stopped taking it as soon as they could. Now, out in the world where they need to write, they are as afraid of writing as I am afraid of science. They have writing anxiety. They don't know how to start.

One way to start is to realize that writing is a craft, like carpentry or cabinet-making, with its own set of tools, which are words. Writing is not some sort of divine act that can only be performed by people of artistic bent, though obviously a gift for words is helpful. Writing is the logical arrangement of thought. Anybody who thinks clearly should be able to write clearly—if he learns how to use the tools. Anybody whose thinking is muddy will never write clearly.

To clarify what we write, it is important to see what we are writing and to constantly ask, "Have I said what I wanted to say?" Usually we haven't. Even for a professional writer very few sentences come out right the first time, or even the second or third time. Almost every sentence has some flaw: it's not clear; it could mean several different things; it's not logical; it's cluttered with unnecessary words or phrases; it has too many words that are long and lifeless; it's pretentious; it lacks rhythm.

These are problems that a writer systematically attacks. Like a watchmaker or any other artisan, he wants to build something that works as simply and as smoothly as possible—with no extra parts to get in the way—and he fiddles with his materials until they are right. Nonwriters don't do this. Nobody has told them that rewriting is the essence of writing—that their first draft is probably poor and that they have a second and a third chance to make it better. The worst offenders tend to be bosses who dictate to a secretary. Most people's spoken sentences are full of repetition and disarray. Therefore the man who dictates should see what he has said after it has been typed. One of the things he will see is that he could have said it in half the number of words.

Seeing is a key to writing. What the word processor could do is to revolutionize

16

17

18

19

20

21

22

[3]A rune is a poem or riddle written in an alphabet used by ancient Germanic peoples.

the way we think about words by displaying them for our consideration and giving us an instant chance to reconsider them. It will also draw far more people into the act of writing. In a few years, professional men and women in every field and at every level will be writing on word processors to conduct their daily business. I hope that as their words appear on the terminal screen they will begin to see them as tools that they can use like any other tools—without fear, and maybe even with pleasure.

23

The fourth block is the typing block.

24

A word processor has the same basic keyboard as a typewriter; therefore, anyone who uses it must know how to type. But a surprising number of otherwise competent professional people—especially men—have never learned this fundamental skill. For many men it's a sexist hang-up: typing is something women do. It's all right for men to type if they are writers; their image has been validated by macho authors like Hemingway and by movies about tough reporters in snap-brim hats. But for a man with executive ambitions to sit down at a typewriter and bang out a memo or a letter is an indignity. Better to have Miss Smithers ("a really wonderful gal") do it, even if she can't get to it until tomorrow.

25

What is lost, among other things, is independence. A person who can type is a person in control of an important area of his life: how he communicates with other people. Most writers, for instance, type their own letters—it's quick, and the writing is warm and direct. I would hate to filter what I say through Miss Smithers, wonderful though she is. What I type is who I am. When a secretary is brought into the act, writing stiffens and loses its spontaneity.

26

These, of course, are subjective reasons, related to my feelings about the writing process and about the role of women in America's offices. But there is a practical reason that is far more compelling. With the advent of computers it will be crucial for managers and other people who work in offices to have "keyboard skills."

27

"Suppose a manager must get in touch with the London or San Francisco office," said a recent piece in *The New York Times* analyzing the office of the future. "To operate at maximum efficiency he or she will not interrupt a secretary for a quick memo but will sit down at the keyboard and type. During a typical day a business manager might use terminals several times to write memos to out-of-town offices. Productivity is the key."

28

Nor will there be as many secretaries to interrupt. "The number of young, semi-skilled people for clerical jobs continues to decline," the *Times* noted. "This means that there will be more direct-support computers for managers who do not have enough people support. Middle management officers will certainly be typing."

29

Ironically, many bright and educated young women have avoided learning how to type—or admitting that they already know how—because they have seen how often this skill gets them deflected from a possible good job into one that is clerical and demeaning. The word processor could be the answer to everybody's problem because it isn't stereotyped by sex. Although it's just a glorified typewriter, it doesn't look like a typewriter. It's modern and sleek. You'd almost expect to see it on the command deck of the starship *Enterprise.* A woman can sit at its keyboard and not be taken for a secretary. So can a man.

    Anybody can learn to type. It's one of those skills that become habitual with   30 practice, like driving a car. If typing is your block, invest in a typing course. Don't get stuck with the hang-ups of today when everyone else is flourishing in the office of tomorrow.

Questions on Content, Structure, and Style

1. What is the principle of classification in this essay?
2. What is Zinsser's purpose in presenting his essay?
3. What kinds of psychological blocks does this essay describe? What simple devices does Zinsser use to show the transition from the discussion of one block to the next?
4. Is each kind of "block" clearly presented? Select some examples and details that help make each one distinct.
5. What does Zinsser gain by using himself as a primary example in his discussion of two kinds of blocks?
6. Why does Zinsser include the business memo and the airline notice in his discussion of the third kind of psychological block?
7. How, according to Zinsser, can a word processor help people with writing anxiety and with revision?
8. What evidence does Zinsser cite to support his belief that business people must acquire word-processing skills?
9. Evaluate the appropriateness of the essay's tone in terms of Zinsser's intended audience. What effects do the author's frequent use of personal examples and his use of expressions such as "the murk of Memoville" (15) have on this tone?
10. Zinsser's essay as reprinted here ends after the discussion of the fourth hang-up. Practice your ability to write a good conclusion by adding a last paragraph that wraps up the discussion of all four blocks and is consistent with Zinsser's emphasis on the importance of clear writing.

Vocabulary

injurious (1)	fathom (7)
papyrus (2)	endemic (16)
phobias (6)	pretentious (20)
arcane (7)	artisan (21)

A Revision Worksheet for Your Classification Essay

As you write your rough drafts, consult Chapter 5 for guidance through the revision process. In addition, here are a few questions to ask yourself as you revise your classification essay:

1. Is the purpose of the classification clear to the reader?
2. Is the principle of division for the classification maintained consistently throughout the essay?
3. If the essay presents a formal classification, has the subject been narrowed so that all the parts of the subject are accounted for?
4. If the essay presents an informal or humorous classification, does the paper nevertheless make a significant or entertaining point?
5. Is each category developed with enough specific detail? Where might more details be effectively added?
6. Is each class distinct, with no overlap among categories?
7. Is the essay organized logically and coherently with smooth transitions between the discussions of the categories?

After you've revised your essay extensively, you might exchange rough drafts with a classmate and answer these questions for each other, making specific suggestions for improvement wherever appropriate.

STRATEGY SIX: DEVELOPMENT BY CAUSAL ANALYSIS

Causal analysis explains the cause-and-effect relationship between two (or more) elements. When you discuss the condition producing something, you are analyzing *cause;* when you discuss the result produced by something, you are analyzing *effect*. To find examples of causal analysis, you need only look around you. If your car stops running on the way to class, for example, you may discover the cause was an empty gas tank. On campus, you may study the causes of the Civil War in your history class, the effects of teenage spending on the cosmetics market in your economics class, and both the causes and effects of heart disease in your biology class. Over dinner you may discuss the effects of some crisis in the Middle East on American foreign policy, and as you drift to sleep, you may ponder the effects of your studying—or *not* studying—for your chemistry test tomorrow.

To express it most simply, *cause* asks:

—why did "X" happen?
or, why does "X" happen?
or, why will "X" happen?

Effect, on the other hand, asks:

—what did "Y" produce?
or, what does "Y" produce?
or, what will "Y" produce?

Some essays of causal analysis focus on the cause(s) of something; others analyze only the effect(s); still others discuss both causes and effects. If, for example, you wanted to concentrate on the major causes of the Wall Street crash of 1929, you might begin by briefly describing the effects of the crash on the economy, then devote your thesis and the rest of your essay to analyzing the major causes, perhaps allotting one major section (or one paragraph, depending on the complexity of the reasons) to each cause. Conversely, an effect paper might briefly describe the causes of the crash and then detail the most important effects. An essay covering both the causes and effects of something usually demands a longer paper so that each part will be clear. (If you can select your own essay topic, ask your teacher which kind of causal analysis essay you should write.)

Developing Your Essay

Whether you are writing an essay that primarily discusses either causes or effects, or one that focuses on both, you should follow these rules:

Present a reasonable thesis statement. If your thesis makes dogmatic, unsupportable claims ("Medicare will lead to a complete collapse of quality medical treatment") or overly broad assertions ("Boredom is the cause of alcoholism among housewives"), you won't convince your reader. Limit or qualify your thesis whenever necessary by using such phrases as "may be," "a contributing factor," "one of the main reasons," "two important factors," and so on ("Boredom is *one of the major causes* of alcoholism among housewives").

Limit your essay to a discussion of recent, major causes or effects. In a short paper you generally don't have space to discuss minor or remote causes or effects. If, for example, you analyzed your car wreck, you might decide that the three major causes were defective brakes, a hidden yield sign, and bad weather. A minor, or remote, cause might include being tired because of too little sleep, too little sleep because of staying out late the night before, staying out late because of an out-of-town visitor, and so on—back to the womb. In some cases you may want to mention a few of the indirect causes or effects, but do be reasonable. Concentrate on the most immediate, most important factors. Often, a writer of a 500–800-word essay will discuss no more than two, three, or four major causes or effects of something; to try to cover more frequently results in an underdeveloped essay.

Organize your essay clearly. Organization of your causal analysis essay will vary, of course, depending on whether you are focusing on the causes of something or the effects, or both. To avoid becoming tangled in causes and effects, you might try sketching out a drawing of your thesis and essay map before you begin your first draft. Here, for instance, are a couple of sketches for essays you might write on your recent traffic accident:

THESIS EMPHASIZING THE CAUSES:

Cause (defective brakes)
Cause (hidden yield sign)   produced > Effect (my car wreck)
Cause (bad weather)

THESIS EMPHASIZING THE EFFECTS:

                                     Effect (loss of car)
Cause (my car wreck)   produced > Effect (doctor bills)
                                     Effect (higher insurance rates)

Sometimes you may discover that you can't isolate "the three main causes/effects of 'X'"; some essays do in fact demand a narrative explaining a chain reaction of causes and effects. For example, a paper on the rebellion of the American colonies might show how one unjust British law or restriction after another led to the war for independence. In this kind of causal analysis essay, be careful to limit your subject so that you'll have the space necessary to show your readers how each step in the chain led to the next. Here's a sketch of a slightly different car-wreck paper presented in a narrative or chain-reaction format:

Cause ⟶ 1st Effect —causes→ 2nd Effect —causes→ 3rd Effect
(bad   (wet   (car   (doctor
weather)   brakes)   wreck)   bills)

Sometimes the plan for organizing your causal analysis paper will be suggested by your subject matter; often, however, you'll have to devote some of your prewriting time to deciding, first, whether you want to emphasize causes or effects and, then, in what order you will present your analysis.

Convince your reader that a causal relationship exists by showing how the relationship works. Let's suppose you are writing an essay in which you want to discuss the three major changes you've undergone since coming to college. Don't just state the changes and describe them; your job is to show the reader how college has brought about these changes. If, for instance, your study habits have improved, then you must show the reader how the academic demands of your college courses caused you to change your habits; a simple description of your new study techniques is not enough. Remember that a causal analysis essay should stress *how* (and sometimes *why*) "X" caused "Y," rather than merely describing "Y" as it now exists.

Problems to Avoid

Don't oversimplify by assigning one all-encompassing cause to some effect. Most complex subjects have more than one cause (or effect), so make your analysis as complete and objective as you can, especially when dealing with your own problems or beliefs. For example, was that car wreck really caused only by the bad weather—or also because of your carelessness? Did your friend do poorly in math only because the instructor didn't like her? Before judging a situation too quickly, investigate your own biases. Then provide a thoughtful, thorough analysis, effectively organized to convince your readers of the validity of your viewpoint.

Avoid the post hoc fallacy. This error in logic (from the Latin phrase *post hoc, ergo propter hoc*, meaning "after this, therefore because of this") results when we mistake a temporal connection for a causal relationship—or, in other words, when we assume that because one event follows another in time, the first event caused the second. Most of our superstitions are *post hoc* fallacies; we now realize that tripping after walking under a ladder is a matter of coincidence, not cause and effect. The *post hoc* fallacy provided the basis for a rather popular joke in the 1960s' debates over decriminalizing marijuana. Those against argued that marijuana led to heroin because most users of the hard drug had first smoked grass. The proponents retorted that milk, then, was the real culprit, because both marijuana and heroin users had drunk milk as babies. The point is this: in any causal analysis, you must be able to prove that one event *caused* another, not just that it preceded it in time.

Avoid circular logic. Often causal essays seem to chase their own tails when they include such circular statements as "There aren't enough parking spaces for students on campus because there are too many cars." Such a statement merely presents a second half that restates what is already implied in the first half. A revision might say, "There aren't enough parking spaces for students on campus because the parking permits are not distributed fairly." This kind of assertion can be argued specifically and effectively; the other is a dead end.

Essay Topics

The suggestions below may be developed into essays emphasizing cause, or effect, or both.

1. a pet peeve or bad habit
2. a change of mind about some important issue or belief

3. an accident
4. a family tradition
5. the popularity of some sport, hobby, fad, or style
6. a trend in T.V. shows or movies (horror, science fiction, cops-and-robbers, etc.)
7. a change in your appearance (losing or gaining weight, dyeing your hair)
8. a form of pollution or crime
9. cheating or dishonesty
10. an important decision
11. an act of heroism or sacrifice or selfishness
12. an important idea or discovery in your field of study
13. a superstition or irrational fear
14. a place that is special to you
15. a disappointment or a success
16. sexism (in your experience) or some kind of discrimination or prejudice
17. a friendship or influential person
18. a political action (campus, local, state, national) or piece of legislation
19. teenage marriage or divorce
20. a campus problem

Sample Student Essay

In the following lighthearted essay, the student writer explains the three main causes of his habit of saving old papers or documents. Note that the writer tries to provide enough detail in each paragraph so that the reader understands how this bad habit developed and why it flourishes still.

TIMELESS ACCUMULATION

Introduction: The habit of saving things

Throughout history people have continued to save things that seem to have little or no value. Cavemen would save their old broken clubs, sultans would hold on to their old wives, and preppies would never think of discarding an old Izod shirt. I, in a similar fashion, indefinitely hold on to every piece of paper given to me. Saving all these papers is not just a bad habit picked up from my father; I also hoard papers because I often think of them as awards and because I'm convinced that one day each one will serve some useful, valuable purpose.

Thesis and essay map: The three causes of his habit

Cause one: Imitation of father

While I was growing up, Dad would constantly warn me of the vices of life; however, not throwing away items like church bulletins, ticket stubs, and newspaper clippings was never mentioned as a vice because he saved these scraps of paper himself. Because I wanted to grow up just like my father, I imitated everything he did. Since my dad's desk was crammed with bills, receipts, and office memos, I had to stuff my desk full of paper (that is, if there was any that had slipped past him). Not only did he save little pieces of paper, but every periodical like *Time, National Geographic,* and *People* that entered our house stayed there. So whenever I purchased a *Sports Illustrated* or *Backpacker* magazine, it was soon jammed into a drawer or shoved into my magazine-laden bookshelf. Thus, by the age of twelve my habit of not throwing anything away was well established through my efforts to be just like my dad.

Cause two: View of papers as ego-pleasing awards

Once I began to collect papers in my youth, I found I could not part with them because so many of them seemed like awards. For example, looking at highly scored old tests and well-written reports from school is like looking over a collection of medals and ribbons; viewing them strokes my ego. Surely no one would be expected to toss his Medal of Valor into the trash can! Even though I wrote my first term paper on the American Federation of Labor when I was in the eighth grade, it is still stashed away in one of the many boxes of old papers that seem to grow exponentially in my closet. When I occasionally dig through those boxes and find that report, I am reminded that my hours spent writing about enormously boring unions were rewarded with an "A" and the memory swells my head. (Not only does pride swell my head, but my enlarged ego usually results in an enlarged collection of papers.) In addition to the boxes full of papers, my bulletin board is another place where little ego-building tidbits tend to crop up. For example, pictures of my chromosomes, which adorn a corner of the board, remind me of all the extra time spent in the biology lab drawing blood, mixing it up, and taking pictures. Because only an elite few were allowed to participate in the nauseating experiment, the resulting photographs help to build my conceit. Consequently, because so many of my papers are conducive to my vanity, there is no way I can bring myself to throw them out.

Cause three: View of papers as potentially valuable

Even though papers like my old bank statements and cash register receipts are not cherished, I hold on to them, too, because I feel strongly that someday they will serve some useful purpose. For instance, if the Internal Revenue Service decided to audit me, their investigation could be thwarted by my simply producing the myriad of receipts, which are buried someplace in my desk, glove box, and other convenient places. Deductions could be verified for anything from pens to boxer shorts to my car battery. Without these receipts I might be continuing my collection in jail. Old papers such as class notes might be extremely helpful if a friend enrolls in a class I have taken before. For a nominal fee, I would be more than willing to allow him to peruse my notes if he thought it would help him with the class. Because of this potential loss of revenue, throwing out old notes would not be very practical.

Conclusion:
Reference to thesis,
ending on humorous
note

Despite the opinions of neatness fanatics, my utter disdain toward throwing away papers is not the product of a warped mind but has been caused by several sensible desires for a better life. My only problem now is that I've either got to become more selective about what to keep or plan to make lots of money to buy a bigger house. I wonder what the caveman did with all those broken clubs. . . .

Professional Essay

THE GREAT AMERICAN COOLING MACHINE
Frank Trippett

Frank Trippett is a journalist, author, and editor who has worked for *Newsweek, Look,* and *Time,* where he is currently an associate editor. His books include *The States: United They Fell* (1967), *The First Horseman* (1974), and *Child Ellen* (1975). This essay appeared in *Time* during the energy crunch of 1979.

"THE GREATEST CONTRIBUTION to civilization in this century may well be air conditioning—and America leads the way." So wrote British Scholar-Politician S. F. Markham 32 years ago when a modern cooling system was still an exotic luxury. In a century that has yielded such treasures as the electric knife, spray-on deodorant and disposable diapers, anybody might question whether air conditioning is the supreme gift. There is not a whiff of doubt, however, that America is far out front in its use. As a matter of lopsided fact, the U.S. today, with a mere 5% of the population, consumes as much man-made coolness as the whole rest of the world put together.   1

Just as amazing is the speed with which this situation came to be. Air conditioning began to spread in industries as a production aid during World War II. Yet only a generation ago a chilled sanctuary during summer's stewing heat was a happy frill that ordinary people sampled only in movie houses. Today most Americans tend to take air conditioning for granted in homes, offices, factories, stores,   2 theaters, shops, studios, schools, hotels and restaurants. They travel in chilled buses, trains, planes and private cars. Sporting events once associated with open sky and fresh air are increasingly boxed in and air cooled. Skiing still takes place outdoors, but such attractions as tennis, rodeos, football and, alas, even baseball are now often staged in synthetic climates like those of Houston's Astrodome and New Orleans' Superdome. A great many of the country's farming tractors are now, yup, air-conditioned.

It is thus no exaggeration to say that Americans have taken to mechanical cooling avidly and greedily. Many have become all but addicted, refusing to go places that are not air-conditioned. In Atlanta, shoppers in Lenox Square so resented having to endure natural heat while walking outdoors from chilled store to chilled store that the mall management enclosed and air-conditioned the whole sprawling shebang. The widespread whining about Washington's raising of thermostats to a mandatory 78°F suggests that people no longer think of interior coolness as an amenity but consider it a necessity, almost a birthright, like suffrage. The existence of such a view was proved last month when a number of federal judges, sitting too high and mighty to suffer 78°, defied and denounced the Government's energy-saving order to cut back on cooling. Significantly, there was no popular outrage at this judicial insolence; many citizens probably wished that they could be so highhanded.

Everybody by now is aware that the cost of the American way is enormous, that air conditioning is an energy glutton. It uses some 9% of all electricity produced. Such an extravagance merely to provide comfort is peculiarly American and strikingly at odds with all the recent rhetoric about national sacrifice in a period of menacing energy shortages. Other modern industrial nations such as Japan, Germany and France have managed all along to thrive with mere fractions of the man-made coolness used in the U.S., and precious little of that in private dwellings. Here, so profligate has its use become that the air conditioner is almost as glaring a symptom as the automobile of the national tendency to overindulge in every technical possibility, to use every convenience to such excess that the country looks downright coddled.

But not everybody is aware that high cost and easy comfort are merely two of the effects of the vast cooling of America. In fact, air conditioning has substantially altered the country's character and folkways. With the dog days at hand and the thermostats ostensibly up, it is a good time to begin taking stock of what air conditioning has done besides lower the indoor temperature.

Many of its byproducts are so conspicuous that they are scarcely noticed. To begin with, air conditioning transformed the face of urban America by making possible those glassy, boxy, sealed-in skyscrapers on which the once humane geometries of places like San Francisco, Boston and Manhattan have been impaled. It has been indispensable, no less, to the functioning of sensitive advanced computers, whose high operating temperatures require that they be constantly cooled. Thus, in a very real way, air conditioning has made possible the ascendancy of computerized civilization. Its cooling protection has given rise not only to moon landings, space shuttles and Skylabs but to the depersonalized punch-cardification of society that regularly gets people hot under the collar even in swelter-proof environments.

It has also reshaped the national economy and redistributed political power simply by encouraging the burgeoning of the sultry southerly swatch of the country, profoundly influencing major migration trends of people and industry. Sunbelt cities like Phoenix, Atlanta, Dallas and Houston (where shivering indoor frigidity became a mark of status) could never have mushroomed so prosperously without air conditioning; some communities—Las Vegas in the Nevada desert and Lake Havasu City on the Arizona-California border—would shrivel and die overnight if it were turned off.

It has, as well, seduced families into retreating into houses with closed doors   7
and shut windows, reducing the commonalty of neighborhood life and all but obsoleting the front-porch society whose open casual folkways were an appealing hallmark of a sweatier America. Is it really surprising that the public's often noted withdrawal into self-pursuit and privatism has coincided with the epic spread of air conditioning? Though science has little studied how habitual air conditioning affects mind or body, some medical experts suggest that, like other technical avoidance of natural swings in climate, air conditioning may take a toll on the human capacity to adapt to stress. If so, air conditioning is only like many other greatly useful technical developments that liberate man from nature by increasing his productivity and power in some ways—while subtly weakening him in others.

Neither scholars nor pop sociologists have really got around to charting and   8
diagnosing all the changes brought about by air conditioning. Professional observers have for years been preoccupied with the social implications of the automobile and television. Mere glancing analysis suggests that the car and TV, in their most decisive influences on American habits, have been powerfully aided and abetted by air conditioning. The car may have created all those shopping centers in the boondocks, but only air conditioning has made them attractive to mass clienteles. Similarly, the artificial cooling of the living room undoubtedly helped turn the typical American into a year-round TV addict. Without air conditioning, how many viewers would endure reruns (or even Johnny Carson) on one of those pestilential summer nights that used to send people out to collapse on the lawn or to sleep on the roof?

Many of the side effects of air conditioning are far from being fully pinned   9
down. It is a reasonable suspicion, though, that controlled climate, by inducing Congress to stay in Washington longer than it used to during the swelter season, thus presumably passing more laws, has contributed to bloated Government. One can only speculate that the advent of the supercooled bedroom may be linked to the carnal adventurism associated with the mid-century sexual revolution. Surely it is a fact—if restaurant complaints about raised thermostats are to be believed—that air conditioning induces at least expense-account diners to eat and drink more; if so, it must be credited with adding to the national fat problem.

Perhaps only a sophist might be tempted to tie the spread of air conditioning   10
to the coincidentally rising divorce rate, but every attentive realist must have noticed that even a little window unit can instigate domestic tension and chronic bickering between couples composed of one who likes it on all the time and another who does not. In fact, perhaps surprisingly, not everybody likes air conditioning. The necessarily sealed rooms or buildings make some feel claustrophobic, cut off

from the real world. The rush, whir and clatter of cooling units annoys others. There are even a few eccentrics who object to man-made cool simply because they like hot weather. Still, the overwhelming majority of Americans have taken to air conditioning like hogs to a wet wallow.

It might be tempting, and even fair, to chastise that vast majority for being spoiled rotten in their cool ascendancy. It would be more just, however, to observe that their great cooling machine carries with it a perpetual price tag that is going to provide continued and increasing chastisement during the energy crisis. Ultimately, the air conditioner, and the hermetic buildings it requires, may turn out to be a more pertinent technical symbol of the American personality than the car. While the car has been a fine sign of the American impulse to dart hither and yon about the world, the mechanical cooler more neatly suggests the maturing national compulsion to flee the natural world in favor of a technological cocoon. **11**

Already architectural designers are toiling to find ways out of the technical trap represented by sealed buildings with immovable glass, ways that might let in some of the naturally cool air outside. Some have lately come up with a remarkable discovery: the openable window. Presumably, that represents progress. **12**

Questions on Content, Structure, and Style

1. When Trippett begins his essay with the Markham quotation followed by his reference to a century that has produced "such treasures as the electric knife, spray-on deodorant and disposable diapers," what tone is being established?
2. Why does Trippett spend several paragraphs describing America's "addiction" to air conditioning? What is his attitude toward America's use of this invention?
3. Where is Trippett's thesis stated? Does his essay analyze the causes or the effects of this country's dependence on air conditioning?
4. What, in Trippett's opinion, are some of the lesser-known effects of air conditioning?
5. What kinds of evidence does Trippett offer to support this analysis? Cite some examples from the essay.
6. Do you think Trippett intended for his audience to take all his speculations on the effects of air conditioning entirely seriously? Why/why not?
7. What is the effect on the reader of such words and phrases as "whiff of doubt" (paragraph 1), "yup" (2), "whole sprawling shebang" (3), "punch-cardification of society" (6), "a sweatier America" (7), and "hogs to a wet wallow" (10)? Is such language appropriate in this essay?
8. Is Trippett generally pleased or unhappy with the effects of air conditioning he describes? Support your answer with specific examples from the essay.
9. What, ultimately, may the air conditioner symbolize about modern Americans? Do you agree?

   10. How does Trippett's concluding paragraph emphasize both the tone and the author's attitude toward his subject as expressed throughout the essay?

Vocabulary

amenity (3)	indispensable (6)
suffrage (3)	burgeoning (6)
profligate (4)	sophist (10)
ostensibly (5)	chastise (11)
conspicuous (6)	hermetic (11)

A Revision Worksheet for Your Causal Analysis Essay

As you write your rough drafts, consult Chapter 5 for guidance through the revision process. In addition, here are a few questions to ask yourself as you revise your causal analysis essay:

   1. Is the thesis limited to a reasonable claim that can be supported in the essay?

   2. Is the organization clear and consistent so that the reader can understand the purpose of the analysis?

   3. Does the essay focus on the most important causes and/or effects?

   4. If the essay has a narrative form, is each step in the chain reaction clearly connected to the next?

   5. Does the essay convincingly show the reader how or why relationships between the causes and effects exist, instead of merely naming and describing them?

   6. Does the essay provide enough evidence to show the connections between causes and effects? Where could additional details be added to make the relationships clearer?

   7. Has the essay avoided the problems of oversimplification, circular logic, and the *post hoc* fallacy?

After you've revised your essay extensively, you might exchange rough drafts with a classmate and answer these questions for each other, making specific suggestions for improvement wherever appropriate.

Argumentation

Almost without exception, each of us, every day, argues for or against something with somebody. The discussions may be short and friendly ("Let's go to this restaurant rather than that one") or long and complex ("Mandatory seat belt laws are an intrusion on civil rights"). Because we do argue our viewpoints so often, most of us realized long ago that shifting into high whine did not always get us what we wanted; on the contrary, we've learned that we usually have a much better chance at winning a dispute or having our plan adopted or changing someone's mind if we present our side of an issue in a calm, logical fashion, giving sound reasons for our position. And this approach is just what a good argumentative essay does: it presents logical reasoning and solid evidence that will persuade your readers to accept your point of view.

Some argumentative essays declare the best solution to a problem ("Raising the drinking age will decrease traffic accidents"); others argue a certain way of looking at an issue ("Beauty pageants degrade women"); still others may urge adoption of a specific plan of action ("Voters should pass ordinance #10 to fund the new ice rink"). Whatever your exact purpose, your argument essay should be composed of a clear thesis and body paragraphs that offer enough sensible reasons and persuasive evidence to convince your readers to agree with you.

DEVELOPING YOUR ESSAY

Here are some suggestions for developing and organizing an effective argumentative essay:

Know why you hold your views. We human beings, being opinionated creatures, frequently voice beliefs that we, when pressed, can't always support effectively. Sometimes we hold an opinion simply because on the surface it seems to make good sense to us or because it fits comfortably with our other social, ethical, or political beliefs. Or we may have inherited some of our beliefs from our families or friends, or perhaps we borrowed ideas from people we admired. In some cases, we may have held an opinion for so long that we can't remember why we adopted it in the first place. We may also have a purely sentimental or emotional attachment to some idea or position. Whatever the original causes of our beliefs, we need to examine the real reasons for thinking what we do before we can effectively convince others.

Once you've selected a topic for your argument essay, try writing down a list of the reasons or points that support your opinion on that subject. Then study the list—are your points logical and persuasive? Which aren't, and why not? After this bit of prewriting, you may discover that although you believe something strongly, you really don't have the kinds of factual evidence or reasoned arguments you need to support your opinion. In some cases, depending upon your topic, you may wish to talk to others who share your position or to research your subject (for help with research, see Chapter 12); in other cases, you may just need to think longer and harder about your topic and your reasons for maintaining your attitude toward it. With or without formal research, the better you know your subject, the more confident you will be about writing your argumentative essay.

Anticipate opposing views. An argument assumes that there is more than one side to an issue. To be convincing, you must be aware of your opposition's views on the subject and then organize your essay to answer or counter those views. If you don't have a good idea of the opposing arguments, you can't effectively persuade your readers to dismiss their objections and see matters your way. Therefore, before you begin your first rough draft, write down all the opposing views you can think of and an answer to each of them so that you will know your subject thoroughly. (For the sake of clarity throughout this chapter, your act of responding to those arguments against your position will be called *refuting the opposition*; "to refute" means "to prove false or wrong," and that's what you will try to do to some of the arguments of those who disagree with you.)

Decide which points of argument to include. Once you have a good sense of both your own position and your opposition's arguments, try making a Pro-and-Con Sheet to help you sort out which points you will discuss in your essay.

Let's suppose you want to write on the sale-of-class-notes controversy at your school. Should professional note-takers be allowed to sit in on a course and then sell their notes to class members? After reviewing the evidence on both sides, you have decided to argue that your school should prohibit professional note-taking services from attending classes and selling notes. To help yourself begin planning your essay, you list all the pro and con arguments you can think of concerning the controversy:

MY SIDE: AGAINST THE SALE OF CLASS NOTES

1. unfair advantage for some students in some classes
2. note-taking is a skill students need to develop
3. rich students can afford and poor can't
4. prevents students from learning to organize for themselves
5. encourages class cutting
6. missing class means no chance to ask questions, participate in discussions
7. notes taken by others are often inaccurate
8. some professors don't like strangers in classroom
9. students need to think for themselves

MY OPPOSITION'S SIDE: FOR THE SALE OF CLASS NOTES

1. helps students to get better test, course grades
2. helps students to learn, organize material
3. helps if you're sick and can't attend class
4. shows students good models for taking notes and outlining them
5. other study guides are on the market, why not these?
6. gives starving graduate students jobs
7. no laws against sale of notes, free country

After making your Pro-and-Con Sheet, look over the list and decide which of your strongest points you want to argue in your paper and also which of your opposition's claims you want to refute. At this point you may also see some arguments on your list that might be combined and some that might be deleted because they're irrelevant or unconvincing. (Be careful not to select more arguments or counter-arguments to discuss than the length of your writing assignment will allow. It's far better to present a persuasive analysis of a few points than it is to give an underdeveloped, shallow treatment of a host of reasons.)

Let's say you want to cover the following points in your essay:

- professional note-taking services keep students from developing own thinking and organizational skills (combination of #4 and 9)
- professional note-taking services discourage class attendance and participation (#5 and 6)
- unfair advantages to some students (#1 and 3).

Your assignment calls for a short essay of 750–1000 words, so you figure you'll only have space to refute your opposition's strongest claim, and you decide that is

- helps students to learn and organize material (#2).

The next step is to formulate a working thesis. At this stage you may find it helpful to put your working thesis in an "although-because" format so you can clearly see both your opposition's arguments and your own. An "although-because" statement for the note-taking essay might look something like this:

Although some students maintain that using professional note-taking services helps them learn more, such services should be banned from our campus *because* they prevent students from developing their own thinking and organizational skills, they discourage class attendance, and they give unfair advantages to some students.

Frequently your "although-because" thesis will be too long and awkward to use in the later drafts of your essay. But for now, it can serve as a guide, allowing you to see your overall position before the writing of the first draft begins.

Organize your essay clearly. While there is no set model of organization for argumentative essays, here are some common patterns that you might use or that you might combine in some effective way.

Important Note: For the sake of simplicity, the first two outlines present two of the writer's points and two opposing ideas. Naturally, your essay may contain any number of points and refuted points, depending upon the complexity of your subject and the assigned length of your essay.

In Pattern A you devote the first few body paragraphs to arguing points on your side and then turn to refute or answer the opposition's claims.

Pattern A: Thesis
Body paragraph 1: you present your first point and its supporting evidence
Body paragraph 2: you present your second point and its supporting evidence
Body paragraph 3: you refute your opposition's first point
Body paragraph 4: you refute your opposition's second point
Conclusion

Sometimes you may wish to clear away the opposition's claims before you present the arguments for your side. To do so, you might select Pattern B:

Pattern B: Thesis
Body paragraph 1: you refute your opposition's first point
Body paragraph 2: you refute your opposition's second point
Body paragraph 3: you present your first point and its supporting evidence
Body paragraph 4: you present your second point and its supporting evidence
Conclusion

In some cases you may find that the main arguments you want to present are the very same ones that will refute or answer your opposition's primary claims. If so, try Pattern C, which allows each of your argumentative points to refute one of your opposition's claims in the same paragraph:

Pattern C: Thesis
Body paragraph 1: you present your first point and its supporting evidence, which also refutes one of your opposition's claims
Body paragraph 2: you present a second point and its supporting evidence, which also refutes a second opposition claim
Body paragraph 3: you present a third point and its supporting evidence, which also refutes a third opposition claim
Conclusion

Now you might be thinking, what if my position on a topic as yet has no opposition? Remember that almost all issues have more than one side, so try to anticipate objections and then answer them. For example, you might first present a thesis that calls for a new traffic signal at a dangerous intersection in your town and then address hypothetical counter-arguments, such as "The City Council may say that a stop light at Lemay and Columbia will cost too much, but the cost in lives will be much greater" or "Commuters may complain that a traffic light there will slow the continuous flow of north-south traffic, but it is precisely the uninterrupted nature of this road that encourages motorists to speed." By answering hypothetical objections, you impress your readers by showing them you've thought through your position thoroughly before you asked them to consider your point of view.[1]

If you are feeling confident about your ability to organize an argumentative essay, you might try some combination of patterns, if your material allows such a treatment. For example, you might have a strong point to argue, another point that simultaneously answers one of your opposition's strongest claims, and another opposition point you want to refute. Your essay organization might look like this:

> **Combination:**   Thesis
> Body paragraph 1: A point for your side
> Body paragraph 2: One of your points, which also refutes an opposition claim
> Body paragraph 3: Your refutation of another opposition claim

In other words, you can organize your essay in a variety of ways as long as your paper is logical and clear. Study your Pro-and-Con Sheet and then decide which organization best presents the arguments and counter-arguments you want to include. Try sketching out your essay following each of the patterns; look carefully to see which pattern (or variation on one of the patterns) seems to put forward your particular material most persuasively, with the least repetition or confusion. Sometimes your essay's material will clearly fall into a particular pattern of organization, so your choice will be easy; more often, however, you will have to arrange and rearrange your ideas and counter-arguments until you see the best approach. Don't be discouraged if you decide to change patterns after you've begun a rough draft; what matters is finding the most effective way to persuade the reader to your side.

If no organizational pattern seems to fit at first, ask yourself which of your points or counter-arguments is the strongest or most important. Try putting that point in one of the two most emphatic places: either first or last. Sometimes your most important discussion will lead the

---

[1]You might also be thinking, "What if my opposition actually has a valid objection, a legitimate point of criticism? Should I ignore it?" Hoping that an obviously strong opposing point will just go away is like hoping the IRS will cancel income taxes this year—a nice thought but hardly likely. Don't ignore your opposition's good point; instead, acknowledge it, but then go on quickly to show your readers why that reason, though valid, isn't compelling enough by itself to motivate people to adopt your opposition's entire position. Or you might concede that one point while simultaneously showing why your position isn't really in conflict with that criticism, but rather with other, more important, parts of your opponent's viewpoint. By admitting that you see some validity in your opposition's argument, you can again show your readers that you are both fair-minded and informed about all aspects of the controversy.

way into your other points and consequently should be introduced first; perhaps more often, effective writers and speakers build up to their strongest point, presenting it last as the climax of their argument. Again, the choice depends on your material itself, though it's rare that you would want to bury your strongest point in the middle of your essay.

After studying the arguments and counter-arguments you selected for the note-taking essay, let's say that you decide that your most important point concerns the development of students' learning skills. Since your opposition claims the contrary, that their service does promote learning, you see that you can make your main point as you refute theirs. But you also wish to include a couple of other points for your side. After trying several patterns, you decide to put the "thinking skills" rebuttal last for emphasis and present your other points first. Consequently, Pattern A best fits your plan. A sketchy outline might look like this:

- Revised working thesis and essay map: Professional note-taking services should be banned from our campus. Not only do they give some students unfair advantages and discourage class attendance, they prevent students from developing and practicing good thinking skills.
- Body paragraph 1 (A first point for the writer's side): services penalize some students—those who haven't enough money or take other sections or enroll in classes without notes.
- Body paragraph 2 (Another point for the writer's side): the service encourages class-cutting and so students miss opportunities to ask questions, participate in discussion, talk to instructor, see visual aids, etc.
- Body paragraph 3 (Rebuttal of the opposition's strongest claim): services claim they help students learn more, but they don't because they're doing the work students ought to be doing themselves. Students must learn to think and organize for themselves.

Once you have a general notion of where your essay is going, plan to spend some more time thinking about ways to make each of your points clear, logical, and persuasive to your particular audience. (If you wish to see how one student actually developed an essay based on the outline above, turn to the sample student paper on pp. 219–221.)

Support your argument effectively. To convince your readers, you must first provide sufficient reasons for your position. You must give more than mere opinion—you must offer logical evidence to back up your assertions. Some of the possible ways of supporting your ideas should already be familiar to you from writing expository essays; listed below are several methods and illustrations:

1. Give Examples (real or hypothetical): "Cutting class because you have access to professional notes can be harmful; for instance, you might miss seeing some slides or graphics essential to your understanding of the lecture."
2. Present a Comparison or Contrast: "In contrast to reading 'canned' notes, outlining your own notes helps you remember the material."
3. Show a Cause-and-Effect Relationship: "Dependence on professional notes may mean that some students will never learn to organize their own responses to classroom discussions."
4. Argue by Definition: "Passively reading through professional notes isn't a learning experience in which one's mind is engaged."

In addition to your reasoned arguments, in some essays you may also want to include the following kinds of evidence:

- personal experiences
- the experiences or testimony of others whose opinions are pertinent to the topic
- factual information you've gathered from research
- statistics from current, reliable sources
- charts, graphs, diagrams
- testimony from authorities and experts

You'll need to spend quite a bit of your prewriting time thinking about the best kinds of evidence to support your case. Not all personal experiences or research materials are persuasive. For instance, the experiences we've had (or that our friends have had) may not be representative of a universal experience and consequently may lead to unconvincing generalizations. Even testimony from an authority may not be convincing if the person is not speaking on a topic from his or her field of expertise; famous football players, for instance, don't necessarily know any more about panty hose or soft drinks than anyone else. Always put yourself in the skeptical reader's place and ask, "Does this point convince me? If not, why not?" (For much more information on gathering, selecting, and incorporating research material into your essays, see Chapter 12.)

Know and remember your audience. While it's important to think about your readers' needs and expectations whenever you write, it is essential to consider carefully the audience of your argumentative essay both before and as you write your rough drafts. Because you are trying to persuade people to adopt some new point of view or perhaps to take some action, you need to decide what kinds of supporting evidence will be most convincing to your particular readers. Try to analyze your audience by asking yourself a series of questions, such as what do they already know about your topic? What information or terms do they need to know to understand your point of view? What biases might they already have for or against your position? What special concerns might your readers have that influence their receptiveness? To be convincing, you should consider these questions and others by carefully reviewing the discussion of audience on pp. 15–18 *before* you start your first rough draft.

One more note on audience: sometimes when we argue, it's easy to get carried away. Remember that your goal is to persuade and perhaps change your readers, not alienate them. Instead of laying on insults or sarcasm, present your ideas in a moderate let-us-reason-together spirit. Such a tone will persuade your readers that you are sincere in your attempts to argue as truthfully and fairly as possible. If your readers do not respect you as a reasonable person, they certainly won't be swayed to your side of an issue. Don't preach or pontificate either; no one likes—or respects—a writer with a superior attitude. Write in your natural "voice"; don't adopt a pseudointellectual tone. In short, to argue effectively you should sound logical, sincere, and informed. (For additional comments on tone, review pp. 111–114.)

Problems to Avoid

Writers of argumentative essays must appear logical or their readers will reject their point of view. Here is a short list of some of the most common *logical fallacies*—that is, errors in reasoning. Check your rough drafts carefully to avoid these problems.

Incidentally, students sometimes ask, "If a logical fallacy works, why not use it? Isn't all fair in love, war, and argumentative essays?" The honest answer is "maybe." It's quite true that speakers and writers do use faulty logical and irrational appeals to persuade people everyday (one needs only to look at advertising or politics to see example after example). But the cost of the risk is high: if you do try to slide one by your readers and they see through your trick, you will lose your credibility instantly. On the whole, it's far more effective to use logical reasoning and strong evidence to convince your readers to accept your point of view.

COMMON LOGICAL FALLACIES

Hasty generalization: The writer bases the argument on insufficient or unrepresentative evidence. . Suppose, for example, you have owned two poodles and they have both attacked you. If you declare that all poodles are vicious dogs, you are making a hasty generalization. There are, of course, thousands of poodles who have not attacked anyone. Similarly, you're in error if you interview only campus athletes and then declare, "University students favor a new stadium." What about the opinions of the students who aren't athletes? In other words, when the generalization is drawn from an unrepresentative or insufficient sample, your conclusion isn't valid.

Non sequitur ("it doesn't follow"): The writer's conclusion is not necessarily a logical result of the facts. An example of a *non sequitur* occurs when you conclude, "Professor Smith is a famous historian, so he will be a brilliant history teacher." As you may have realized by now, just that someone knows a subject well does not automatically mean that he or she can communicate the information clearly; hence, the conclusion is not necessarily valid.

Begging the question: The writer presents as truth what is supposed to be proven by the argument. For example, in the statement, "All useless laws such as Reform Bill 13 should be repealed," the writer has already assumed the bill is useless without assuming responsibility for proving that accusation. Similarly, the statement "Japan's immoral slaughter of whales ought to be condemned by the United Nations" begs the question (that is, tries like a beggar to get something for nothing from the reader) because the writer gives no evidence for what must first be argued, not merely asserted—that Japan's actions are immoral.

Red herring: The writer introduces an irrelevant point to divert the readers' attention from the main issue. This term originates from the old tactic, used by escaped prisoners, of dragging a smoked herring, a strong-smelling fish, across their trail to confuse tracking dogs by making them follow the wrong scent. For example, roommate A might be criticizing roommate B for his repeated failure to do the dishes when it was his turn. To escape facing the charges, roommate B brings up times in the past when the other roommate failed to repay some money he borrowed. While roommate A may indeed have a problem with remembering his debt, that discussion isn't relevant to the original argument about sharing the responsibility for the dishes.

Post hoc, ergo propter hoc: See p. 197.

Argument ad hominem ("to the man"): The writer attacks the opponent's character rather than the opponent's argument. The statement

"Dr. Bloom can't be a competent marriage counselor because she's been married twice" may not be valid; Bloom's advice to her clients may be excellent regardless of her own marital status.

Faulty use of authority: See pp. 258–259.

Argument <u>ad populum</u> ("to the people"): The writer evades the issues by appealing to readers' emotional reactions to certain subjects. For example, instead of arguing the facts of an issue, a writer might play upon the readers' negative response to such words as "communism" and "fascism" or their positive response to words and concepts like "God," "country," and "liberty." In the statement "If you are a true American, you will vote against the referendum on busing," the writer avoids any discussion of the merits or weaknesses of the bill and merely substitutes an emotional appeal. (Advertisers, of course, play on consumers' emotions by filling their ads with pictures of babies, animals, status objects, and sexually attractive men and women.)

Circular thinking: See p. 197.

Either/or: The writer tries to convince the readers that there are only two sides to an issue—one right, one wrong. The statement "If you don't go to war against Iceland, you don't love your country" is irrational because it doesn't consider the other possibilities, such as patriotic people's right to oppose war as an expression of love for their country. A classic example of this sort of oversimplification was illustrated in the 1960s' bumper sticker that was popular during the debate over the Vietnam War: "America: Love It or Leave It." Obviously, there are other choices ("Change It or Lose It," for instance).

Hypostatization: The writer uses an abstract concept as if it were a concrete reality. Always be suspicious of a writer who uses statements beginning, "History has taught us . . .," "Science has proven . . .," or "Medicine has discovered. . . ." The implication in each case is that history or science or medicine has only one voice, one opinion. On the contrary, "history" is written by a multitude of historians who hold a variety of opinions; doctors and scientists also frequently disagree. Instead of generalizing about a particular field, quote a respected authority or simply qualify your statement by referring to "many" or "some" scientists, historians, or whatever.

Bandwagon appeal: The writer tries to validate a point by intimating that "Everyone else believes in this." Such a tactic evades discussion of the issue itself. Advertising often uses this technique: "Everyone who demands real taste smokes Phooey cigarettes"; "Discriminating women use Smacky-Mouth lipstick." (The ultimate in "bandwagon" humor may have appeared on a recent Colorado bumper sticker: "Eat lamb— could 1000s of coyotes be wrong?")

Faulty analogy: The writer uses an extended comparison as proof of a point. Look closely at all extended comparisons and metaphors to see if the two things being compared are really similar. For example, in a recent editorial a woman protested the new laws requiring parents to use car seats for small children, arguing that if the state could require the seats they could just as easily require mothers to breastfeed instead of using formula. Are the two situations alike? Car accidents are the leading cause of death of children under four; is formula dangerous? Or perhaps you've read that Politician X's plan for aid to Transylvania (or somewhere) is just like Russia's control of Poland. If the opinion isn't supported by factual evidence, then the analogy isn't persuasive. Remember that even though an analogy might suggest similarities, it alone cannot *prove* anything.

Quick fix: The writer leans too heavily on catchy phrases or empty slogans. A clever turn-of-phrase may be an attention-grabber, but it may lose its persuasiveness when scrutinized closely. For instance, a banner at a recent rally to protest a piece of anti-gun legislation read "When guns are outlawed, only outlaws will have guns." While the sentence has nice balance, it oversimplifies and thus misleads. The legislation was not trying to outlaw all guns, just the sale of the infamous Saturday Night Specials, most often used in crimes and domestic violence; the sale of guns for sport, such as hunting rifles, would remain legal. Other slogans sound good but are simply irrelevant; a particular soft drink, for example, may be "the real thing," but what drink isn't? Look closely at clever lines substituted for reasoned argument; always demand clear terms and logical explanations.[2]

Practicing What You've Learned

Errors in reasoning can cause your reader to doubt your credibility. In the following mock essay, for example, the writer includes a variety of fallacies that undermine his argument; see if you can identify all his errors.

---

[2]Sometimes advertisers get more for their slogans than they bargained for. According to one news source, a popular soft drink company had to spend millions to revise its slogan after introducing its product into parts of China. Apparently the slogan "Come alive! Join the Blah-Blah-Cola Generation!" translated into some dialects as "Blah-Blah Cola Brings Your Ancestors Back from the Dead"!

BAN THOSE BOOKS!

A serious problem faces America today, a problem of such grave importance that our very existence as a nation is threatened. We must either cleanse our schools of evil-minded books, or we must reconcile ourselves to seeing our children become welfare moochers and bums.

History has shown time and time again that placement of immoral books in our schools is part of a *bona fide* Communist plot designed to weaken the moral fiber of our youth from coast to coast. In Wettuckett, Ohio, for example, the year after books by Mark Twain such as *Tom Sawyer* and *Huckleberry Finn* were introduced into the school library by liberal free-thinkers and radicals, the number of students cutting classes rose by ten percent. And in that same year the number of high school seniors going on to college dropped from thirty to twenty-two.

The reason for this could either be a natural decline in intelligence and morals or the influence of those dirty books that teach our beloved children disrespect and irresponsibility. Since there is no evidence to suggest a natural decline, the conclusion is inescapable: once our children read about Twain's characters skipping school and running away from home, they had to do likewise. If they hadn't read about such undesirable characters as Huckleberry Finn, our innocent children would never have behaved in those ways.

Now, I am a simple man, a plain old farm boy—the pseudointellectuals call me redneck just like they call you folks. But I can assure you that, redneck or not, I've got the guts to fight the Communist conspiracy everywhere I find it, and I urge you to do the same. For this reason I want all you good folks to come to the ban-the-books rally this Friday so we can talk it over. I can promise you all your right-thinking neighbors will be there.

Assignment

Search for the following:
1. Two examples of advertisements that illustrate one or more of the fallacies or appeals discussed on pp. 214–216.
2. One example of illogical or fallacious reasoning in a piece of writing (you might try looking at the editorial page or letters-to-the-editor column of your local or campus newspaper).
3. One example of a logical, persuasive point in a piece of writing.

Be prepared to explain your analyses of your samples, but do not write any sort of identifying label or evaluation on the samples themselves. Bring your ads and pieces of writing to class and exchange them with those of a classmate. After ten minutes, compare notes. Do you and your classmate agree on the evaluation of each sample? Why or why not?

Essay Topics

Write a convincing argument attacking or defending one of the following statements. Narrow the topic when necessary. (Note that essays on some of the topics presented below would profit from library research material; see Chapter 12 for help.)

1. Students who fail their academic courses should/should not be allowed to participate in athletic programs.
2. Throwaway bottles and cans should/should not be outlawed.
3. Televised instant replays should/should not be used to call plays in football and other sports.
4. The foreign language requirement (or any requirement) at this school is worthwhile/useless.
5. Children with AIDS should/should not be prevented from attending public school.
6. High school competency tests in math and English should/should not be adopted across the country.
7. Education in computer literacy should/should not begin in grade school.
8. The CIA (or any controversial organization) should/should not be allowed to recruit on campus.
9. Lie detector tests for employees should/should not be prohibited in all states.
10. Vitamin C (or herbal healing or any kind of nontraditional treatment) can/cannot help relieve illness.
11. In the event of a compulsory military draft, men and women should/should not be equally liable.
12. Homosexuals should/should not be allowed to become teachers of young children.
13. Prostitution should/should not be legalized.
14. Students should/should not be employed for two years before they are admitted to college.
15. Convicted murderers who committed their crime as juveniles should/should not face the death penalty.
16. Persons over twelve should/should not have the right to see the movies of their choice.
17. Student evaluations should/should not be a major consideration in the promotion of a professor.
18. Insurance rates for males under 25 are unfair in this state.

19. Conscientious objectors should/should not have the right to object to a particular war.

20. State lotteries (or some other form of gambling) should be outlawed because they encourage crime.

Sample Student Essay

The student who wrote the essay below followed the steps for writing an argumentative paper that are discussed in this chapter. His intended audience were the readers of his school newspaper, primarily fellow students but also instructors as well. To argue his case, he chose Pattern A, presenting two of his own points and then concluding with a rebuttal of an important opposing view. Notice that this writer uses a variety of methods to convince his readers, including hypothetical examples, causal analysis, analogy, and testimony. Does the writer persuade you to his point of view? Which are his strongest and weakest arguments? What might you change to make his essay even more persuasive?

STUDENTS, TAKE NOTE!

Introduction: Presenting the controversy

A walk across campus this week will reveal students, professors, and administrators arguing about class notes like never before. But they're not engaged in intellectual debates over chemical formulas or literary images; no, they're fighting over the taking of the notes themselves, as professional note-taking services in town are applying for permission to sit in on courses and then sell their notes to the students in those classes. Although the prospect of having "canned" notes looks inviting to many students, our administration should nevertheless ban these services from campus. Not only do such businesses give certain students unfair advantages and discourage class attendance, but they also prohibit the development of students' important learning skills, despite the services' claims to the contrary.

Thesis

Essay map

A point for the writer's position

What is bothered for many of us about the professional-notes option is our sense of fair play. Let's face it: like it or not, school is, among other things, a place of competition, as students vie for the best academic records to send to prospective employers, graduate and professional schools, and, in some cases, paying parents. In today's classes all students have an equal opportunity to come to class, take notes, study, and pass or fail on their own merits. But the expensive professional notes, already organized and outlined, may give those with plenty of money some advantages that poorer students—those on scholarships or with families, for example—just can't afford. In addition, the notes may be available only to those students who take certain sections of a course and not others, thus giving some students an extra option. The same is true for students who satisfy a requirement by taking one course that has notes available rather than another which has not. Knowing that you're doing your own work may make you feel morally superior to a classmate who isn't, but frankly, seeing others buy notes just plain feels irritating and unfair, sort of like watching your roommate plagiarize his paper for a class after you spent weeks researching yours.

Another point for the writer's position

In addition to being a potential source of conflict among students, the professional-note services aren't winning many friends among the faculty either. Several instructors have complained that the availability of notes will encourage many students, especially the weaker ones, to cut classes, assuming that they have all the material necessary to understanding the lecture, discussion, or lab. But anyone who has ever had to use borrowed notes knows something vital is not there. Someone else's interpretations of the information is often hard or impossible to follow, especially if you must understand complex relationships and problems. Moreover, skipping class may mean missed opportunities for students to ask questions or to participate in experiments or in group discussions, all of which often help clarify concepts under study. Not seeing visual aids or diagrams in person can also result in problems understanding the material. And, last, missing class can mean failure to become comfortably acquainted with your teacher, which, in turn, may discourage a student from asking for individual help when it's needed. All these possibilities are real; even Jeff Allridge, owner of the Quotable Notes service, has admitted to a campus reporter, "There *is* an incentive to skip class."

Presentation and rebuttal of the opposition's claim

Despite the admission that professional note-taking encourages class-cutting, the services still promote themselves by claiming that students using their notes learn more. They support this claim by arguing that their notes offer students clearly organized information and, according to one advertising brochure, "good models" for students to follow in other classes. But such arguments miss the larger point: students should be learning how to develop their own note-taking, organizing, and thinking skills rather than swallowing the material whole as neatly packaged and delivered. Memorizing class material as outlined can be important, but it's not really as valuable in the long run as learning how to think about the material and use it to solve problems or come up with new ideas later. Taking your own notes teaches you how to listen and how to spot the important concepts; organizing your own notes teaches you how to pull ideas together in a logical way, all skills students will need in other classes, on jobs, and in life in general. Having memorized the outlines but not really mastered the thinking skills won't help the medical student whose patient's symptoms vary from the textbook description or the engineer whose airplane's wings suddenly fail the stress test for no apparent reason.

Conclusion:
Restatement of thesis, ending on pun to emphasize the main idea

By appealing to students who believe professional notes will help them accomplish their educational goals easier and quicker, a variety of note-taking services now have franchises across the country. But our campus shouldn't allow them to move in. CU students need to recognize that the difference between the services' definition of "learning" and the real learning experiences college can provide is of notable importance.

The following professional essays present conflicting views of the proposal to lower the minimum wage for young people during the summer months. As you read the essays, notice how each writer tries to support his own points and how each responds to the concerns of those who oppose his position. Which essay do you find the most convincing? Why? Which points are the most persuasive? The least persuasive? Why?

Professional Essay

SHOULD YOUTH BE PAID SUBMINIMUM WAGE?

Yes: Lowered Wage Gives Youth Entry into Job Market

William E. Brock

William E. Brock is the United States Secretary of Labor. His essay advocating subminimum wage for young people was published in a number of newspapers in the spring of 1985.

AMERICA needs to take a deep breath and do something positive—something it   1
hasn't tried before—about our youth unemployment problem.

Reprinted by permission of Scripps Howard News Service.

I believe one part of the solution is simple: Offer a pay differential for young-   2
sters hired in first jobs during summer months as an incentive for employers.

We've tried other approaches to no avail. We've thrown billions of dollars at   3
this problem, to no avail.

I think we can all agree that youth unemployment is not a temporary or recent   4
problem resulting from cyclical fluctuations in the economy. Unemployment rates
for 16-to-19-year-olds have increased steadily over the past 30 years. They've gone
from 12.6 percent in 1954 (overall rate 5 percent) to 17.8 percent in 1980 (overall
7.1 percent), to 18.9 percent last year, still more than double the overall rate. For
black teenagers, the rate soared steadily from 17 percent in 1954 to 39 percent
today.

The Reagan administration is trying for the second year to urge Congress to   5
give this new approach a chance to prove its merit. It has proposed to lower the
minimum wage to $2.50 an hour for youth jobs during the summer months only—
with stiff penalties for employers who attempt substitution for adult workers.

I do not regard the proposed Youth Employment Opportunity Wage as a pan-   6
acea. But I do regard it as an intelligent, logical avenue to pursue to see if we can
indeed offer some hope and opportunity to those young men and women.

I share some of the concerns voiced by labor. They have legitimate concerns   7
about lowering the minimum wage for any reason, as well as job displacement
concerns we must take fully into account.

The administration's proposal contains two basic safeguards: (1) the minimum   8
wage will not be undercut, and (2) someone already working will not be replaced
by someone at a lower wage.

We do owe unemployed—many hopelessly unemployed—youth a chance.   9
This country has nothing to lose by providing that chance to what has been estimated to be 400,000 youngsters in the first year.

The administration's proposal is direct: Hire youth age 16 through 19, from   10
May 1 through Sept. 30, and pay them $2.50 an hour, or about 75 percent of the
current minimum wage. No special paperwork requirements would be imposed on
employers beyond normal payroll record-keeping; and no new government bureau-
cracy would be needed to administer and market the program. Limiting the proposal to summer months makes it unlikely that employers would discharge current
workers and then have to rehire them later.

Employers would be prohibited from discharging, demoting or transferring cur-   11
rent employees and replacing them with youth hired at the opportunity wage. There
is also a provision prohibiting reductions in pay below the basic $3.35 for any youth
age 19 or under who is employed at any time during the 90 days before May 1
each year. Stiff fines or imprisonment face those who might engage in such
practices.

Although it is always difficult to make country-to-country comparisons, it   12
is important to note that other western democracies have made use of various
youth differential wage programs as part of an overall approach to youth unemployment.

By and large, these wage programs have increased employment opportun- 13
ities for young people in these nations for a number of years. The Netherlands,
Sweden, Canada, New Zealand and Australia have different plans based on the
same concept, and their experience can be of use to our own limited, test program.

I believe it is important to note that a summer youth opportunity wage has 14
been strongly endorsed by a variety of concerned groups such as the National Conference of Black Mayors, the Boys Clubs of America with their 1,100 centers,
the Fraternal Order of Police, the National Association for Equal Opportunity in
Higher Education, SER-Jobs for Progress Inc., the American GI Forum and many
others.

Let me say again: Let's give this youth opportunity wage a trial run and see 15
how it affects our youth unemployment problem.

If it works—a lot of kids currently cooling their heels on street corners will 16
have a chance for that all-important first job.

Questions on Content, Structure, and Style

1. What problem does this essay address?
2. What kind of evidence does Brock offer to show that this problem is not a temporary one?
3. What partial solution to the problem does Brock argue for?
4. Describe the pattern of organization used in this essay. Is the essay clearly organized?
5. What opposition concerns does Brock address? Is he effective?
6. In Brock's description of the administration's proposal, what is the effect of using specific details, statistics, and dates?
7. Why does Brock refer to Canada, Australia, and several other foreign countries?
8. Why does Brock mention the Boys Clubs of America and the National Conference of Black Mayors? What do these and the other groups named in paragraph 14 have in common?
9. Characterize the tone of Brock's essay. Pick out several lines that clearly present this tone.
10. Overall, how effective is Brock's argumentative essay? Which points are the most convincing? the least? Why?

Vocabulary

differential (2)   fluctuations (4)
incentive (2)   panacea (6)
avail (3)   displacement (7)
cyclical (4)

Professional Essay

SHOULD YOUTH BE PAID SUBMINIMUM WAGE?

No: Lower Wage Would Hurt Adults But Not Help Youth

Julian Dixon

Julian Dixon is a Democratic congressman from California and is the former chair of the Congressional Black Caucus. His essay opposing the lower wage for youth appeared in newspapers around the country in the spring of 1985.

———

THAT there is a youth employment problem in this country, we are all agreed. 1
With total youth unemployment at 18 percent and black youth unemployment at 39 percent, the question is "What should be done?"

One thing we should not do is implement President Reagan's "Youth Oppor- 2
tunity Wage." This proposal, its name as malapropos as calling the MX missile "Peacekeeper," is more an "Employers Opportunity Wage"; the biggest losers will be the young people it purports to help and adult workers who are discriminated against because of this subminimum wage.

I strongly disagree with the implication that somehow the minimum wage is 3
responsible for young people, and particularly low-income young people, being out of work.

The Targeted Jobs Tax Credit program, which provides a tax credit totaling 4
85 percent of wages for employers who hire disadvantaged young people, has been on the books since 1979. It is estimated that only one young person has been placed with an employer receiving the tax credit for every three certified for this program. This demonstrates that the problem young people face is not high minimum wages.

I also challenge the administration's contention that introduction of this lower 5
wage will generate as many as 400,000 new summer jobs.

Within the Fair Labor Standards Act there are provisions whereby colleges, 6
retail and service businesses can pay full-time high school and college students 85 percent of the minimum wage ($2.75 an hour). Approximately 3 percent of all students are employed under this program. It is unlikely that reducing this wage by only 25 cents will stimulate an additional 400,000 jobs.

Proponents of lowering the minimum wage argue that the lesser wages will be 7
offset by the training youths receive and their entry into the labor market. However, minimum wage jobs are by their very nature low-skill. Most of the training for a job canning peaches or clearing tables can be accomplished the first day and does not generally lead to upward job mobility.

A subminimum wage, even on a seasonal basis, will not prevent the substitu- 8
tion of youth for adult workers. Moreover, it would not prevent the substitution of youth earning the subminimum for those youth already on the payroll at the minimum wage.

———

If this wage rate is enacted, older workers, particularly black women, will be 9
the principal losers. In addition, young people in urban areas will be least likely to
accrue any benefits. The middle-class suburban youths who currently get these jobs
will continue to do so, only at the lower hourly wage.

Despite the apparent shortcomings of the youth subminimum wage proposal, 10
the concept would deserve some support if it seriously addressed the unemployment problem of the nation's youth, particularly minority youth.

Black and white teen-agers currently make the same wage, yet unemployment 11
among black youths is more than twice that of their white counterparts. The subminimum wage proposal does nothing to specifically address this disparity.

It is my opinion that the solution rests with efforts that stimulate training and 12
hiring of disadvantaged youth without reversing the principle of equal pay for equal
work.

One such program, the Youth Incentive Entitlement Pilot Projects, which 13
employed 76,000 poor teen-agers in 17 regions on the condition they would continue to go to school, was very successful.

Of those who had heard of the program, four of five eligible youths enrolled. 14
Black youths enjoyed the highest participation rates, and, according to post-pro-
gram analysis, experienced a significant increase in employment and earnings.

Private businesses, mostly small firms, accounted for more than half of all 15
work sponsors in the project. Of the youths these businesses employed, one-fifth
were hired permanently after they finished the program.

Rep. Augustus Hawkins, D-Calif., has introduced legislation that would imple- 16
ment the Youth Incentive Employment Program on a national basis. Now is the
time for the federal government to move ahead.

Youths will not be served by the president's subminimum wage. Minority com- 17
munities that depend on minimum wage jobs will not be served. I suspect the only
people who will benefit from the youth subminimum wage will be the employers.

Questions on Content, Structure, and Style

1. What is Dixon's thesis? How is his thesis introduced?
2. Why does Dixon compare the "Youth Opportunity Wage" to
   the MX missile?
3. Describe the pattern of organization used in this essay. Is the
   essay clearly organized?
4. What opposition claims does Dixon challenge? Are his
   refutations effective? Why/why not?
5. In addition to countering his opposition's claims, Dixon offers
   what other arguments against the youth-wage proposal?
6. What, according to Dixon, is a better solution to the youth
   unemployment problem?
7. Why does Dixon describe the Youth Incentive Entitlement
   Pilot Projects? What is the effect of the statistics he presents?
8. Overall, how effective is Dixon's argumentative essay? Which
   points are the most convincing? the least? Why?

9. Characterize the tone of Dixon's essay. How does it compare to that of Brock's essay on the same subject?
10. Compare and contrast the effectiveness of the essays by Brock and Dixon. In your opinion which essay is the most persuasive? Be prepared to defend your answer.

Vocabulary

implement (2)	contention (5)
malapropos (2)	mobility (7)
purports (2)	accrue (9)
implication (3)	

A Revision Worksheet for Your Argumentative Essay

As you write your rough drafts, consult Chapter 5 for guidance through the revision process. In addition, here are a few questions to ask yourself as you revise your argumentative essay:

1. Does this essay present a clear thesis limited to fit the assigned length of this paper?
2. Does this essay contain a number of strong, persuasive points in support of its thesis?
3. Is the essay organized in an easy-to-follow pattern that avoids repetition or confusion?
4. Does the essay present enough supporting evidence to make each of its points convincing? Where could additional examples, factual information, testimony, or other kinds of supporting material be added to make the arguments even more effective?
5. Will all the supporting evidence be clear to the essay's particular audience? Do any terms or examples need additional explanation or special definition?
6. Have the opposing arguments been refuted?
7. Does the essay avoid any logical fallacies or problems in tone?

After you've revised your essay extensively, you might exchange rough drafts with a classmate and answer these questions for each other, making specific suggestions for improvement wherever appropriate.

10

Description

The writer of description creates a word-picture of persons, places, objects, and emotions, using a careful selection of details to make an impression on the reader. If you have already written expository or argumentative essays in your composition course, then you almost certainly have written some descriptive prose. Nearly every essay, after all, calls for some kind of description; for example, in the student comparison/contrast essay (pp. 163–165), the writer describes two kinds of stores; in the professional process essay (pp. 152–156), the writer describes the embalming procedure in great detail. To help you write better description in your other essays, however, you may want to practice writing descriptive paragraphs or a short descriptive essay.

HOW TO WRITE EFFECTIVE DESCRIPTION

Regardless of the kind of description you are writing, you should follow the three basic suggestions below:

Recognize your purpose. Description is not free-floating; it appears in your writing for a particular reason—to help you explain, persuade, create a mood, or whatever. In some essays you will want your description as *objective* as you can make it; for example, you might describe a scientific experiment or a business transaction in straight factual detail. Most of the time, however, you will want to convey a particular attitude toward your subject; this approach to description is called *subjective* or *impressionistic*. Note the differences between the following two descriptions of a tall, thin boy: the objective writer sticks to the facts by saying, "The eighteen-year-old boy was 6'1" and weighed 125 pounds," whereas the subjective writer gives an impressionistic description, "The young boy was as tall and scrawny as a birch tree in winter." Therefore, before you begin describing anything, you must first decide on your purpose and then whether it calls for objective or subjective reporting.

Describe clearly, using specific details. To make any description clear to your reader, you must include a sufficient number of details that are specific rather than fuzzy or vague. If, for example, your family dog had become lost, you wouldn't call the animal shelter and ask if they'd seen a "big brown dog with a short tail"—naturally, you'd mention every distinguishing detail about your pet you could think of: size, color, breed, cut of ears, special markings, etc. Similarly, if your car was stolen, you'd give the police as clear and as complete a description of your vehicle as possible.

Look at the two paragraphs below; which more fully answers the question, "What's a vaulting horse?"?

A vaulting horse is a thing usually found in gyms that has four legs and a beam and is used by gymnasts to make jumps.

If you didn't already know what a vaulting horse was, you might have trouble picking it out in a gymnasium crowded with equipment. A description with additional details would help you locate it:

A vaulting horse is a piece of equipment used by gymnasts during competition to help propel them into the air when they perform any of a variety of leaps known as vaults. The gymnasts usually approach the vaulting horse from a running start and then place their hands on the horse for support or for a push off as they perform their vaults. The horse itself resembles a carpenter's sawhorse, but the main beam is composed of padded leather rather than wood. The rectangular beam is approximately five feet, three inches long and thirteen-and-a-half inches wide. Supported by four legs usually made of steel, the padded leather beam is approximately four feet, one-half inch above the floor in men's competitions and three feet, seven inches in women's competitions. The padded leather beam has two white lines marking off three sections on top: the croup, the saddle, and the neck. The two end sections—the croup and the neck—are each fifteen and one-half inches long. Gymnasts place their hands on the neck or croup depending on the type of vault they are attempting.

Moreover, the reader cannot imagine your subject clearly if your description is couched in vague generalities. The sentence below, for example, presents only a hazy picture:

Larry is so overweight that his clothes don't fit him right.

Revised, the picture is now sharply in focus:

Larry is so fat that his shirt constantly bulges over his belt, his trousers will not stay snapped, and his countless chins spill over his collar like dough rising out of a too-small pan.

Specific details can turn cloudy prose into crisp, clear images that can be reproduced in the mind like photographs.

Select only appropriate details. In any description the choice of details depends largely on the writer's purpose and audience. However, many descriptions—especially the more subjective ones—will present a *dominant impression;* that is, the writer selects only those details that communicate a particular mood or feeling to the reader. The dominant impression is the controlling focus of a description; for example, if you wrote a description of your grandmother to show her thoughtfulness, then you would select only those details that convey an impression of a sweet, kindly old lady. Below are two brief descriptions illustrating the concept of dominant impression. The first writer tries to create a mood of mystery:

Down a black winding road stands the abandoned old mansion, silhouetted against the cloud-shrouded moon, creaking and moaning in the wet chill wind.

The second writer tries to present a feeling of joy and innocence.

A dozen kites filled the spring air, and around the bright picnic tables spread with hot dogs, hamburgers, and slices of watermelon, Tom and Annie played away the warm April day.

In the description of the deserted mansion, the writer would have violated the impression of mystery had the sentence read:

Down the black winding road stands the abandoned old mansion, surrounded by bright, multicolored tulips in early bloom.

Including the cheerful flowers as a detail in the description destroys the dominant mood of bleakness and mystery. Similarly, example two would be spoiled had the writer ended it this way:

. . . Tom and Annie played away the warm April day until Tom got so sunburned he became ill and had to go home.

Therefore, remember to select only those details that advance your descriptive purpose. Omit any details you consider unimportant or distracting.

See if you can determine the dominant impression of each description below:

The wind had curled up to sleep in the distant mountains. Leaves hung limp and motionless from the silent trees, while birds perched on the branches like little statues. As I sat on the edge of the clearing, holding my breath, I could hear a squirrel scampering through the underbrush. Somewhere far away a dog barked twice, and then the woods were hushed once more.

This poor thing has seen better days, but one should expect the sofa in a fraternity house den to be well worn. The large, plump, brown corduroy pillows strewn lazily on the floor and propped comfortably against the threadbare arms bear the pencil-point scars of frustrated students and foam-bleeding cuts of multiple pillow wars. No less than four pairs of rotting Nikes stand twenty-four-hour guard at the corners of its carefully mended frame. Obviously the relaxed, inviting appearance masks the permanent odors of cheap cigars and Michelob from Thursday night poker parties; at least two or three guests each weekend sift through the popcorn kernels and Doritos crumbs, sprawl facedown, and pass out for the duration. However, frequent inhabitants have learned to avoid the dark stains courtesy of the house pup and the red-punch designs of the chapter klutz. Habitually, they strategically lunge over the back of the sofa to an unsoiled area easily identifiable in flight by the large depression left by previous regulars. The quiet *hmmph* of the cushions and harmonious squeal of the exhausted springs signal a perfect landing and utter a warm greeting from an old and faithful friend.

Make your descriptions vivid. By using clear, precise words, you can improve any kind of writing. Chapters 6 (on words) and 7 (on sentences) offer a variety of tips on clarifying your prose style. In addition to the advice given there, here are two other ways to enliven your descriptions, particularly those that call for a subjective approach:

Use sensory details. If it's appropriate, try using images that appeal to your readers' five senses. If, for example, you are describing your broken leg and the ensuing stay in a hospital, tell your readers how the place smelled, how it looked, what your cast felt like, how your pills tasted, and what noises you heard. Below are some specific examples using sensory details:

Sight The clean white corridors of the hospital resembled the set of a sci-fi movie, with everyone scurrying around in identical starched uniforms.

Hearing At night, the only sounds I heard were the quiet squeakings of sensible white shoes as the nurses made their rounds.

Smell The green beans on the hospital cafeteria tray smelled stale and waxy, like crayons.

Touch   The hospital bed sheet felt as rough and heavy as a feed sack.

Taste   Every four hours they gave me an enormous gray pill whose aftertaste reminded me of the castor oil my grandmother insisted on giving me when I was a kid.

By appealing to the readers' senses, you better enable them to identify with and imagine the subject you are describing. Joseph Conrad, the famous nineteenth-century novelist, agreed, believing that all art "appeals primarily to the senses, and the artistic aim when expressing itself in written words must also make its appeal through the senses, if its highest desire is to reach the secret spring of responsive emotions." In other words, to make your readers feel, first make them "see."

Use figurative language when appropriate. As you may recall from Chapter 7, figurative language produces images or pictures in the readers' minds, helping them to understand unfamiliar or abstract subjects. Here are some devices you might use to clarify or spice up your prose:

1. Simile: a comparison between two things using the words "like" or "as" (see also pp. 124–125)

Example   Seeing exactly the shirt he wanted, he moved as quickly as a starving teenager finding a piece of favorite pie in a refrigerator full of leftover vegetables.

2. Metaphor: a direct comparison between two things that does not use "like" or "as" (see also pp. 124–125)

Example   After the holidays her body resembled all the "before" shots in every diet ad she'd ever seen.

3. Personification: the attribution of human characteristics and emotions to inanimate objects, animals, or abstract ideas

Example   The old stuffed teddy bear sat in a corner, dozing before the fireplace.

4. Hyperbole: intentional exaggeration or overstatement

Example   "Bring me a steak that's still mooing," roared the cowboy.

5. Understatement: intentional representation of a subject as less important than the facts would warrant (see also irony, p. 112)

Example   "The reports of my death are greatly exaggerated."— Mark Twain

6. Synecdoche: a part of something is used to represent the whole

Example   A hundred tired feet hit the dance floor for one last jitterbug. (Here "feet" stand for the dancing couples themselves.)

Using figures of speech in appropriate places can make your descriptions clear, lively, and memorable.

Problems to Avoid

Keep in mind these three bits of advice to solve problems that frequently arise in description:

Remember your audience. Sometimes the object of our description is so clear in our minds we forget that our readers haven't seen it too. Consequently, the description we write turns out to be vague, bland, or skimpy. Ask yourself about your audience: what do they need to know to see this sight as clearly as I do? Then fill in your description with ample, precise details that reveal the best picture possible. Don't forget to define or explain any terms you use that may be puzzling to your audience.

Avoid an erratic organization of details. Too often descriptions are a hodgepodge of details, jotted down randomly. When you write a lengthy description, you should select a plan that will arrange your details in an orderly fashion. Depending upon your subject matter and your purpose, you might adopt a plan calling for a description of something from top to bottom, left to right, front to back, etc. For example, a description of a woman might begin at the head and move to the feet; furniture in a room might be described as your eyes move from one side of the room to another. A second plan for arranging details presents the subject's outstanding characteristics first and then fills in the lesser information; a child's red hair, for example, might be his most striking feature and therefore would be described first. A third plan presents details in the order you see them approaching: dust, then a car, then details about the car, its occupants, and so on. Or you might describe a subject as it unfolds chronologically, as in some kind of a process or operation. Regardless of which plan of organization you choose, the reader should feel a sense of order in your description.

Avoid any sudden change in perspective. If, for example, you are describing the White House from the outside, don't suddenly include details that could be seen only from inside. Similarly, if you are describing a car from a distance, you might be able to tell the car's model, year, and color, but you could hardly describe the upholstery or reveal the mileage. It is, of course, possible for you—or your observer—to approach or move around the subject of your description, but the reader must be aware of this movement. Any shift in point of view must be presented clearly and logically, with no sudden, confusing leaps from a front to a back view, from outside to inside, and so on.

Essay Topics

Here are some suggestions for a descriptive essay or paragraph; narrow your topic to fit your assignment. Don't forget that every description, whether objective or subjective, has a purpose and that every detail should support that purpose.

1. a campus character
2. your room or roommate
3. a piece of equipment important to your major or to a hobby or favorite sport
4. a building or place you're fond of (such as a "haunted" house in your neighborhood or even a childhood tree house)
5. a sports event
6. a family member or family pet
7. your most valuable material possession
8. the ugliest/most beautiful building on your campus or in town
9. a typical family dinner at your home
10. your first or worst car (or your dream car)
11. a place where you've worked
12. a strange-but-wonderful friend or relative
13. a computer, microscope, or some other complex machine
14. a favorite painting, sculpture, or photograph
15. your most unforgettable character
16. a laboratory experiment
17. a doctor's or dentist's waiting room
18. your face—or your face after plastic surgery
19. a special day in your life (birthday, holiday, graduation, etc.)
20. a dead cockroach

Sample Student Essay

In his descriptive essay, this student tries to capture the changes in his hometown that he saw after having been away for several years. Notice the use of metaphor that runs throughout the essay. Is it effective or overdone?

THE BATTLE OF PROGRESS

Introduction: Contrast of old and new presented in battlefield imagery

When I went home for the first time after a tour of duty in Vietnam and then a couple of years bumming around, I was struck by a scene at the city limits. On the left of the highway was a group of brand-new, look-alike houses, all mobbed together like they were plotting something secret. Directly across the highway were two falling-down farm houses, each at least eighty years old. There they were, the old and the new, enemies staring at each other across the road. As I drove between them, I felt strange, as if I were entering a battlefield that was temporarily quiet.

Elaboration of the "battle" metaphor

My town, you see, is, like other small places, caught in the battle of progress. I see the victims everywhere, as the old falls before the new. Old wooden buildings with hand-carved faces are torn down everyday to make way for impersonal, mirrored high-rises. The rain-fed creeks and streams like the ones I played in as a kid are being bulldozed and replaced by sidewalks and artificial fountains that spray the same water day after day. Everywhere I look I see evidence of the struggle, and everywhere I see that the inevitable victor, progress, is winning skirmishes.

Note the clear point of view as the writer moves through the town.

A simile

After turning off the highway, I head for the town square; the impression of the invasion grows stronger. All along the main drag, the old hamburger joints have been replaced by fast-food restaurants with red and green flashing neon signs exploding like rockets in the air. Where once there was a group of sturdy old homes with wide white porches and big rolling yards, I now see a washateria and hear the loud grumblings of its machines. The sound reminds me of a huge stomach, and the stale smell of old detergent and dirty clothes fills the air. The intruders have taken over and devoured the block.

An extended metaphor

Invasion imagery continues

When I reach the square, I can see that it too has been sacked. The small brown stores—Duke and Ayres Hardware, Woolworth's, Smith's Dry Goods—all have been remodeled into modern boutiques and video-game dives, decorated in glaring victory colors of orange, blue, green.

Personification

The stores' once-solemn, comfortable faces grin ridiculously at me now. I don't recognize them, and they sure don't know me. The dark little bookstore on the southeast corner, where I grew up reading men's magazines on the sly, is now a jolly ice cream parlor, decked out with fake red-and-white barber poles and a big, lighted plate-glass window filled with giant pictures of nineteen weird flavors of ice cream. I move on. The three-story, castle-like pink granite courthouse is gone too, and in its place is a functional, unfriendly red-brick office building with humming air conditioners in its small windows and a sign on its automatic door that says "no solicitors or dogs allowed." As I look around the square without recognizing a single old face, I feel like a stranger. I have gone away and come back to find my little town overrun by barbarians who've done away with all I once knew.

More war imagery

Leaving the square and heading back to the highway, I pass through the poor section on the edge of town. Here, I find, the battle rages. Half the little rundown, unpainted, grey shanties are gone, replaced by a squat tire factory, mud-colored and sooty. Where are the people who used to sit out on their tumble-down steps? The kids that played kick-the-can in the streets and grassless yards? Casualties of war. The black smoke tumbles out of the factory, smelling like gunpowder.

I drive on.

Conclusion: A return to the images of the introduction

Leaving town on the main highway, I once again see the armies peering at each other in the afternoon glare as I drive between them. I shake my head a little sadly. The old will fight, but it is useless. The new always win—they are younger and stronger. I glance in my rear view mirror at the faded two-story farmhouses sitting proudly on their green acres of alfalfa, while the army of track houses across the way grows larger and stronger. Soon the highway will be no barrier. I look closely in my mirror at the farmhouses, because I know I may never see them again.

Professional Essay

DOWN IN THE COAL MINES

George Orwell

George Orwell is the pseudonym of Eric Arthur Blair, a British novelist and essayist. Some of his best-known works include *Down and Out in Paris and London, Animal Farm, Nineteen Eighty-Four,* and *Shooting an Elephant.* This essay is an excerpt from *The Road to Wigan Pier.*

═══════

WHEN you go down a coal mine it is important to try and get to the coal face 1 when the "fillers" are at work. This is not easy, because when the mine is working visitors are a nuisance and are not encouraged, but if you go at any other time, it is possible to come away with a totally wrong impression. On a Sunday, for instance, a mine seems almost peaceful. The time to go there is when the machines are roaring and the air is black with coal dust, and when you can actually see what the miners have to do. At those times the place is like hell, or at any rate like my own mental picture of hell. Most of the things one imagines in hell are there—heat, noise, confusion, darkness, foul air, and above all, unbearably cramped space.

From *The Road to Wigan Pier* by George Orwell. Reprinted by permission of Harcourt Brace Jovanovich, Inc.

Everything except the fire, for there is no fire down there except the feeble beams of Davy lamps[1] and electric torches which scarcely penetrate the clouds of coal dust.

When you have finally got there—and getting there is a job in itself: I will   2
explain that in a moment—you crawl through the last line of pit props and see opposite you a shiny black wall three or four feet high. This is the coal face. Overhead is the smooth ceiling made by the rock from which the coal has been cut; underneath is the rock again, so that the gallery you are in is only as high as the ledge of coal itself, probably not much more than a yard. The first impression of all, overmastering everything else for a while, is the frightful, deafening din from the conveyor belt which carries the coal away. You cannot see very far, because the fog of coal dust throws back the beam of your lamp, but you can see on either side of you the life of half-naked kneeling men, one to every four or five yards, driving their shovels under the fallen coal and flinging it swiftly over their left shoulders. They are feeding it on to the conveyor belt, a moving rubber belt a couple of feet wide which runs a yard or two behind them. Down this belt a glittering river of coal races constantly. In a big mine it is carrying away several tons of coal every minute. It bears it off to some place in the main roads where it is shot into tubs holding half a ton, and thence dragged to the cages and hoisted to the outer air.

It is impossible to watch the "fillers" at work without feeling a pang of envy   3
for their toughness. It is a dreadful job that they do, an almost superhuman job by the standards of an ordinary person. For they are not only shifting monstrous quantities of coal, they are also doing it in a position that doubles or trebles the work. They have got to remain kneeling all the while—they could hardly rise from their knees without hitting the ceiling—and you can easily see by trying it what a tremendous effort this means. Shoveling is comparatively easy when you are standing up, because you can use your knee and thigh to drive the shovel along; kneeling down, the whole of the strain is thrown upon your arm and belly muscles. And the other conditions do not exactly make things easier. There is the heat—it varies, but in some mines it is suffocating—and the coal dust that stuffs up your throat and nostrils and collects along your eyelids, and the unending rattle of the conveyor belt, which in that confined space is rather like the rattle of a machine gun. . . .

Probably you have to go down several coal mines before you can get much   4
grasp of the processes that are going on round you. This is chiefly because the mere effort of getting from place to place makes it difficult to notice anything else. In some ways it is even disappointing, or at least is unlike what you have expected. You get into the cage, which is a steel box about as wide as a telephone box and two or three times as long. It holds ten men, but they pack it like pilchards in a tin, and a tall man cannot stand upright in it. The steel door shuts upon you, and somebody working the winding gear above drops you into the void. You have the usual

---

[1]One of the earliest safety lamps designed to prevent explosions in the British mines. Named for its inventor, Sir Humphrey Davy (1778–1829), the English chemist who discovered sodium and potassium.

momentary qualm in your belly and a bursting sensation in the ears, but not much sensation of movement till you get near the bottom, when the cage slows down so abruptly that you could swear it is going upward again. In the middle of the run the cage probably touches sixty miles an hour; in some of the deeper mines it touches even more. When you crawl out at the bottom you are perhaps four hundred yards underground. That is to say you have a tolerable-sized mountain on top of you; hundreds of yards of solid rock, bones of extinct beasts, subsoil, flints, roots of growing things, green grass and cows grazing on it—all this suspended over your head and held back only by wooden props as thick as the calf of your leg. But because of the speed at which the cage has brought you down, and the complete darkness through which you have traveled, you hardly feel yourself deeper down than you would at the bottom of the Piccadilly tube.[2]

What is surprising, on the other hand, is the immense horizontal distances that   5 have to be traveled underground. Before I had been down a mine I had vaguely imagined the miner stepping out of the cage and getting to work on a ledge of coal a few yards away. I had not realized that before he even gets to his work he may have to creep through passages as long as from London Bridge to Oxford Circus. In the beginning, of course, a mine shaft is sunk somewhere near a seam of coal. But as that seam is worked out and fresh seams are followed up, the workings get farther and farther from the pit bottom. If it is a mile from the pit bottom to the coal face, that is probably an average distance; three miles is a fairly normal one; there are even said to be a few mines where it is as much as five miles. But these distances bear no relation to distances above ground. For in all that mile or three miles as it may be, there is hardly anywhere outside the main road, and not many places even there, where a man can stand upright.

You do not notice the effect of this till you have done a few hundred yards.   6 You start off, stooping slightly, down the dim-lit gallery, eight or ten feet wide and about five feet high, with the walls built up with slabs of shale, like the stone walls in Derbyshire.[3] Every yard or two there are wooden props holding up the beams and girders; some of the girders have buckled into fantastic curves under which you have to duck. Usually it is bad going underfoot—thick dust or jagged chunks of shale, and in some mines where there is water it is as mucky as a farmyard. Also there is the track for the coal tubs, like a miniature railway track with sleepers[4] a foot or two apart, which is tiresome to walk on. Everything is gray with shale dust; there is a dusty fiery smell which seems to be the same in all mines. You see mysterious machines of which you never learn the purpose, and bundles of tools slung together on wires, and sometimes mice darting away from the beam of the lamps. They are surprisingly common, especially in mines where there are

---

[2]"Tube" is the common name for London's underground subway system, the largest in the world; Piccadilly is the name of a popular subway station located near the famous landmark Piccadilly Circus. The average depth of London's subways is no more than forty-five feet.
[3]A county in north central England known for its formations of carboniferous rocks. Derbyshire contains fields divided by stone walls, which give the county a checkerboard appearance.
[4]The British word for railroad ties.

or have been horses. It would be interesting to know how they got there in the first place; possibly by falling down the shaft—for they say a mouse can fall any distance uninjured, owing to its surface area being so large relative to its weight. You press yourself against the wall to make way for lines of tubs jolting slowly toward the shaft, drawn by endless steel cable operated from the surface. You creep through sacking curtains and thick wooden doors which, when they are opened, let out fierce blasts of air. These doors are an important part of the ventilation system. The exhausted air is sucked out of one shaft by means of fans, and the fresh air enters the other of its own accord. But if left to itself the air will take the shortest way round, leaving the deeper workings unventilated; so all shortcuts have to be partitioned off.

At the start to walk stooping is rather a joke, but it is a joke that soon wears off. I am handicapped by being exceptionally tall, but when the roof falls to four feet or less it is a tough job for anybody except a dwarf or a child. You have not only got to bend double, you have also got to keep your head up all the while so as to see the beams and girders and dodge them when they come. You have, therefore, a constant crick in the neck, but this is nothing to the pain in your knees and thighs. After half a mile it becomes (I am not exaggerating) an unbearable agony. You begin to wonder whether you will ever get to the end—still more, how on earth you are going to get back. Your pace grows slower and slower. You come to a stretch of a couple of hundred yards where it is all exceptionally low and you have to work yourself along in a squatting position. Then suddenly the roof opens out to a mysterious height—scene of an old fall of rock, probably—and for twenty whole yards you can stand upright. The relief is overwhelming. But after this there is another low stretch of a hundred yards and then a succession of beams which you have to crawl under. You go down on all fours; even this is a relief after the squatting business. But when you come to the end of the beams and try to get up again, you find that your knees have temporarily struck work and refuse to lift you. You call a halt, ignominiously, and say that you would like to rest for a minute or two. Your guide (a miner) is sympathetic. He knows that your muscles are not the same as his. "Only another four hundred yards," he says encouragingly; you feel that he might as well say four hundred miles. But finally you do somehow creep as far as the coal face. You have gone a mile and taken the best part of an hour; a miner would do it in not much more than twenty minutes. Having got there, you have to sprawl in the coal dust and get your strength back for several minutes before you can even watch the work in progress with any kind of intelligence.

Coming back is worse than going, not only because you are already tired out but because the journey back to the shaft is probably slightly uphill. You get through the low places at the speed of a tortoise, and you have no shame now about calling a halt when your knees give way. Even the lamp you are carrying becomes a nuisance and probably when you stumble you drop it; whereupon, if it is a Davy lamp, it goes out. Ducking the beams becomes more and more of an effort, and sometimes you forget to duck. You try walking head down as the miners do, and then you bang your backbone. Even the miners bang their backbones fairly often. This is the reason why in very hot mines, where it is necessary to go about half naked, most of the miners have what they call "buttons down the back"—

that is, a permanent scab on each vertebra. When the track is downhill the miners sometimes fit their clogs,[5] which are hollow underneath, on to the trolley rails and slide down. In mines where the "traveling" is very bad all the miners carry sticks about two and a half feet long, hollowed out below the handle. In normal places you keep your hand on top of the stick and in the low places you slide your hand down into the hollow. These sticks are a great help, and the wooden crash-helmets—a comparatively recent invention—are a godsend. They look like a French or Italian steel helmet, but they are made of some kind of pith and very light, and so strong that you can take a violent blow on the head without feeling it. When finally you get back to the surface you have been perhaps three hours underground and traveled two miles, and you are more exhausted than you would be by a twenty-five-mile walk above ground. For a week afterward your thighs are so stiff that coming downstairs is quite a difficult feat; you have to work your way down in a peculiar sidelong manner, without bending the knees. Your miner friends notice the stiffness of your walk and chaff you about it. ("How'd ta like to work down pit, eh?" etc.) Yet even a miner who has been long away from work—from illness, for instance—when he comes back to the pit, suffers badly for the first few days.

Questions on Content, Structure, and Style

1. What is Orwell's purpose in writing this description? Is his description primarily objective or subjective?
2. What is the dominant impression Orwell tries to convey? Point out words and passages to support your answer.
3. What is Orwell's attitude toward the coal miners? Again select words and passages to support your opinion.
4. Analyze Orwell's use of specific detail. Are there enough details to give you a clear understanding of what is being described? In paragraph 4, for example, how does Orwell use specific detail to make you aware of the true depth—and possible danger—of the mine?
5. Many of Orwell's descriptive passages affect the senses. Point out specific examples of language that are meant to trigger your sense of smell, sight, touch, or hearing.
6. Orwell often uses figurative language. Select some examples of metaphors and similes and explain how each one helps you to understand his description more clearly.
7. Notice Orwell's frequent choice of action verbs (for instance, in paragraph 2: "driving," "flinging," "races," "shot," "dragged," "hoisted"). How do these verbs contribute to the vividness of his descriptions?
8. Orwell describes the trip into the mine largely in terms of "you" rather than "I." What effect is he trying to produce by using the second-person point of view?

---

[5]Heavy shoes that have thick wooden soles.

9. By what organizational plan does Orwell order his details in paragraphs 4 through 8?
10. This description may also be viewed as an essay developed by what other expository strategy?

Vocabulary

trebles (3)	ignominiously (7)
pilchards (4)	vertebra (8)
qualm (4)	pith (8)
girders (6)	chaff (8)
shale (6)	

A Revision Worksheet for Your Descriptive Essay

As you write your rough drafts, consult Chapter 5 for guidance through the revision process. In addition, here are a few questions to ask yourself as you revise your description:

1. Is the descriptive essay's purpose clear to the reader?
2. Are there enough specific details in the description to make the subject matter distinct to readers who are unfamiliar with your scene, person, or object? Where might more detail be added?
3. Are the details arranged in an order that's easy to follow?
4. If the assignment called for an objective description, are the details as "neutral" as possible?
5. If the assignment called for a subjective description, does the writer's particular attitude come through clearly with a consistent use of well-chosen details or imagery?
6. Could any sensory details or figurative language be added to help the reader "see" the subject matter?
7. What is the strongest part of this essay? How could you make the rest of the essay as good as that part?

After you've revised your essay extensively, you might exchange rough drafts with a classmate and answer these questions for each other, making specific suggestions for improvement wherever appropriate.

Narration

When many people hear the word "narrative," they think of a made-up story. But not all stories are fiction. In this chapter we are not concerned with writing literary short stories—that's a skill you may work on in a creative writing class—but rather with non-fiction *narratives*, stories that may be used in your essays to explain or prove a point. We most often use two kinds of these stories:

1. the *extended narrative*—a long episode that by itself illustrates or supports an essay's thesis
2. the *brief narrative*—a shorter incident that is often used in a body paragraph to support or illustrate a particular point in an expository or argumentative essay.

Let's suppose, for example, you wanted to write an essay showing how confusing the registration system is at your school. To illustrate the problems vividly, you might devote your entire essay to the retelling of a friend's horrible experience signing up for classes last fall, thus making use of extended narration. Or take another example: in an argumentative essay advocating the nationwide use of automobile air-bags, you might use a brief narrative about a car wreck to support a paragraph's point about air-bags' ability to save lives. Regardless of which type of narrative you decide best fits your purpose, the telling of a story or incident can be an informative, persuasive means of swaying your readers to your point of view.

HOW TO WRITE EFFECTIVE NARRATION

Know your purpose. Because narratives in most essays are intended to support or illustrate a thesis or paragraph's point, you must be careful not to allow your story to run on until the reader wonders, "Where is this going? What is the reason for this story?" Once you have decided on your thesis or paragraph point, tailor all the events and details in your narrative to fit your purpose. On the other hand, don't let your narrative turn into a sermonette—support your thesis with a story that informs and illustrates rather than preaches.

Maintain a consistent point of view. This subject is complex, and teachers of literature courses often spend much time explaining it in detail. For your purposes, however, a brief treatment will suffice. In the first place, you should decide whether the narrative will be told by you in the first person, by a character involved in the action, or by an omniscient ("all-knowing") narrator who may reveal the thoughts, feelings, and actions of any character. The selection of a point of view is important because it determines whose thoughts or actions will be described. If, for example, one of your female characters narrates an event, she is limited to giving only the information that she can know; that is, she cannot reveal another character's thoughts or describe actions that took place across town, out of her sight. Once you have decided which point of view is best for your purpose, be consistent; don't abruptly change point of view in mid-story.

Follow a logical time sequence. Many extended narrative essays—and virtually all brief stories used in other kinds of essays—follow a chronological order, presenting events as they naturally occur in the story. Occasionally, however, a writer will use the flashback technique, which takes the readers back in time to reveal an incident that occurred before the present scene of the story. Many novelists and short story writers use a variety of techniques to alter time sequences in their fiction; Joseph Heller's famous novel *Catch-22*, for example, contains chaotic time shifts to emphasize the absurd nature of war. If you decide to use shifts in time, make certain your readers don't become confused or lost.

Use details to present the setting. Most extended narratives are set in particular times and places. If the setting plays an important role in your story, you must describe it in vivid terms so that your readers can imagine it easily. For example, let's suppose you are pointing out the necessity of life preservers on sailboats by telling the story of how you spent a horrible, stormy night in the lake, clinging to your capsized boat. To convince your readers, let them "feel" the stinging rain and the icy current trying to drag you under; let them "see" the black waves, the dark menacing sky; let them "hear" the howling wind and the gradual splitting apart of the boat. Effective narration often depends upon effective description, and effective description depends upon vivid, specific detail. (For more help on writing description, see Chapter 10.)

Make your characters believable. Again, the use of detail is crucial. Your readers should be able to visualize the people in your narrative clearly; if your characters are drawn too thinly, or if they seem phony or stereotyped, your readers will not fully grasp the intensity of your story, and thus its meaning will be lost. Show the readers a realistic picture of the major characters by commenting unobtrusively on their appearances, speech, and actions. In addition, a successful narrative depends upon the reader's understanding of people's motives—why they act the way they do in certain situations. A narrative about your hometown's grouchiest miser who suddenly donated a large sum of money to a poor family isn't very believable unless we know the motive behind the action. In other words, let your readers know what is happening to whom by explaining why.

Use dialogue realistically. If your story calls for dialogue, be sure the word choice and the manner of speaking are in keeping with the character's education, background, age, location, and so forth. Don't, for example, put a sophisticated philosophical treatise into the mouth of a ten-year-old boy or the latest campus slang into the speeches of an auto mechanic from Two Egg, Florida. Also, make sure that your dialogue doesn't sound "wooden" or phony. The right dialogue can help make your characters more realistic and interesting, provided that the conversations are essential to the plot and are not merely substituted for dramatic action. (For help in punctuating dialogue, see pp. 316–317 in Part Three.)

Problems to Avoid

Unconvincing, boring narratives are often the result of problems with subject matter or poor pacing; therefore, you should keep in mind the following advice:

Choose your subject carefully. Most of the best narrative essays come from personal experience, and the reason is fairly obvious; it's much more difficult to write convincingly about something you've never seen or done or read about. You probably couldn't, for instance, write a realistic account of a bullfight unless you'd seen one or at least had studied the subject in great detail. The simplest, easiest, most interesting non-fiction narrative you can write is likely to be about an event with which you are personally familiar. This doesn't mean that you can't improvise many details or occasionally create a brief hypothetical story to illustrate a point. Even so, you will probably still have better luck basing your narrative—real or hypothetical—on something or someone you know well.

Limit your scope. If you wish to use an extended narrative to illustrate a thesis, don't select an event or series of actions whose retelling will be too long or complex for your assignment. In general, it's better to select one episode and flesh it out with many specific details so that your readers may clearly see your point. For instance, you may have had many rewarding experiences during the summer you worked as a lifeguard, but you can't tell them all. Instead, you might focus on one experience that captures the essence of your attitude toward your job— say, the time you saved a child from drowning—and present the story so vividly that the readers can easily understand your point of view.

Don't let your story lag with insignificant detail. At some time you've probably listened to a storyteller who became stuck on some insignificant detail ("Was it Friday or Saturday the letter came? Let's see now . . ." "Then Joe said to me—no, it was Sally—no, wait, it was . . ."). And you've probably also heard bores who insist on making a short story long by including too many unimportant details or digressions. These mistakes ruin the *pacing* of their stories; in other words, the story's tempo or movement becomes bogged down until the readers are bored witless. To avoid putting your readers to sleep, dismiss all unessential details and focus your attention—and use of detail—on the important events, people, and places. Skip uneventful periods of time by using such phrases as "A week went by before Mr. Smith called . . ." or "Later that evening, around nine o'clock . . ." In short, keep the story moving quickly enough to hold the readers' interest. Moreover, you should use a variety of transition devices to move the readers from one action to another; don't rely continuously on the childish "and then . . . and then . . ." method.

Essay Topics

Use one of the topics below to suggest an essay that is at least partially, if not entirely, supported by narration. Remember that each essay must have a clear purpose or thesis.
1. a loyal pet or friend
2. the worst mix-up of your life
3. your best Christmas (birthday or any holiday)
4. your worst accident or brush with death
5. an act of courage or cowardice
6. your most frightening or wonderful childhood experience
7. a memorable event governed by nature

8. meeting a celebrity
9. an event that changed your thinking on a particular subject
10. challenging an authority
11. an event that influenced your choice of career (or some other important decision)
12. your first introduction to prejudice or sexism
13. being hired or fired from your first or most important job
14. a triumph in sports or in some artistic endeavor
15. a risk that paid off
16. a non-academic lesson learned at school
17. a trip or special time spent by yourself
18. a bad habit that got you into (or out of) trouble
19. a family story passed down through the generations
20. an episode marking your passage from adolescence to adulthood

Sample Student Essay

In this extended narrative a student uses a story about a sick but fierce dog to show how she learned a valuable lesson in her job as a veterinarian's assistant. Notice the student's good use of vivid details that makes this well-paced story both clear and interesting.

NEVER UNDERESTIMATE THE LITTLE THINGS

Introduction: A misconception

When I went to work as a veterinarian's assistant for Dr. Sam Holt and Dr. Jack Gunn last summer, I was under the false impression that the hardest part of veterinary surgery would be the actual performance of an operation. What might transpire before or after this feat didn't occur to me as being of any importance. As it happened, I had been in the veterinary clinic only a total of four hours before

Thesis

I met a little animal who convinced me that the operation itself was probably the easiest part of treatment. This animal, to whom I owe thanks for so enlightening me, was a chocolate-colored chihuahua of tiny size and immense perversity named Smokey.

Description of the story's main character: His appearance

Now Smokey could have very easily passed for some creature from another planet. It wasn't so much his gaunt little frame and overly large head, or his bony paws with nearly saberlike claws, as it was his grossly infected eyes. Those once-shining eyes were now distorted and swollen into grotesque balls of septic, sightless flesh. The only vague similarity they had to what we'd normally think of as the organs of vision was a slightly upraised dot, all that was left of the pupil, in the center of a pink and purply marble. As

His personality

if that were not enough, Smokey had a temper to match his ugly sight. He also had surprisingly good aim, considering his largely diminished vision, toward any moving object that happened to place itself unwisely before his ever-inquisitive nose, and with sudden and wholly vicious intent he would snap and snarl at whatever blocked the little light that could filter through his swollen and ruptured blood vessels. Truly, in many respects, Smokey was a fearful dog to behold.

Beginning of the
story: Dog in the cage

Such an appearance and personality did nothing to encourage my already flagging confidence in my capabilities as a vet's assistant. How was I supposed to get that little demon out of his cage? Jack had casually requested that I bring Smokey to the surgery room, but did he really expect me to put my hands into the mouth of the cage of that devil dog? I suppose it must have been my anxious expression that saved me, for as I turned uncertainly toward the kennel, Jack chuckled nonchalantly and accompanied me to demonstrate how professionals in his line of business dealt with professionals in Smokey's. He took a small rope about four feet long with a slipnoose at one end and began to unlatch Smokey's cage. Then cautiously he reached in and dangled the noose before the dog's snarling jaws. Since Smokey could only barely see what he was biting at, his attacks were directed haphazardly in a semicircle around his body. The tiny area of his cage led to his capture, for during one of Smokey's forward lunges, Jack dropped the noose over his head and dragged the struggling creature out onto the floor. The fight had only just begun for Smokey, however, and he braced his feet against the slippery linoleum tiling and forced us to drag him, like a little pull toy on a string, to the surgery.

In the surgery room

Once in the surgery, however, the question that hung before our eyes like a veritable presence was how to get the dog from the floor to table. Simply picking him up and plopping him down was out of the question. One glance at the quivering little figure emitting ominous and throaty warnings was enough to assure us of that. Realizing that the game was over, Jack grimly handed me the rope and reached for a muzzle. It was a doomed attempt from the start; the closer Jack dangled the tiny leather cup to the dog's nose the more violent did Smokey's contortions and rage-filled cries become and the more frantic our efforts became to try to keep our feet and fingers clear of the angry jaws. Deciding that a firmer method had to be used, Jack instructed me to raise the rope up high enough so that Smokey'd have to stand on his hind legs. This greatly reduced his maneuverability but served to increase his tenacity, for at this the little dog nearly went into paroxysms of frustration and rage. In his struggles, however, Smokey caught his forepaw on his swollen eye, and the blood that had been building up pressure behind the fragile cornea burst out and dripped to the floor. In the midst of our surprise and the twinge of panic startling the three of us, Jack saw his chance and swiftly muzzled the animal and lifted him to the operating table.

During the operation   Even at that point it wasn't easy to put the now terrified dog to sleep. He fought even the local anesthesia and caused Jack to curse as he was forced to give Smokey far more of the drug than should have been necessary for such a small beast. After what seemed an eternity, Smokey lay prone on the table, breathing deeply and emitting soft snores and gentle whines. We also breathed deeply in relief, and I relaxed to watch fascinated, while Jack performed a very delicate operation quite smoothly and without mishap.

Conclusion:
Restatement of thesis   Such was my harrowing induction into the life of a veterinary surgeon. But Smokey did teach me a valuable lesson that has proven its importance to me many times since, and that is that wherever animals are concerned, even the smallest detail should never be taken for granted.

Professional Essay

SHAME

Dick Gregory

Dick Gregory is a comedian, civil-rights activist, lecturer, and author of a number of books, including *The Shadow That Scares Me, From the Back of the Bus,* and *Dick Gregory's Political Primer.* This story is taken from *nigger: An Autobiography.*

———————

I never learned hate at home, or shame. I had to go to school for that. I was   1
about seven years old when I got my first big lesson. I was in love with a little girl named Helene Tucker, a light-complected little girl with pigtails and nice manners. She was always clean and she was smart in school. I think I went to school mostly to look at her. I brushed my hair and even got me a little old handkerchief. It was

a lady's handkerchief, but I didn't want Helene to see me wipe my nose on my hand. The pipes were frozen again, there was no water in the house, but I washed my socks and shirt every night. I'd get a pot, and go over to Mr. Ben's grocery store, and stick my pot down into his soda machine. Scoop out some chopped ice. By evening the ice melted to water for washing. I got sick a lot that winter because the fire would go out at night before the clothes were dry. In the morning I'd put them on, wet or dry, because they were the only clothes I had.

Everybody's got a Helene Tucker, a symbol of everything you want. I loved her for her goodness, her cleanliness, her popularity. She'd walk down my street and my brothers and sisters would yell, "Here comes Helene," and I'd rub my tennis sneakers on the back of my pants and wish my hair wasn't so nappy and the white folks' shirt fit me better. I'd run out on the street. If I knew my place and didn't come too close, she'd wink at me and say hello. That was a good feeling. Sometimes I'd follow her all the way home, and shovel the snow off her walk and try to make friends with her Momma and her aunts. I'd drop money on her stoop late at night on my way back from shining shoes in the taverns. And she had a Daddy, and he had a good job. He was a paper hanger. 2

I guess I would have gotten over Helene by summertime, but something happened in that classroom that made her face hang in front of me for the next twenty-two years. When I played the drums in high school it was for Helene and when I broke track records in college it was for Helene and when I started standing behind microphones and heard applause I wished Helene could hear it, too. It wasn't until I was twenty-nine years old and married and making money that I really got her out of my system. Helene was sitting in that classroom when I learned to be ashamed of myself. 3

It was on a Thursday. I was sitting in the back of the room, in a seat with a chalk circle drawn around it. The idiot's seat, the troublemaker's seat. 4

The teacher thought I was stupid. Couldn't spell, couldn't read, couldn't do arithmetic. Just stupid. Teachers were never interested in finding out that you couldn't concentrate because you were so hungry, because you hadn't had any breakfast. All you could think about was noontime, would it ever come? Maybe you could sneak into the cloakroom and steal a bite of some kid's lunch out of a coat pocket. A bite of something. Paste. You can't really make a meal out of paste, or put it on bread for a sandwich, but sometimes I'd scoop a few spoonfuls out of the paste jar in the back of the room. Pregnant people get strange tastes. I was pregnant with poverty. Pregnant with dirt and pregnant with smells that made people turn away, pregnant with cold and pregnant with shoes that were never bought for me, pregnant with five other people in my bed and no Daddy in the next room, and pregnant with hunger. Paste doesn't taste too bad when you're hungry. 5

The teacher thought I was a troublemaker. All she saw from the front of the room was a little black boy who squirmed in his idiot's seat and made noises and poked the kids around him. I guess she couldn't see a kid who made noises because he wanted someone to know he was there. 6

It was on a Thursday, the day before the Negro payday. The eagle always flew on Friday. The teacher was asking each student how much his father would give 7 to the Community Chest. On Friday night, each kid would get the money from his father, and on Monday he would bring it to the school. I decided I was going to buy me a Daddy right then. I had money in my pocket from shining shoes and selling papers, and whatever Helene Tucker pledged for her Daddy I was going to top it. And I'd hand the money right in. I wasn't going to wait until Monday to buy me a Daddy.

I was shaking, scared to death. The teacher opened her book and started calling out names alphabetically.   **8**

"Helene Tucker?"   **9**

"My daddy said he'd give two dollars and fifty cents."   **10**

"That's very nice, Helene. Very, very nice indeed."   **11**

That made me feel pretty good. It wouldn't take too much to top that. I had almost three dollars in dimes and quarters in my pocket. I stuck my hand in my pocket and held onto the money, waiting for her to call my name. But the teacher closed her book after she called everybody else in the class.   **12**

I stood up and raised my hand.   **13**

"What is it now?"   **14**

"You forgot me."   **15**

She turned toward the blackboard. "I don't have time to be playing with you, Richard."   **16**

"My Daddy said he'd . . ."   **17**

"Sit down, Richard, you're disturbing the class."   **18**

"My Daddy said he'd give . . . fifteen dollars."   **19**

She turned and looked mad. "We are collecting this money for you and your kind, Richard Gregory. If your Daddy can give fifteen dollars you have no business being on relief."   **20**

"I got it right now, I got it right now, my Daddy gave it to me to turn in today, my Daddy said . . ."   **21**

"And furthermore," she said, looking right at me, her nostrils getting big and her lips getting thin and her eyes opening wide, "we know you don't have a Daddy."   **22**

Helene Tucker turned around, her eyes full of tears. She felt sorry for me. Then I couldn't see her too well because I was crying, too.   **23**

"Sit down, Richard."   **24**

And I always thought the teacher kind of liked me. She always picked me to wash the blackboard on Friday, after school. That was a big thrill, it made me feel important. If I didn't wash it, come Monday the school might not function right.   **25**

"Where are you going, Richard?"   **26**

I walked out of school that day, and for a long time I didn't go back very often. There was shame there.   **27**

Now there was shame everywhere. It seemed like the whole world had been inside that classroom, everyone had heard what the teacher had said, everyone had turned around and felt sorry for me. There was shame in going to the Worthy Boys Annual Christmas Dinner for you and your kind, because everybody knew what a worthy boy was. Why couldn't they just call it the Boys Annual Dinner, why'd they have to give it a name? There was shame in wearing the brown and orange and   **28** white plaid mackinaw the welfare gave to 3,000 boys. Why'd it have to be the same for everybody so when you walked down the street the people could see you were on relief? It was a nice warm mackinaw and it had a hood, and my Momma beat me and called me a little rat when she found out I stuffed it in the bottom of a pail full of garbage way over on Cottage Street. There was shame in running over to Mister Ben's at the end of the day and asking for his rotten peaches, there was shame in asking Mrs. Simmons for a spoonful of sugar, there was shame in running out to meet the relief truck. I hated that truck, full of food for you and your kind. I ran into the house and hid when it came. And then I started to sneak through alleys, to take the long way home so the people going into White's Eat Shop wouldn't see me. Yeah, the whole world heard the teacher that day, we all know you don't have a Daddy.

Questions on Content, Structure, and Style

1. What is Gregory's purpose in telling this story from his childhood? What information about himself is he trying to explain to the reader?
2. For Gregory, who was Helene Tucker, and why was it important to "buy" himself a Daddy? Why did Helene's face hang before Gregory until he was twenty-nine? How did he finally get her "out of his system"?
3. Are the events in this story told in strict chronological order? If not, where are the deviations and why are they included?
4. Does Gregory use enough vivid detail to help you visualize the people and events of his story? Support your answer by citing specific passages.
5. Which characters are most developed in this story? How does Gregory help you understand the motivations for their actions? Is there any one character more fully developed than the others? If so, why?
6. Evaluate Gregory's use of dialogue. What does it add to the story?
7. Comment on Gregory's use of parallel construction in paragraphs 5 and 28.
8. Point out examples of slang and colloquial language in this story. Why did Gregory use such language?
9. How effective is Gregory's conclusion?
10. Describe Gregory's "voice" in this narrative. Is it effective or too full of self-pity?

Vocabulary

nappy (2)   pregnant (5)   mackinaw (28)

A Revision Worksheet for Your Narrative Essay

As you write your rough drafts, consult Chapter 5 for guidance through the revision process. In addition, here are a few questions to ask yourself as you revise your narrative:

1. Is the narrative essay's purpose clear to the reader?
2. Is the thesis plainly stated or at least clearly implied?
3. Does the narrative convincingly support or illustrate its intended point? If not, how might the story be changed?
4. Does the story maintain a consistent point of view and an understandable order of action?
5. Are the characters, actions, and settings presented in enough vivid detail to make them clear and believable? Where could more detail be effectively added?
6. Is the story coherent and well-paced or does it wander or bog down in places because of irrelevant or repetitious details? What might be condensed or cut?
7. What is the strongest part of your essay? How could you make the rest of your essay as good as that part?

After you've revised your essay extensively, you might exchange rough drafts with a classmate and answer these questions for each other, making specific suggestions for improvement wherever appropriate.

Writing the Research Paper

Although the words "upcoming research paper" have been known to produce anxiety equal to or worse than that caused by the sound of the dentist's drill or the news that the Huns have invaded Manhattan, you should try to relax. A research paper is similar to the kinds of expository and argumentative essays described in the earlier parts of this book, with the primary difference being the use of documented source material to support, illustrate, or expand your ideas. Research papers still call for thesis statements, logical sequences of paragraphs, well-developed supporting evidence, smooth conclusions—or in other words, all the skills you've been practicing throughout this book. By citing sources in your essays or reports, you merely show your readers that you have researched your ideas and found support for them; in addition, using sources affords your readers the opportunity to look into your subject further if they so desire, following your references as a guide to additional readings.

The process described in the next few pages should help you write a research paper that is carefully and effectively documented. This chapter also contains sample documentation forms (pp. 268–273) and a sample student paper (pp. 275–285).

SEARCHING FOR YOUR TOPIC

In some cases you will be assigned your topic, and you will be able to begin your research right away. In other classes, however, you may be encouraged to select your own subject, or you may be given only a general subject ("cults," "pornography," "violence on T.V.") that you must narrow and then focus on a particular manageable topic. If the topic is your choice, you need to do some preliminary thinking about what interests you; as in any assignment, you should make the essay a learning experience from which both you and your readers will profit. Therefore, you may want to brainstorm for a while on your general subject before you go to the library, asking yourself questions about what you already know and don't know. Some of the most interesting research papers are problem-solving essays in which writers set about to find an answer to a controversy or to find support for a solution they suspect might work. Other research papers expose or illuminate a situation or a problem for its audience. Whatever the goal of your particular research, remember that your readers want to finish your paper knowing more about a significant subject than when they started.

Once you have at least a general topic in mind, your next step is to familiarize yourself with the school or public library where you will do your research. Most libraries have handouts, maps, or librarians who will help you locate the important parts of the library; do not be shy about asking for such information *before* you start your search.

After you become comfortable in the library, you can begin to compile a *working bibliography*, that is, a list of possible sources for your topic. You may find it useful to start by investigating one or more of the following reference room tools:

The card catalog

The card catalog is usually a series of cabinets containing alphabetized index cards; in some libraries the card catalog is divided into three parts so that you may look up information under "subject," "author," and "titles."[1] Unless you are already familiar with authorities or their books on your subject, you will most likely begin with the "subject" catalog. If your subject is "acupuncture," you might find a typical subject card that looks like the sample on page 254.

You may have to look under several headings in the subject catalog to find the one your library uses for your topic.

Periodical indexes

Periodical indexes list magazines and journals that may contain articles you will wish to consult. There are several kinds of periodical indexes, and your library will carry a number of them to help you with your search. If your subject is of interest to a general audience, you might begin by checking *The Reader's Guide to Periodical Literature*, an index that lists 160 magazines of general interest, such as *Time* and *Newsweek*. *The New York Times Index* is also useful if your subject has

---

[1]If your library has become computerized, the traditional card catalog may now be on microfiche. Since libraries today are often in a state of transition, you may need to consult your reference librarian about the system in use at your school.

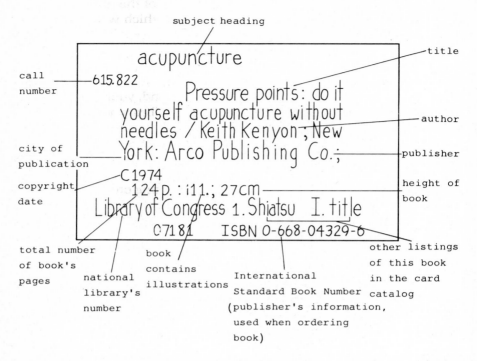

subject heading

call number

title

author

city of publication

publisher

copyright date

height of book

acupuncture

615.822

Pressure points: do it yourself acupuncture without needles / Keith Kenyon ; New York: Arco Publishing Co. ;

C1974

124 p. : ill. ; 27cm

Library of Congress 1. Shiatsu I. title

C7181   ISBN 0-668-04329-6

total number of book's pages

book contains illustrations

national library's number

International Standard Book Number (publisher's information, used when ordering book)

other listings of this book in the card catalog

been in the national or international news. However, if your subject is particular to a field of study, you may wish to try first those indexes that list only magazines and journals in specific areas, such as the *Business Periodicals Index,* the *Humanities Index,* the *Applied Science and Technology Index,* or the *Social Sciences Index.* Note too that your topic may be listed under slightly different headings from index to index (for instance, "wife abuse" in one index might be "battered wife syndrome" in another). If you can't find your subject under the headings that first come to your mind, ask your librarian for the *Library of Congress Subject Headings,* a common reference book that will suggest other names for your topic.

Special collections

Your library may also contain special collections that will help you research your subject. Some libraries, for example, have extensive collections of government documents or educational materials or newspapers from certain cities. Other libraries may have invested in manuscripts from famous authors or in a series of works on a particular subject, such as your state's history, a Vietnam War collection, or studies on human rights in post-World War II Latin America. Consult your librarian or the handouts describing your library's special holdings.

Looking through the card catalog and periodical indexes may take time, but seeing what's been published on your subject may help you focus on a specific topic. You may also find it useful at this point to skim a number of articles on your subject, so that eventually you reach the idea you want to research and write about. (And don't underestimate the value of browsing—sometimes the most interesting book on your subject is on the shelf next to the book you were looking for.)

Once you have a narrowed topic, you are ready to prepare a *working bibliography*, a list of the most promising sources for your paper. To compile a working bibliography, you should note on an index card the following information for each source: author's name, title of work, publisher, date and city of publication, page numbers of the material you're interested in, and library call number.

TAKING NOTES

Begin to look up the sources listed in your working bibliography and take notes on *content cards*. Most researchers recommend that you take notes on index cards rather than on notebook paper because the cards can be shuffled around more easily later when you are organizing your paper. In addition, you may find it helpful to use cards of a different color or size from the bibliography cards, just for ease of sorting. When you find a useful book, be sure you have a bibliography card for it that contains the author's name, the book's full title, publisher, city and date of publication, and the page numbers from which your notes are taken. If your notes are from a magazine or journal, the card should contain the author's name, journal's name, article's name, volume number, issue number, date of issue, page numbers of the article within the journal, and the page numbers from which you took your notes. Plan to use several content cards for each book or article because you may wish to divide your notes into categories of ideas that will later help you organize your paragraphs. Write on one side of the content cards only, to avoid having some material out of sight and mind while you're organizing your notes for your first rough draft.

Your notes will probably be of four kinds:

Direct quotations. When you lift material word-for-word,[2] you must always use quotation marks and note the precise page number of the quotation. If the quoted material runs from one page onto another, always use some sort of signal to yourself such as a slash bar (child/abuse) or arrow (→ p. 10) at the break so if you only use part of the

---

[2]Please note that all tables, graphs, and charts that you copy must also be directly attributed to their sources, though you do not enclose graphics in quotation marks.

quoted material in your paper, you will know on which page it appeared. If the quoted material contains odd, archaic, or incorrect spelling, punctuation marks, or grammar, insert the word [*sic*] in brackets next to the item in queston; [*sic*] means "this is the way I found it in the original text," and such a symbol will remind you later that you did not miscopy the quotation. Otherwise, always double check to make sure you did copy the material accurately and completely to avoid having to come back to the source as you prepare your essay. If the material you want to quote is lengthy, you will find it easier— though not cheaper—to photocopy the material rather than transcribe it (almost all libraries have one or more photocopy machines, but be prepared to bring your own bag of correct change).

Paraphrase. You paraphrase when you put into your own words what someone else has written or said. Please note: *Paraphrased ideas are borrowed ideas, not your original thoughts, and consequently they must be attributed to their owner just as direct quotations are!* To remind yourself that certain information on your notecards is para-phrased, always leave space in the lefthand margin for some sort of notation such as a circled Ⓟ; quotation marks will always tell you what you borrowed directly, but sometimes when writers take notes one week and write their first draft a week or two later, it's hard to remem-ber if a note was paraphrased or if it's original thinking. Writers occa-sionally plagiarize unintentionally because they believe only direct quotations and statistics must be attributed to their proper sources, so make your notes as clear as possible (for more information on avoiding plagiarism, see pp. 261–263).

Summary. You may wish to condense a piece of writing so that you may offer it as support for your own ideas. Using your own words, you should present in shorter form the writer's thesis and supporting ideas. In addition, you may find it helpful to include a few direct quotations in your summary to retain the flavor of the original work. Of course, you will tell your readers what you are summarizing and by whom it was written. Remember to make a note in the margin to indicate sum-marized, rather than original, material.

Your own ideas. Your note cards should also contain your personal comments (judgments, flashes of brilliance, notions of how to use some-thing you've just read, notes to yourself about connections between sources, and so forth) that will aid you in the writing of your paper. It might be helpful to jot these down in a different colored pen or put them in brackets that you've initialed, so that you will recognize them later as your own responses when your note cards are cold.

DISTINGUISHING PARAPHRASE FROM SUMMARY

Because novice writers sometimes have a hard time telling the difference between paraphrase and summary, here is a sample of each.

First, here is a paragraph from an article suggesting a way to stop juvenile delinquency that might be pertinent in a research paper you're preparing on the current theories for controlling juvenile crime.

> Another successful approach to the prevention of criminality has been to target very young children in a school setting before problems arise. The Perry Preschool Program, started 22 years ago in a low socioeconomic area of Ypsilanti, Michigan, has offered some of the most solid evidence to date that early intervention through a high-quality preschool program can significantly alter a child's life. A study released this fall tells what happened to 123 disadvantaged children from preschool age to present. The detention and arrest rates for the 58 children who had attended the preschool program was 31 percent, compared to 51 percent for the 65 who did not. Similarly, those in the preschool program were more likely to have graduated from high school, have enrolled in postsecondary education programs and be employed, and less likely to have become pregnant as teenagers.
>
> —from "Arresting Delinquency,"
> Dan Hurley, *Psychology Today*,
> March 1985, p. 66.

A *paraphrase* puts the information in the researcher's own words, but it does follow the order of the original text, and it does include the important details.

PARAPHRASE

> Quality preschooling for high-risk children may help stop crime before it starts. A recent study from the twenty-two-year-old Perry Preschool Program located in a poor area of Ypsilanti, Michigan, shows that of 123 socially and economically disadvantaged children the 58 who attended preschool had an arrest rate of 31% as compared to 51% for those 65 who did not attend. The adults with preschool experience had also graduated from high school in larger numbers; in addition, more of them had attended postsecondary education programs, were employed, and had avoided teenage pregnancy (Hurley 66).

A *summary* is generally much shorter than the original; the researcher picks out the key ideas but often omits many of the supporting details.

SUMMARY

A recent study from the Perry Preschool Program in Michigan suggests that disadvantaged children who attend preschool are less likely to be arrested as adults. Those in this study with preschool experience also chose more education, had better employment records, and avoided teenage pregnancy more often than those without preschool (Hurley 66).

Remember: both paraphrased and summarized ideas must be attributed to their sources, even if you did not reproduce exact words or figures.

CHOOSING YOUR SOURCES

Once you have collected and reviewed your notes, you may be ready to begin sketching out your outline and first draft. In doing so, you must decide which sources to use, where to use them, and in what form: paraphrase, summary, or direct quotation.

To help you choose your sources, here are some questions to consider as you try to decide which facts, figures, and testimonies will best support or illustrate your ideas.

Are your sources reliable? Newspapers are frequently faulted for basing entire stories on unnamed, so-called "reliable sources." Be sure that your sources are dependable and well-respected in the particular area under discussion. An expert in organic chemistry, for example, might know an enormous amount about his or her own field but actually very little about genetics.

Are your sources unreasonably biased? Some authorities stand to gain economically or politically from taking a particular point of view. The president of a tobacco company, for instance, might insist that secondary smoke from the cigarettes of others will not harm non-smokers, but does he or she have an objective opinion? Try to present testimony from those authorities whose views will sway your readers.

Is your research sensibly balanced? Your treatment of your subject—especially if it's a controversial one—should show your readers that you investigated all sides of the issue before reaching a conclusion. If your sources are drawn only from authorities well known for voicing one position, your readers will tend to become skeptical about the quality of your research. For instance, if on a paper on prayer in the schools, you refer only to the opinions of William Buckley, Phyllis Schaefly, and the president of the Eagle Forum, all well-known conservatives, you may antagonize the reader who wants a thorough analysis of all sides of the question. Do use sources that support your position— but don't overload your argument with only obviously biased sources. (Be careful with certain publications, too; check the origins and publishers of your magazines and pamphlets. Naturally, a brochure on abortion printed by Planned Parenthood will have a different point of view from one printed by the local right-to-life organization.)

Are your sources reporting valid research? Is your source the original researcher or is he or she reporting someone else's study? If the information is being reported secondhand, has your source been accurate and clear? Is the original source named or footnoted in some way so that the information could be checked? Look too at the way the information was obtained in the first place. Did the original researchers themselves draw the logical conclusions from their evidence? Did they run their study or experiment (or whatever) in a fair, impartial way? For example, a survey of people whose names were obtained from the rolls of the Democratic Party will hardly constitute a representative sampling of voters' opinion on an upcoming election. Moreover, be especially careful with statistics as they can be manipulated quite easily to give a distorted picture. A recent survey, for instance, asked a large sample of people to rate a number of American cities on questions dealing with quality of life. Pittsburgh—a lovely city, to be sure—came out the winner, but only if one agrees that all the questions should be weighted equally; that is, the figures averaged out with Pittsburgh boasting the highest score only if one rates "weather" as equally important as "educational opportunities," "amount of crime," "cultural opportunities," and other factors. In short, always evaluate the quality of your sources' research and the validity of their conclusions before you decide to incorporate their findings into your own paper. (And don't forget Mark Twain's reference to "lies, damned lies, and statistics.")

Are your sources still current? While it's true that some famous experiments or studies have withstood the years, for many controversial topics you should use as current research as possible. What may have been written ten, or even five, years ago may have been disproved or surpassed since, especially in some of our rapidly expanding fields of technology. If they're appropriate, journals and other periodicals may contain more up-to-date reports than books printed several years ago. Readers usually appreciate hearing the current word on the topic under examination, though you certainly shouldn't ignore a "classic" study on your subject, especially if it is the one against which all the other studies are measured.

Are you using your sources in a clear, logical way?   First, make certain that you understand your source material well enough to use it in support of your own thoughts. Once you have selected the best references to use, be as convincing as possible. Ask yourself if you're using enough evidence and if the information you're offering really does clearly support your point. As in any essay, you need to avoid oversimplification, hasty generalizations, *non sequiturs*, and other problems in logic (for a review of common logical fallacies, see pp. 213–216). Resist the temptation to add quotations, facts, or statistics that are interesting but not really relevant to your paper.

INCORPORATING YOUR SOURCE MATERIAL

Remember that a research paper is not a massive collection of quotations and paraphrased ideas glued together with a few transition phrases. It is, instead, an essay in which you offer your thesis and ideas based upon and supported by your research. Consequently, you will need to incorporate and blend in your reference material in a variety of smooth, persuasive ways. Here are some suggestions:

Don't overuse direct quotations. It's best to use a direct quotation *only* when it expresses a point in a far more impressive, emphatic, or concise way than you could say it yourself. Suppose, for instance, you were analyzing the films of a particular director and wanted to include a sample of critical reviews:

As one movie critic wrote, "This film is really terrible, and people should ignore it" (Dennison 14).

(This direct quotation isn't remarkable and could be easily paraphrased.)

As one movie critic wrote, "This film's plot is so inane that the director must have intended it for people who move their lips not only when they read but also when they watch T.V." (Dennison 14).

(You might be tempted to quote this line to show your readers an emphatically negative review of this movie.)

When you do decide to use direct quotations, don't merely drop them in next to your prose.   Instead, lead into them smoothly so that they obviously support or clarify what you are saying.

Dropped in   Scientists have been studying the ill effects of nitrites on test animals since 1961. "Nitrites produced malignant tumors in 62 percent of the test animals within six months" (Smith 109).

Better   Scientists have been studying the ill effects of nitrites on test animals since 1961. According to Dr. William Smith, head of the Farrell Institute of Research, "Nitrites produced malignant tumors in 62 percent of the test animals within six months" (109).

Don't use the same pattern again and again to introduce your quotations. Here are some sample lead-in phrases for quotations:

In his introduction to *The Great Gatsby*, Professor William Smith points out that "Fitzgerald wrote about himself and produced a narcissistic masterpiece" (5).

William Smith, author of *Impact*, summarized the situation this way: "Eighty-eight percent of the sales force threaten a walkout" (21).

"Only the President controls the black box," according to the White House Press Secretary (Smith 129).

As drama critic William Smith observed last year in *The Saturday Review*, the play was "a rousing failure" (212).

Perhaps the well-known poet William Smith expressed the idea best when he wrote, "Love is a spider waiting to entangle its victims" (14).

Congressman William Smith presented the opposing view when he claimed, "Employment figures are down ten percent from last year" (32).

In other words, don't simply repeat "William Smith said," "John Jones said," "Mary Brown said."

Don't let reference material dominate your essay. Remember that your reader is interested in your thesis and your conclusions, not just in a string of references. Use your researched material wisely whenever your statements need clarification, support, or amplification. But don't use quotations, paraphrased, or summarized material at every turn, just to show that you've done your homework.

Punctuate your quotations correctly. The proper punctuation will help your reader understand who said what. For information on the appropriate uses of quotation marks and commas, see pp. 309 and 315.

AVOIDING PLAGIARISM

Unfortunately, most discussions of research papers must include a brief word about plagiarism. Novice writers often unintentionally plagiarize, as noted before, because they fail to recognize the necessity to attribute paraphrased, summarized, and borrowed ideas to their original owners. And indeed it is difficult sometimes after days of research to know exactly what one has borrowed and what one originally thought. Also, there's frequently a thin line between general or common knowledge ("Henry Ford was the father of the automobile industry in America") that does not have to be documented and those ideas and statements that do ("U.S. Steel reported an operating loss of four million in its last quarter"). As a rule of thumb, ask yourself whether the majority of your readers would recognize the fact or opinion you're expressing or if it's repeatedly found in commonly used sources; if so, you may not need to document it. For example, most people would acknowledge that the Wall Street Crash of 1929 ushered in the Great Depression of the 1930s, but the exact number of bank foreclosurers in 1933 is not common knowledge and needs documenting. Similarly, a well-known quotation from the Bible or Mother Goose or even the Declaration of Independence might pass without documentation, but a line from the vice-president's latest speech needs a reference to its source. When in doubt, the best choice is to document anything that you feel may be in question.

To help you understand the difference between plagiarism and proper documentation, here is an original passage and both incorrect and correct ways to use it in a paper of your own:

Original   It is a familiar nightmare: a person suffers a heart attack, and as the ambulance fights heavy traffic, the patient dies. In fact, 350,000 American heart-attack victims each year die without ever reaching a hospital. The killer in many cases is ventricular fibrillation, uncoordinated contraction of the heart muscle. Last week a team of Dutch physicians reported in *The New England Journal of Medicine* that these early deaths can often be prevented by administration of a common heart drug called lidocaine, injected into the patient's shoulder muscle by ambulance paramedics as soon as they arrive on the scene.
                            —From "First Aid for Heart Attacks," *Newsweek*, November 11, 1985, page 88

Plagiarized   It is a common nightmare: a person with a heart attack dies as the ambulance sits in heavy traffic, often a victim of ventricular fibrillation, uncoordinated contraction of the heart muscle. Today, however, these early deaths can often be prevented by an injection into the patient's shoulder of a common heart drug called lidocaine, which may be administered by paramedics on the scene.

This writer has changed some of the words and sentences, but the passage has obviously been borrowed and must be attributed to its source.

Also plagiarized   According to *Newsweek*, 350,000 American heart attack victims die before reaching help in hospitals ("First

Aid for Heart Attacks" 88). However, a common heart drug called lidocaine, which may be injected into the patient by paramedics on the scene of the attack, may save many victims who die en route to doctors and sophisticated life-saving equipment.

This writer did attribute the statistic to its source, but the remainder of the paragraph is still borrowed and must be documented.

Properly documented   Ambulance paramedics can, and often do, play a vital life-saving role today. They are frequently the first medical assistance available, especially to those patients or accident victims far away from hospitals. Moreover, according to a recent *Newsweek* report, paramedics are now being trained to administer powerful drugs to help the sick survive until they reach doctors and medical equipment. For instance, paramedics can inject the common heart drug lidocaine into heart attack victims on the scene, an act that may save many of the 350,000 Americans who die of heart attacks before ever reaching a hospital ("First Aid for Heart Attacks" 88).

This writer used the properly documented information to support her own point about paramedics and has not tried to pass off any of the article as her own.

Although plagiarism is often unintentional, it's your job to be as honest as possible. If you're in doubt about your use of a particular idea, consult your instructor for a second opinion.

Practicing What You've Learned

To practice some of the skills you've learned so far, read the following passage on Alexander II of Russia (1855-1881) and do the tasks listed below it.

Alexander's greatest single achievement was his emancipation of some forty million Russian serfs, a deed which won him the title of "Tsar Liberator." To visit a rural Russian community in the earlier nineteenth century was like stepping back into the Middle Ages. Nine-tenths of the land was held by something less than one hundred thousand noble families. The serfs, attached to the soil, could be sold with the estates to new landlords, conscripted into the nobleman's household to work as domestic servants, or even sent to the factories in the towns for their master's profit. Though some nobles exercised their authority in a kindly and paternal fashion, others overworked their serfs, flogged them cruelly for slight faults, and interfered insolently in their private affairs and family relations. A serf could not marry without his master's consent, could not leave the estate without permission, and might be pursued, brought back, and punished if he sought to escape. He lived at the mercy of his master's caprice.

1. The book from which the above passage was taken contains the information listed below. Select the appropriate information and prepare a bibliography card.

> *A Survey of European Civilization Part Two, Since 1660*
> Third Edition
> Houghton Mifflin Company, Publishers
> Boston
> First edition, 1936
> 853.21
> 1012 pages
> Authors:
>   Wallace K. Ferguson, The University of Western Ontario
>   Geoffrey Brun, Formerly Visiting Professor of History, Cornell
>   University
> Indexes: general, list of maps
> Picture Acknowledgments, xxvii
> copyright 1962
> p. 716
> 44 chapters

2. Paraphrase the passage.

3. Summarize the passage, but do not quote from it.

4. Select an important idea from the passage to quote directly and lead into the quotation with a smooth acknowledgment of its source.

5. Select an idea or a quotation from the passage and use it as support for a point of your own, being careful not to plagiarize the borrowed material.

Assignment

In your school or local library, look up a newspaper from any city or state and find the issue published on the day of your birth. Prepare a bibliography card for the issue you chose. Then summarize the most important or "lead" article located on the front page. (Don't forget to acknowledge the source of your summary.)

FINDING THE PROPER FORMAT FOR YOUR DOCUMENTATION

Once you've begun to write your paper incorporating your source material, you need to know how to show your readers where your material came from. You may have already learned a system for using footnotes (or endnotes), but since today's researchers and scholars use a number of different documentation forms, it's important that you know which form is appropriate for your essay. In some cases your instructors (or the audience for whom you are writing) will designate a particular form; at other times, the choice will be yours.

New MLA Form

Many instructors of writing across the country assign the documentation form prescribed by the Modern Language Association of America (MLA). Beginning in 1984, the MLA recommended a new form of documentation that no longer uses traditional footnotes or endnotes to show references.[3] This new form calls for *parenthetical documentation*, most often consisting of the author's last name and the appropriate page number(s) in parentheses immediately following the source material in your paper. The information in the parentheses is then keyed to a "Works Cited" page at the end of your essay, a list of the sources used in your essay (see pp. 268–274 for more explanation and samples).

Here are some guidelines for using the new parenthetical reference form within your paper:

1. If you use a source by one author, place the author's name and page number right after the quoted, paraphrased, or summarized material. Note that the parentheses go *before* the end punctuation, and there is no punctuation between the author's name and page number.

Example   Although pop art often resembles the comic strip, it owes a debt to such painters as Magritte, Matisse, and de Kooning (Rose 184).

2. If you use a source by one author and give credit to that author by name within your paper, you need only give the page number in the parentheses.

Example   According to art critic Barabara Rose, pop art owes a large debt to such painters as Magritte, Matisse, and de Kooning (184).

---

[3]If you wish a more detailed description of the new MLA form, you should ask your local bookstore for the *MLA Handbook for Writers of Research Papers*, 2nd ed. (New York: MLA, 1984) by Joseph Gibaldi and Walter S. Achtert.

3. If you are directly quoting material longer than five typed lines, set off the material by five spaces on the left margin and do not use quotation marks. Note that in this case, the parentheses appears *after* the puncutation that ends the quoted material.

Example   In addition to causing tragedy for others, Crane's char-
                           acters who are motivated by a desire to appear heroic to
                           their peers may also cause themselves serious trouble. Col-
                           lins, in "A Mystery of Heroism," for example, almost
                           causes his own death because of his vain desire to act
                           bravely in front of his fellow soldiers. (Hall 16)

4. If you are citing more than one work by the same author, include a short title in the parentheses.

Example   Within 50 years the Inca and Aztec civilizations were
                           defeated and overthrown by outside invaders (Thomas,
                           Lost Cultures 198).

5. If you are citing a work by more than one author, use both last names and page number.

Example   Prisons today are overcrowded to the point of emer-
                           gency; conditions could not be worse, and the state budget
                           for prison reform is at an all-time low (Smith and Jones 72).

6. If you cite a work that has no author given, use the work's title and the page number.

Example   Each year 350,000 Americans will die of a heart attack
                           before reaching a hospital ("First Aid for Heart Attacks"
                           88).

7. If the work you are citing appears in a series, include the volume and page number with the author's name.

Example   The most common view camera format is 4″ by 5,″
                           though many sizes are available on today's market (Pursell
                           1:29).

If the material you are citing contains a quoted passage from another source, indicate the use of the quotation in the parentheses.

Example   According to George Orwell, "Good writing is like a
                           window-pane" (qtd. in Murray 142).

Footnote/Endnote Form

In case your assignment calls for traditional footnotes rather than for the new MLA format, here is a brief description of that form.

Each idea you borrow and each quotation you include must be

attributed to its author(s) in a footnote that appears at the bottom of the appropriate page.[4] Number your footnotes consecutively throughout the essay (do not start over with "1" on each new page), and place the number in the text to the right of and slightly above the end of the passage, whether it is a direction quotation, a paraphrase, or a summary. Place the corresponding number, indented (five spaces) and slightly raised, before the footnote at the bottom of the page. Double-space each entry, and double-space after each footnote if more than one appears on the same page. See below for sample footnote entries.

Once you have provided a first full reference, subsequent footnotes for that source may only include the author's last name and page number. However, some authorities still require the use of Latin abbreviations such as *ibid.* ("in the same place") and *op. cit.* ("in the work cited"); if your assignment does require these Latin abbreviations, use *ibid.* immediately after the original footnote to substitute for the author's name, the title, and the publication information; add a page number only if it differs from the one in the original footnote. Use *op. cit.* with the author's name to substitute for the title in later references.

First reference   [5]Barbara Tuchman, <u>A Distant Mirror: The</u>

<u>Calamitous Fourteenth Century</u> (New York:

Knopf, 1978), p. 77.

Next footnote   [6]Ibid., p. 82.

Later reference   [12]Tuchman, <u>op. cit.</u>, p. 120.

Using Supplementary Notes

Sometimes when writers of research papers wish to give their readers additional information about their topic or about a particular piece of source material, they include *supplementary notes.* If you are using the MLA format, these notes should be indicated by using a raised number in your text (The study seemed incomplete at the time of its publication.[2]); the explanations appear on a page called "Notes" that follows the end of your essay. If you are using traditional footnote form, simply include the supplementary notes in your list of footnotes at the bottom of the page or in the list of endnotes following your essay's conclusion.

Supplementary notes can offer a wide variety of additonal information. *Examples:*

[1]For a different interpretation of this imagery, see Robert

Spiller, <u>Literary History of the United States</u> (New York:

Macmillian, 1953), 1021.

---

[4]Some writing situations permit the use of endnotes, a list of your footnotes that appears following the essay or report. Consult your teacher or the person (or publication) for whom you are writing to see if endnotes are permissible or even preferred.

[2]Simon and Brown have also contributed to this area of investigation. For a description of their results, see <u>Report on the Star Wars Project</u> (Chicago: Indigo, 1985), 98-102.

[3]It is important to note here that Brown's study followed Smith's by at least six months.

[4]Later in his autobiography Louis himself contradicts his earlier evaluation by saying, "Our experiment was contaminated from the beginning" (319).

Don't, of course, overdo supplementary notes; use them only when you think the additional information would be truly valuable to your readers. Obviously, information critical to your essay's points should go in the appropriate body paragraphs.

COMPILING A WORKS CITED LIST[5]

If you are using the MLA format, at the end of your essay (or following a list of supplementary notes if you have one) you should include a *works cited list*—a formal listing of the sources you used in your essay. Arrange the entries alphabetically by the authors' last names; if no name is given, arrange your sources by the first important word of the title. Double-space each entry, and double-space after each one. If an entry takes more than one line, indent the subsequent lines five spaces. See the sample entries that follow.

Sample Entries for a List of References

Here are some sample entries to help you prepare a Works Cited page according to the MLA guidelines. Please note that if you type your paper the titles of books and journals should be underlined (even though you may see them printed in books or magazines in italics), and the titles of articles, essays, and chapters should be enclosed in quotation marks.[6]

BOOKS

- Book with one author

Tuchman, Barbara. <u>A Distant Mirror: The Calamitous Fourteenth Century</u>. New York: Knopf, 1978.

[5]Please note that if you're using the footnote format, this page has traditionally been called a *bibliography page*.

[6]The new MLA style recommends shortened forms of publishers' names: Holt for Holt, Rinehart and Winston; Harper for Harper & Row; and so forth. Also, omit business descriptions, such as "Inc.," "Co.," "Press," or "House."

- Two books by same author

Tuchman, Barbara. A Distant Mirror: The Calamitous
    Fourteenth Century. New York: Knopf, 1978.
---. Stillwell and the American Experience in China. New
    Jersey: Macmillan, 1971.

- Book with two or three authors

Weider, Ben, and David Hapgood. The Death of Napoleon. New
    York: Congdon, 1982.

- Book with more than three authors

Guerin, Wilfred L., et al. A Handbook of Critical
    Approaches to Literature. New York: Harper, 1979.

- Book with author and editor

Chaucer, Geoffrey. The Tales of Canterbury. Ed. Robert
    Pratt. Boston: Houghton, 1974.

- Book with corporate authorship

United States Council on Fire Prevention. Stopping Arson
    Before It Starts. Washington: Edmondson, 1982.

- Book with an editor

Baugh, Albert C., ed. A Literary History of England. New
    York: Appleton, 1974.

- Selection or chapter from an anthology or collection with an
  editor

Chopin, Kate. "La Belle Zoraide." Classic American Women
    Writers. Ed. Cynthia Griffin Wolff. New York: Harper,
    1980. 250-273.

- Work in more than one volume

Sharp, Harold. Handbook of Pseudonyms and Personal
     Nicknames. Vol. 1. New York: Scarecrow, 1972. 2
     vols.

- Work in a series

Berg, Barbara L. The Remembered Gate: Origins of American
     Feminism. Urban Life in America Series. New York:
     Oxford UP, 1978.

(Note that the new MLA style recommends using "UP" instead of
the words "University Press.")

- Translation

Proust, Marcel. Remembrance of Things Past. Trans. C. K.
     S. Moncrieff. New York: Random, 1970.

- Reprint

Thaxter, Celia. Among the Isles of Shoals. 1873. Hampton,
     N.H.: Heritage, 1978.

MAGAZINES AND PERIODICALS

- Signed article in magazine

Dellinger, Walter. "Another Route to the ERA." Newsweek 2
     Aug. 1982: 8.

- Unsigned article in magazine

"Men's and Women's Trenchcoats." Consumer Reports Oct.
     1982: 491-97.

- Signed article in periodical

Lockwood, Thomas. "Divided Attention in Persuasion."
     Nineteenth-Century Fiction 33 (1978): 309-23.

- A review

Musto, Michael. Rev. of Goddess, The Secret Lives of
     Marilyn Monroe, by Anthony Summers. Saturday Review
     Dec. 1985: 65-66.

NEWSPAPERS

- Signed article in newspaper

Branscombe, Art. "American Students Not Getting 'Basics.'"
     Denver Post 19 Sept. 1982: A17.

- Unsigned article in newspaper

"Soviet Union Buys 7.6 Million Metric Tons of Grain from
     Canada." Wall Street Journal 14 Oct. 1982: A18.

- Unsigned editorial

"Give Life after Death." Editorial. Coloradoan [Ft.
     Collins, CO] 23 Dec. 1985: A4.
(If the newspaper's city of publication is not clear from the title, put
the location in brackets following the paper's name, as shown above.)

- A letter to the newspaper

Franklin, Charles. Letter. Denver Post 10 Sept. 1985: B10.

ENCYCLOPEDIAS, PAMPHLETS, DISSERTATIONS

- Signed article in an encyclopedia

Langlotz, Ernst. "Greek Art." Encyclopedia of World Art.
     1963.

- Unsigned article in an encyclopedia

"Sailfish." The International Wildlife Encyclopedia. 1970
     ed.

- A pamphlet

Young, Leslie. Baby Care Essentials for the New Mother.

   Austin: Hall, 1985.

- A government document

Department of Health. National Institute on Drug Abuse.

   Drug Abuse Prevention. Washington: GPO, 1980.

- Unpublished dissertations and theses

Harmon, Gail A. "Poor Writing Skills at the College Level: A

   Program for Correction." Diss. U of Colorado, 1982.

FILMS, TELEVISION, RADIO, PERFORMANCES, RECORDS

- A film

La Cage aux Folles. Dir. Edouard Molinaro. With Ugo

   Tognazzi and Michel Serrault. United Artists, 1979.

If you are referring to the contribution of a particular individual, such as the director, writer, actor, or composer, begin with that person's name:

Molinaro, Edouard, dir. La Cage aux Folles. With Ugo

   Tognazzi and Michel Serrault. United Artists, 1979.

- A television or radio show

Innovation. WNET, Newark. 12 Oct 1985.

If your reference is to a particular episode or person associated with the show, cite that name first, before the show's name:

"A Tribute to Beethoven." Sounds Alive. CBS. WXYZ,

   Dallas. 10 May 1983.

Moyers, Bill, writ. and narr. <u>Bill Moyers' Journal</u>. PBS.

WABC, Denver. 30 Sept. 1980.

• Performances (plays, concerts, ballets, operas)

<u>Julius Caesar</u>. By William Shakespeare. With Royal

Shakespeare Company. Booth Theater, New York. 13 Oct.

1982.

If you are referring to the contribution of a particular person associated with the performance, put that person's name first:

Shostakovich, Maxim, cond. New York Philharmonic Orch.

Concert. Avery Fisher Hall, New York. 12 Nov. 1982.

• A record

Seger, Bob. "Night Moves." Rec. 20 May 1980. <u>Nine</u>

<u>Tonight</u>. Capitol, 7777-12182-1, 1981.

LETTERS, LECTURES, AND SPEECHES

• A letter

Moore, Thomas. To Lord Byron. 28 Oct. 1821. Letter 112 in

<u>Memoirs, Journals and Correspondence</u>. Ed. Lord John

Russell. Vol. 3. London: Longman, 1853. 352-53. 8

vols. 1953-55

• A lecture or speech

Give the speaker's name and the title of the talk first, before the sponsoring organization (or occasion) and location. If there is no title, substitute the appropriate label, such as "lecture" or "speech."

Dippity, Sarah N. "The Importance of Prewriting." CLAS

Convention. Colorado Springs, 15 Feb. 1984.

INTERVIEWS

- A published interview

Cite the person interviewed first. Use the word "Interview" if the interview has no title.

Mailer, Norman. "Dialogue with Mailer." With Andrew Gordon.
Berkeley Times 15 Jan. 1969.

- A personal interview

Johns, Professor Henry. Dept. of Political Science,
Colorado State University. Personal interview. 4
Sept. 1982.

Clay, Marilyn. City Council Office, Loveland, CO.
Telephone interview. 13 April 1985.

Sample Student Paper

The "problem-solving" assignment that resulted in this paper asked students to select a current controversy in a professional or personal area of interest and research possible solutions. They were then to report on their findings: was there a feasible answer to a particular problem? If not, why not?

The student writer of this paper is, as she indicates in her introduction, both fascinated and repelled by boxing. At first, she wanted to write a paper banning boxing entirely, but, after some thought, she decided to research the most-often suggested reforms. Firmly convinced that the thesis of her paper would call *for* the reforms, she was amazed to discover, after some weeks in the library, that her evidence was mounting *against* adopting the reforms. Consequently, she wrote a rather controversial essay to support a position only discovered after her research. As you read her essay, ask yourself how effectively she uses supporting evidence to back up her analysis. Where might she have used other sources to support her claims? Other kinds of evidence? Do you find her essay convincing or not? Why?

Introduction: the writer's involvement with the subject

The controversy

THE CASE AGAINST BOXING REFORMS

For years I've been one of the millions of people who a half-dozen times a year witness the brutality and savagery of a sport whose principal purpose is to incapacitate or maim the opponent: boxing. Although every bit of sense I have tells me I shouldn't approve of this demoralizing contest, some instinctive appeal urges me to sit through the fifteen rounds of bashing blows and paralyzing punches. Yes, I was at television's ringside in 1971 when the hammering left hook of defending heavyweight champion Joe Frazier sent the once-champ Muhammad Ali to the canvas in the fourteenth round to clinch a unanimous decision over the no-longer skipping and dancing Ali, in what the whole world referred to as "The Fight." I witnessed the bout between former champion Larry Holmes and his courageous, although inept, challenger Randall "Tex" Cobb, in what proved to be a massacre of the worst sort. And then there was the knock out (and eventual death) of twenty-three-year-old Duk Koo Kim after a thirty-nine blow bombardment from Boom Boom Mancini in the fourteenth round of his challenge for the WBA championship. Indeed, I saw all of these. I cheered. I cringed. I grieved.

Since the death of Kim many prominent people have called for the banning of professional boxing, including sports authorities such as announcer Howard Cosell and sports writer George Vecsey of The New York Times ("Abolish Boxing?" 1528). Such powerful organizations as the American Medical Association have called for an end to the sport (Leershen and Katz 67).[1] But cooler heads have pointed out the uselessness of demanding the extinction of one of the world's oldest and most popular sports; instead, they have offered a series of proposals to reduce the number of boxing fatalities caused by head injuries (Axthelm 60). Those

Narrowing the focus to three proposals

Thesis

First reform: weight of gloves

Conflicting testimony

Supporting study

Second reform: headgear

proposals most often suggested include changing the weight of gloves, using protective headgear, and requiring rigorous medical tests before and after each match. But while such reforms sound beneficial, they will not, unfortunately, significantly reduce the number of boxing deaths; consequently, they would only be an unnecessary and expensive burden on the sport.

Perhaps the most widely voiced proposal calls for an increase in the padding of the gloves. Back in the early 1960s when the deaths of Benny Paret and Davey Moore, among others, raised questions about glove reform, boxers were fighting with six-ounce gloves. After many deaths occurred while fighters were using this glove, the New York State Athletic Commission set down a new rule for the use of a more heavily padded, eight-ounce glove ("Ring Safety" 16). At the time, however, many people associated with the sport agreed that the eight-ounce glove was actually more dangerous because the increase in weight made the glove a heavier weapon, and because the boxer's hands would be better protected, the fighters would be apt to strike with more force ("Ring Safety" 18). Since then, boxers have fought with various glove weights ranging from six-ounce to fourteen-ounce, and the number of ring deaths has continued with no significant change (Goldman 100). Because fatal head injuries occur as often with light gloves as heavier ones, imposing larger gloves is not the solution for minimizing the number of unfortunate deaths.

A second proposal to reduce the number of fatal injuries calls for the use of protective headgear. But because the record shows that deadly head injuries occur despite the use of head protection, this promising solution takes its own fatal blow. To cite a few cases: in the fight that resulted in the 1960 death of

Supporting examples

Third reform: medical exams and tests

Supporting examples

Testimony from medical authority

Supporting fact

Writer reassesses the problem

Charlie Mohr, a middleweight from the University of Wisconsin, and the subsequent banning of collegiate boxing, the fighters were wearing protective headpieces (Boyle and Ames 54). In 1982 twenty-two-year-old Benjamin Davis died after a fight during which he was required to wear headgear; Charles Love died wearing headgear at the hands of Daryl Stitch that same year (Deford 70). The list goes on. There just isn't any significant correlation between the use of protective headgear and the reduction of fatal head injuries.

A third proposal, raised more recently, demands more rigorous medical exams before and after matches. A prefight exam, for instance, would include an EEG and a CAT scan in order to trace changes or abnormalities in the brain that might mean vulnerability to a blow to the head. But do these exams really help identify potential problems? Both Benny Peret and Davey Moore had taken and passed a prefight EEG examination (Boyle and Ames 55); similarly, Koo had no diagnosed medical vulnerabilities ("Abolish Boxing?" 1528). Even the Council on Scientific Affairs of the American Medical Association admits that there exists no reliable test that could identify boxers who are at risk of sudden death ("Brain Injury in Boxers" 256). In addition to the tests' lack of accuracy, one must also consider the high costs of CAT scans and full neurological exams in terms of a fighter's time and money. While the top prize-winners might be able to afford the expensive tests, could fighters just starting out afford the CAT scan that carries a $300 price tag for each use (Boyle and Ames 67)? Once again, the proposed extensive exams don't seem the answer to the problem.

Before requiring new equipment or expensive tests, perhaps one needs to take a closer look at the extent of the problem itself. Boxing does occasionally result in death, but

Supporting studies

Testimony

Supporting statistics

Conclusion: admission of boxing as violent sport but rejection of current reform proposals

the fatality rate is actually not as bad as in other high risk
sports. In studies reported in <u>Sporting News</u> and substantiated
by two other studies described in the <u>Journal of the American
Medical Association</u>, popular sports such as mountaineering,
sky diving, hang gliding, horse racing, and even scuba diving
had higher fatality rates for a given period ("Brain Injury"
255).[2] Dr. Bennet Derby of the New York State Boxing
Commission has also pointed out that while football and ice
hockey also produce head injuries, they have escaped the furor
directed at boxing (Leershen and Katz 67). Moreover, according
to <u>Ring Magazine</u>, 439 deaths have occurred between 1918 and
and 1982 among amateur and professional boxers worldwide
(Callahan 84).[3] This is fewer than seven deaths per year for
sixty-four years. Even one death from boxing is deplorable, of
course--but when one considers the hundreds of thousands of
young men, participating in a sport found virtually in every
country on the globe, seven deaths per year seems relatively
small, especially compared to the number of annual swimming
accidents, for instance.

   Obviously, no one wants to see a sporting event result in
a death. And boxing <u>is</u> violent and it <u>is</u> dangerous--that's the
nature of the sport. Perhaps Sugar Ray Robinson said it best at
the 1947 inquest after the death of Jimmy Doyle. When the
judge asked Robinson if he knew Doyle was in trouble,
Robinson replied softly, "Sir, getting people in trouble is my
business" (qtd. in Callahan 84). If the critics believe a sport
that demands "getting people in trouble" is immoral, they
should work for its abolition on ethical grounds. But the
flurry of recently proposed reforms that have followed the
latest tragedy in the ring will do nothing to stop the number
of fatalities. If the sport of boxing continues, perhaps we must
resign ourselves to looking at the tragic deaths as the few,
unfortunate accidents they really are.

Supplementary Notes

[1]Interestingly, the critics themselves don't always agree on <u>why</u> boxing should be banned. Popular columnist George Will, for example, called for an end to the sport to "protect the audience from a brutalizing spectacle," rather than to save the fighters (qtd. in "Abolish Boxing?" 1528).

[2]The sporting fatalities per 1,000 participants were as follows: boxing: 0.13; mountaineering: 5.1; hang gliding: 5.6; sky diving: 12.3; horse racing: 12.8; and scuba diving: 1.1 ("Brain Injury" 255).

[3]Figures vary slightly as authorities disagree on whether some deaths were the result of the boxing matches. Deford, for example, cites 353 deaths since 1945 (70).

Works Cited

"Abolish Boxing?" National Review 10 Dec. 1982: 1528-29.

Axthelm, Pete. "Don't Count Boxing Out." Newsweek 20 Dec. 1982: 60.

Boyle, Robert and Wilmur Ames. "Too Many Punches, Too Little Concern." Sports Illustrated 11 April 1983: 44-67.

Callahan, Tom. "Boxing Shadows." Time 29 Nov. 1982: 84-86.

Council on Scientific Affairs. "Brain Injury in Boxers." Journal of the American Medical Association 14 Jan. 1983: 254-57.

Deford, Frank. "An Encounter to Last an Eternity." Sports Illustrated 11 April 1983: 70-82.

Goldman, Herbert G., ed. The Ring, 1982 Record Book and Boxing Encyclopedia. New York: Ring, 1982.

Leershen, Charles and Susan Katz. "The AMA Tries to KO Boxing." Newsweek 17 Dec. 1984: 67.

"The Search for Ring Safety." Sports Illustrated. 15 April 1963: 16-18.

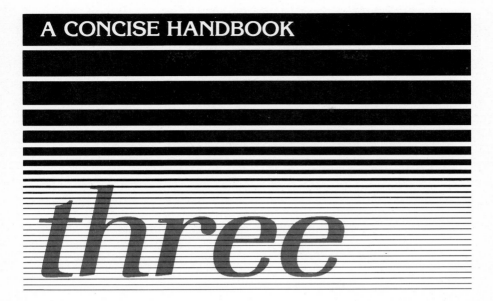

A CONCISE HANDBOOK

three

P A R T   T H R E E

In this section you will learn to recognize and correct the most common errors in grammar, punctuation, and mechanics. Each error will be explained as simply as possible, with a minimum of technical language. Beside each rule you will find the mark most teachers use to indicate that error in your essays.

Major Errors in Grammar

ERRORS WITH VERBS

Faulty Agreement   S-V Agr

Make your verb agree in number with its subject; a singular subject takes a singular verb, and a plural subject takes a plural verb.

Incorrect *Lester Peabody*, principal of the Kung Fu School of Grammar, *don't* agree that gum chewing should be banned in the classroom.

Correct *Lester Peabody*, principal of the Kung Fu School of Grammar, *doesn't* agree that gum chewing should be banned in the classroom.

Incorrect The *actions* of the new Senator *hasn't* been consistent with his campaign promises.

Correct The *actions* of the new Senator *haven't* been consistent with his campaign promises.

A compound subject takes a plural verb, unless the subject denotes a single person or a single unit.

Examples *Bean sprouts* and *tofu are* dishes Jim Bob won't consider eating. ["Bean Sprouts" and "tofu" are two elements in a compound subject; therefore, use a plural verb.]
The *winner* and new *champion refuses* to give up the microphone at the news conference. ["Winner" and

"champion" denote a single person; therefore, use a singular verb.]

Listed below are some of the most confusing subject-verb agreement problems:

1. With a collective noun: a singular noun referring to a collection of elements as a unit generally takes a singular verb.

Incorrect During boring parts of the Reverend Hung Moon's sermons, the *congregation* often *chant* dirty mantras.
Correct During boring parts of the Reverend Hung Moon's sermons, the *congregation* often *chants* dirty mantras.
Incorrect The *army* of the new nation *want* shoes, bullets, and weekend passes.
Correct The *army* of the new nation *wants* shoes, bullets, and weekend passes.

However, you sometimes use a plural verb when the collective noun refers to its members as parts rather than to the group as a unit.

Incorrect After Sticky Fingers O'Hoolihan visited the Queen, a *number of the crown jewels was* missing.
Correct After Sticky Fingers O'Hoolihan visited the Queen, a *number of the crown jewels were* missing.
Incorrect A small *group of the actors has* forgotten their lines.
Correct A small *group of the actors have* forgotten their lines.

2. With a relative pronoun ("that," "which," "who" used as a subject: the verb agrees with its antecendent.

Incorrect The boss rejected a shipment of *shirts* that *was* torn.
Correct The boss rejected a shipment of *shirts* that *were* torn.

3. With "each," "none," "everyone," "neither" as the subject: use a singular verb even when followed by a plural construction.

Incorrect *Each* of the children *think* Mom and Dad are automatic teller machines.
Correct *Each* of the children *thinks* Mom and Dad are automatic teller machines.
Incorrect All the students saw the teacher pull out his hair, but *none know* why he did it.
Correct All the students saw the teacher pull out his hair, but *none knows* why he did it.

Incorrect   *Neither have* a dime left by the second of the month.
Correct   *Neither has* a dime left by the second of the month.

4. With "either . . . or," "neither . . . nor": the verb agrees with the nearer item.

Incorrect   Neither rain nor dogs nor *gloom of night keep* the mailman from delivering bills.
Correct   Neither rain nor dogs nor *gloom of night keeps* the mailman from delivering bills.

Incorrect   Either Betty or her *neighbors is* hosting a come-as-you-are breakfast.
Correct   Either Betty or her *neighbors are* hosting a come-as-you-are breakfast.

5. With "here is (are)," "there is (are)": the verb agrees with the number indicated by the subject following the verb.

Incorrect   *There is* only two good *reasons* for missing this law class: death and jury duty.
Correct   *There are* only two good *reasons* for missing this law class: death and jury duty.

Incorrect   To help you do your shopping quickly, Mr. Scrooge, *here are* a *list* of gifts under a dollar.
Correct   To help you do your shopping quickly, Mr. Scrooge, *here is* a *list* of gifts under a dollar.

6. With plural nouns intervening between subject and verb: the verb still agrees with the subject.

Incorrect   The *jungle,* with its poisonous plants, wild animals, and biting insects, *make* Herman long for the sidewalks of Topeka.
Correct   The *jungle,* with its poisonous plants, wild animals, and biting insects, *makes* Herman long for the sidewalks of Topeka.

7. With nouns plural in form but singular in meaning: a singular verb is usually correct.

Examples   *News travels* slowly if it comes through the post office.
Charades is the exhibitionist's game of choice.
Politics is often the rich person's hobby.

Subjunctive   *V Sub*

When you make a wish or a statement that is contrary to fact, use the subjunctive verb form "were."

Incorrect My mother always wished she *was* queen so she could levy a tax on men who cursed.

Correct My mother always wished she *were* queen so she could levy a tax on men who cursed. [This expresses a wish.]

Incorrect If "Fightin' Henry" *was* a foot taller and thirty pounds heavier, we would all be in trouble.

Correct If "Fightin' Henry" *were* a foot taller and thirty pounds heavier, we would all be in trouble. [This proposes a statement contrary to fact.]

Tense Shift   *T*

In most cases the first verb in a sentence establishes the tense of any later verb. Keep your verbs within the same time frame.

Incorrect Big Joe *saw* the police car coming up behind, so he *turns* into the next alley.

Correct Big Joe *saw* the police car coming up behind, so he *turned* into the next alley.

Incorrect Horace *uses* an artificial sweetener in his coffee all day, so he *felt* a pizza and a hot-fudge sundae were fine for dinner.

Correct Horace *uses* an artificial sweetener in his coffee all day, so he *feels* a pizza and a hot-fudge sundae are fine for dinner.

Incorrect Rex the Wonder Horse *was* obviously very smart because he *taps* out the telephone numbers of the stars with his hoof.

Correct Rex the Wonder Horse *was* obviously very smart because he *tapped* out the telephone numbers of the stars with his hoof.

Split Infinitive   *Sp I*

Many authorities insist that you never separate *to* from its verb; today, however, some grammarians allow the split infinitive except in the most formal kinds of writing. Nevertheless, because it offends some readers, it is probably best to avoid the construction unless clarity or emphasis is clearly served by its use.

Traditional A swift kick is needed to *start* the machine properly.

Untraditional A swift kick is needed *to* properly *start* the machine.

Traditional The teacher wanted Lori *to communicate* her ideas clearly.

Untraditional The teacher wanted Lori *to* clearly *communicate* her ideas.

Double Negatives   D Neg

Don't use a negative verb and a negative qualifier together.

Incorrect I *can't hardly* wait until Jim Bob gets his jaw out of traction, so I can challenge him to a bubble gum blowing contest again.

Correct I *can hardly* wait until Jim Bob gets his jaw out of traction, so I can challenge him to a bubble gum blowing contest again.

Incorrect Even when he flew his helicopter upside-down over her house, she *wouldn't scarcely* look at him.

Correct Even when he flew his helicopter upside-down over her house, she would *scarcely* look at him.

Passive Voice   Pass

For the most part, your prose style will improve if you choose strong, active voice verbs over wordy or unclear passive constructions.

Wordy passive construction It is obvious that dirty words are being written on the rest room walls by the company's junior executives.

Strong active verb The company's junior executives write dirty words on the rest room walls.

Wordy passive construction After the successful nose-transplant operation, the surgeon and his staff were given a round of applause by the malpractice lawyers in attendance.

Strong active verb After the successful nose-transplant operation, the malpractice lawyers in attendance applauded the surgeon and his staff.

Unclear passive construction Much protest is being voiced over the new Z.A.P. bomb. [Who is protesting?]

Strong active verb   Members of the Fuse Lighters
                                    Association are protesting the
                                    new Z.A.P. bomb.

(For more examples of active and passive voice verbs, see pp. 92–
93.)

Practicing What You've Learned

Errors with Verbs

Correct the sentences below.

1. None of the students know that both mystery writer Agatha
   Christie and inventor Thomas Edison was dyslexic.
2. For years Johnny Appleseed was considered a mythical figure
   by many scholars, but now two local historians, the authors
   of a well-known book, argues he was a real person named
   John Chapman.
3. Either the cocker spaniel or the poodle hold the honor of
   being the most popular breed of dog in the United States, say
   the American Kennel Club.
4. The team from Houston College are considering switching
   from basketball to volleyball because passing athletics are
   required for graduation.
5. Observation of Cuban land crabs show they can run faster
   than horses.
6. The folklore professor's articles on modern horror stories
   reminds me of the tale often referred to as "The Hook."
7. In the story of the hook, a couple of teenagers are parked on a
   lonely road, but neither realize that a crazy man with a hook
   instead of an arm was lurking nearby.
8. Each of us have heard how the couple decides to quickly
   drive away and later discover that there is a hook hanging on
   the car door.
9. Neither Clyde nor his brothers can hardly believe that such
   stories are being collected by university anthropologists, who
   refers to them as "urban legends."
10. Tammy wishes she was teaching the class on urban legends,
    so she could tell the story of the window viper.

ERRORS WITH NOUNS   N

Possessive with "-ing" Nouns

When the emphasis is on the action, use the possessive pronoun plus
the "-ing" noun.

Example He hated *my* singing around the house, so I made him live in the garage. [The emphasis is on *singing*.]

When the emphasis is not on the action, you may use a noun or pronoun plus the "-ing" noun.

Example He hated *me* singing around the house, so I made him live in the garage. [The emphasis is on the person singing—*me*—not the action; he might have liked someone else singing.]

Misuse of Nouns as Adjectives

Some nouns may be used as adjectives modifying other nouns: "horse show," "movie star," "theater seats," etc. But some nouns used as adjectives sound awkward or like jargon. To avoid such awkwardness, you may need to change the noun to an appropriate adjective or reword the sentence.

Awkward The group decided to work on local *environment* problems.

Better The group decided to work on local *environmental* problems.

Jargon The executive began a *cost estimation comparison study* of the two products.

Better The executive began to *study a comparison* of the two products' costs.

(For more information on ridding your prose of jargon, see pp. 119–121)

ERRORS WITH PRONOUNS

Faulty Agreement   P Agr

A pronoun should agree in number and gender with its antecedent (that is, the word the pronoun stands for).

Incorrect To get a temperamental *actress* to sign a contract, the director would lock *them* in their dressing room.

Correct To get a temperamental *actress* to sign a contract, the director would lock *her* in her dressing room.

Use the singular pronoun with "everyone," "anyone," and "each."

Incorrect When the belly dancer asked for a volunteer partner from the audience, *everyone* in the YMCA raised *their* hand.

Correct   When the belly dancer asked for a volunteer partner from the audience, *everyone* in the YMCA raised *his* hand.

Incorrect *Each* of the new wives decided to keep *their* own name.

Correct   *Each* of the new wives decided to keep *her* own name.

In the past, writers have traditionally used the masculine pronoun "he" when the gender of the antecedent is unknown, as in the following: "If a *spy* refuses to answer questions, *he* should be forced to watch James Bond movies until *he* cracks." Today, however, many authorities prefer the nonsexist "she/he" even though the construction can be awkward when maintained over a stretch of prose. Perhaps the best solution is to use the impersonal "one" when possible or simply rewrite the sentence in the plural: "If *spies* refuse to answer questions, *they* should be forced to watch James Bond movies until *they* crack." (For more examples, see pp. 122–124.)

Vague Reference   Ref

Your pronoun references should be clear.

Vague If the trained seal won't eat its dinner, throw *it* into the lion's cage. [What goes into the lion's cage?]

Clear If the trained seal won't eat its dinner, throw *the food* into the lion's cage.

Vague After the dog bit Harry, he raised such a fuss at the police station that the sergeant finally had *him* impounded. [Who was impounded?]

Clear After being bitten, Harry raised such a fuss at the police station that the sergeant finally had the *dog* impounded.

Sometimes you must add a word or rewrite the sentence to make the pronoun reference clear:

Vague   I'm a lab instructor in the biology department and am also taking a composition course. *This* has always been difficult for me. [What is difficult?]

Clear   I'm a lab instructor in the biology department and am also taking composition, *a course* that has always been difficult for me.

Also clear I'm a lab instructor in the biology department and am also taking a composition course. Being a teacher and a student at the same time is difficult for me.

Shift in Pronouns   P Sh

Be consistent in your use of pronouns; don't shift from one person to another.

Incorrect One shouldn't eat pudding with your fingers.
Correct   One shouldn't eat pudding with one's fingers.
Correct   You shouldn't eat pudding with your fingers.

Incorrect *We* left-handed people are at a disadvantage because most of the time *you* can't rent left-handed golf clubs or bowling balls.
Correct   *We* left-handed people are at a disadvantage because most of the time *we* can't rent left-handed golf clubs or bowling balls.

(For additional examples, see p. 99.)

Incorrect Case   *Ca*

The case of a pronoun is determined by its function. If the pronoun is a subject, use the nominative case: "I," "he," "she," "we," "they"; if the pronoun is an object, use the objective case: "me," "him," "her," "us," "them." To check your usage, all you need to do in most cases is isolate the pronoun in the manner shown here and see if it makes sense alone.

Incorrect Give the treasure map to Frankie and *I*.
Isolated   Give the treasure map to *I*.
Correct   Give the treasure map to Frankie and *me*.

Incorrect Bertram and *her* suspect that the moon is hollow.
Isolated   *Her* suspects that the moon is hollow.
Correct   Bertram and *she* suspect that the moon is hollow.

In other cases, to determine the correct pronoun, you will need to add implied but unstated sentence elements:

Examples Mother always liked Dickie more than *me*. [Mother liked Dickie more than *she liked* me.]
She is younger than *I* by three days. [She is younger than I *am* by three days.]

To solve the confusing *who/whom* pronoun problem, first determine the case of the pronoun in its own clause in each sentence.

1. If the pronoun is the subject of a clause, use "who" or "whoever."

Examples I don't know *who* spread the peanut butter on my English paper. ["Who" is the subject of the verb "spread" in the clause "who spread the peanut butter on my English paper."]
Rachel is a librarian who only likes books with pictures. ["Who" is the subject of the verb "likes" in

the clause "who only likes books with pictures."]

He will sell secrets to *whoever* offers the largest sum of money. ["Whoever" is the subject of the verb "offers" in the clause "whoever offers the largest sum of money."]

2. If the pronoun is the object of a verb, use "whom" or "whomever."

Examples *Whom* am I kicking? ["Whom" is the direct object of the verb "kicking."]
Sid is a man *whom* I distrust. ["Whom" is the direct object of the verb "distrust."]
Whomever he kicked will probably be angry. ["Whomever" is the direct object of the verb "kicked."]

3. If the pronoun occurs as the object of a preposition, use "whom," especially when the preposition immediately precedes the pronoun.

Examples *With whom* am I speaking?
To whom does the credit belong for spreading peanut butter on my English paper?
Do not ask *for whom* the bell tolls.

Practicing What You've Learned

Errors with Nouns and Pronouns

Correct the sentences below. Skip any correct sentences.

1. The executive knew she was in trouble when her salary underwent a modification reduction adjustment of fifty percent.
2. Of whom did Oscar Wilde once say, "He hasn't a single redeeming vice"?
3. It was a surprise to both Mary and I to learn that Switzerland didn't give women the right to vote until 1971.
4. Each of the young women in the Family Life class decided not to marry after they read that couples today have 2.3 children.
5. Jim Bob explained to Frankie that the best way for him to avoid his recurring nosebleeds was to stay out of his cousin's marital arguments.
6. Those of us who'd had the flu agreed that one can always get your doctor to return your call quicker if you get in the shower.
7. The stranger gave the free movie tickets to Louise and I after he saw people standing in line to leave the theater.

8. The personnel director told each of the employees, most of who opposed him, to signify their "no" vote by saying, "I resign."

9. Clarence and me have an uncle who is so mean he writes the name of the murderer on the first page of mystery novels that are passed around the family.

10. The first movie to gross over one million dollars was *Tarzan of the Apes* (1932) starring Johnny Weismuller, a former Olympic star who became an actor. This didn't happen often in the movie industry at that time.

ERRORS WITH ADVERBS AND ADJECTIVES

Incorrect Usage   Adv   Adj

Incorrect use of adverbs and adjectives often occurs when you confuse the two modifiers. Adverbs qualify the meaning of verbs, adjectives, and other adverbs; they frequently end in "-ly," and they often answer the question "how?"

Incorrect After Kay argued with the mechanic, her car began running *bad.*

Correct After Kay argued with the mechanic, her car began running *badly.*

Adjectives, on the other hand, describe or qualify the meanings of nouns only.

Example The *angry* mechanic neglected to put oil into Kay's car.

One of the most confusing pairs of modifiers is "well" and "good." We often use "good" as an adjective modifying a noun and "well" as an adverb modifying a verb.

Examples *A Sap's Fables* is a *good* book for children, although it is not *well* organized.
Bubba was such a *good* liar his wife had to call in the children at suppertime.
After eating the Rocky Mountain oysters, Susie did not feel *well.*
Did you do *well* on your math test?

If you cannot determine whether a word is an adverb or adjective, consult your dictionary.

Faulty Comparison   *Comp*

When you compare two elements to a higher or lower degree, you often add "-er" or "-r" to the adjective.

> **Incorrect** Of the two sisters, Sarah is the *loudest.*
> **Correct**   Of the two sisters, Sarah is the *louder.*

When you compare more than two elements, you often add "-est" to the adjective.

> **Example** Sarah is the loudest of the four children in the family.

Other adjectives use the words "more," "most," "less," and "least" to indicate comparison.

> **Examples** Bela Lugosi is *more* handsome than Lon Chaney but *less* handsome than Vincent Price.
> Boris Karloff is the *most* handsome, and Christopher Lee is the *least* handsome of all the horror film stars.

ERRORS IN MODIFYING PHRASES

Dangling Modifiers   *DM*

A modifying—or descriptive—phrase must have a logical relationship to some specific words in the sentence. When those words are omitted, the phrase "dangles" without anything to modify. Dangling modifiers frequently occur at the beginnings of sentences and often may be corrected by adding the proper subjects to the main clauses.

> **Dangling** Not knowing how to swim, buying scuba gear was foolish.
> **Correct** Not knowing how to swim, *I decided that* buying scuba gear was foolish.
> **Dangling** After seeing a number of flying saucers, pinching the waitress seemed a bad idea.
> **Correct** After seeing a number of flying saucers, Jim Bob admitted that pinching the waitress had been a bad idea.

(For additional examples, see pp. 87–88.)

Misplaced Modifiers   *MM*

When modifying words, phrases, or clauses are not placed near the word they describe, confusion or unintentional humor often results.

Misplaced	Teddy swatted the fly still dressed in his pajamas.
Correct	Still dressed in his pajamas, Teddy swatted the fly.
Misplaced	The cook prepared turkey tartu for his guests made primarily of spinach.
Correct	The cook prepared turkey tartu, made primarily of spinach, for his guests.

(For additional examples, see pp. 86–87.)

Practicing What You've Learned

Errors with Adverbs, Adjectives, and Modifying Phrases

Correct the errors in the sentences below.

1. Squeezing the can, it was hard to tell if the tomatoes were ripe.
2. While liver is probably the worse food in the world, buttermilk is hardly more better.
3. After the optometrist pulled her eye tooth, Hortense didn't behave very (good/well) in the waiting room.
4. He didn't think the car would make it over the mountains, being eight years old.
5. The James brothers decided to have their cattle engraved instead of branded, since they were so rich.
6. In the Death Valley Swim Meet, Maria could use the back stroke or side stroke in the first race, whichever was best for her.
7. I didn't do (good/well) on my nature project because my bonsai sequoia tree grew real bad in its small container.
8. After boarding Hard Luck Airways, the meals we were offered convinced us to return by ship.
9. I've read that a number of modern sailors, like Thor Heyerdahl, have sailed primitive vessels across the ocean in a book from the public library.
10. We are enclosing with this letter the new telephone number for notifying the fire department of any fires that may be attached to your telephone.

ERRORS IN SENTENCES

Fragments   Frag

A complete sentence must contain a subject and a verb. A fragment is an incomplete sentence; it is often a participial phrase or dependent clause that belongs to the preceding sentence. To check for fragments, try reading your prose, one sentence at a time, starting at the *end* of your essay. If you find a "sentence" that makes no sense alone, it's probably a fragment that should either be rewritten or connected to another sentence.

Incorrect Bubba's parents refuse to send him to a psychiatrist. Although they both know he eats shoelaces and light bulbs.

Correct Bubba's parents refuse to send him to a psychiatrist although they both know he eats shoelaces and light bulbs.

Incorrect This tape recording of the symphony's latest concert is so clear you can hear every sound. Including the coughs and whispers of the audience.

Correct This tape recording of the symphony's latest concert is so clear you can hear every sound, including the coughs and whispers of the audience.

Incorrect At Liz's most recent wedding, the photographer used an instant camera. Because her marriages break up so fast.

Correct At Liz's most recent wedding, the photographer used an instant camera because her marriages break up so fast.

You can also try this test to see if a group of words is a fragment: say the phrase "It is true that" in front of the words in question; a complete sentence will still make sense, but a fragment won't.

Example At Liz's most recent wedding, the photographer used an instant camera. Because her marriages break up so fast. [Which is a fragment?]
It is true that *at Liz's most recent wedding the photographer used an instant camera.* [This sentence makes sense, so there's no fragment.]
It is true that *because her marriages break up so fast.* [Yes, this is a fragment.]

Comma Splice   CS

A comma splice occurs when two sentences are linked with a comma. To correct this error, you can (1) separate the two sentences with a period, (2) separate the two sentences with a semicolon, (3) insert a coordinating conjunction (such as "and," "or," "nor," "so," "yet") after the comma, (4) subordinate one clause.

Incorrect	Grover won a stuffed gila monster at the church raffle, his mother threw it away the next day while he was in school.
Correct	Grover won a stuffed gila monster at the church raffle. His mother threw it away the next day while he was in school.
Correct	Grover won a stuffed gila monster at the church raffle; his mother threw it away the next day while he was in school.
Correct	Grover won a stuffed gila monster at the church raffle, but his mother threw it away the next day while he was in school.
Correct	Although Grover won a stuffed gila monster at the church raffle, his mother threw it away the next day while he was in school.

(For more help on correcting comma splices, see p. 308; subordination is discussed in detail on pp. 103–104.)

Run-on Sentence   R-O

Don't run two sentences together without any punctuation. Use a period, a semicolon, a comma plus a coordinating conjunction (if appropriate), or subordinate one clause.

Incorrect	The indicted police chief submitted his resignation the mayor accepted it gratefully.
Correct	The indicted police chief submitted his resignation. The mayor accepted it gratefully.
Correct	The indicted police chief submitted his resignation; the mayor accepted it gratefully.
Correct	The indicted police chief submitted his resignation, and the mayor accepted it gratefully.
Correct	When the indicted police chief submitted his resignation, the mayor accepted it gratefully.

Faulty Parallelism   //

Parallel thoughts should be expressed in parallel constructions.

Awkward	Boa constrictors like *to lie* in the sun, *to hang* from limbs, and *swallowing* small animals.
Better	Boa constrictors like *to lie* in the sun, *to hang* from limbs, and *to swallow* small animals.
Awkward	Whether *working* on his greasy car, *fistfighting* at the hamburger joint, or in bed, my brother always kept his hair combed.

> **Better**   Whether *working* on his greasy car, *fistfighting* at the hamburger joint, or *lounging* in bed, my brother always kept his hair combed.

False Predication   Pred

This error occurs when the predicate (that part of the sentence that says something about the subject) doesn't fit properly with the subject. Illogical constructions result.

> **Incorrect**   The meaning of the sermon deals with love. [A "meaning" cannot deal with anything; the author, speaker, or work itself can, however.]
>
> **Correct**   The sermon deals with love.
>
> **Incorrect**   Energy is one of the world's biggest problems. ["Energy" itself is not a problem.]
>
> **Correct**   The lack of fuel for energy is one of the world's biggest problems.
>
> **Incorrect**   True failure is when you make an error and don't learn anything from it. [Avoid all "is when" and "is where" constructions. The subject does not denote a time, so the predicate is faulty.]
>
> **Correct**   You have truly failed only when you make an error and don't learn anything from it.
>
> **Incorrect**   Her first comment after winning the lottery was exciting. [Her comment wasn't exciting; her feeling was.]
>
> **Correct**   Her first comment after winning the lottery expressed her excitement.

(For other examples of faulty predication, see p. 88.)

Mixed Structure   Mix S

"Mixed structure" is a catchall term that applies to a variety of sentence construction errors. Usually, the term refers to a sentence in which the writer begins with one kind of structure and then shifts to another in mid-sentence. Such a shift often occurs when the writer is in a hurry, and the mind has already jumped ahead to the next thought.

> **Confused**   By the time one litter of cats is given away seems to bring a new one.
>
> **Clear**   Giving away one litter of cats seems to tell the mother cat that it's time to produce a new batch.
>
> **Confused**   The bank robber realized that in his crime spree how very little fun he was having.

Clear   The bank robber realized that he was having very little fun in his crime spree.

Confused The novel is too confusing for what the author meant.

Clear   The novel is too confused for me to understand what the author meant.

Confused Being a poet won't ever make much money.

Clear   Poets don't ever make much money.

(For other examples of mixed structure, see pp. 88–89.)

Practicing What You've Learned

Errors in Sentences

Correct the following sentences; skip any that are correct.

1. Mary Lou decided not to eat the alphabet soup the letters spelled out "botulism."
2. An example of his intelligence is when he brought home a twenty-pound block of ice after ice fishing all day.
3. A friend of mine offers this definition of nasty theater critics on opening night, according to him, they're the people who can't wait to stone the first cast.
4. My father told me never to ask people where they're from because if they're from Texas they'll tell you, however, if they're not, don't embarrass them.
5. The mother of the triplets got rid of her headache by following the advice on the aspirin bottle of taking two pills and keep away from children.
6. Americans forget how large the Soviet Union is, for example, they don't realize that it encompasses eleven time zones.
7. The new baby kept the textbook author awake all night. Thus causing her to conclude that people who say they sleep like a baby don't have one in the house.
8. Is it true that Superman could leap tall buildings, run faster than a locomotive, and that bullets would bounce off his skin?
9. People always find the time to complain about how busy they are. Despite the fact that they say they are too busy to stop.
10. According to a study by the Fish and Wildlife Service, Americans' favorite animals are dogs, horses, swans, robins, and butterflies. Whereas their least favorites are cockroaches, mosquitos, rats, wasps, and rattlesnakes.

A Concise Guide to Punctuation

Punctuation marks do not exist, as one student recently complained, to make your life miserable. They are used to clarify your written thoughts so that the reader understands your meaning. Just as traffic signs and signals tell a driver to slow down, stop, or go faster or slower, so punctuation is intended to guide the reader through your prose. Look, for example, at the confusion in the sentences below when the necessary punctuation marks are omitted:

Confusing	Has the tiger been fed Bill? [Bill was the tiger's dinner?]
Clear	Has the tiger been fed, Bill?
Confusing	After we had finished raking the dog jumped into the pile of leaves. [Raking the dog?]
Clear	After we had finished raking, the dog jumped into the pile of leaves.
Confusing	The teacher called the students names. [Was the teacher fired for verbally abusing the students?]
Clear	The teacher called the students' names.

Because punctuation helps you communicate clearly with your reader, you should familiarize yourself with the following rules.

THE PERIOD (.)   P

1. Use a period to end a sentence.

Examples Ralph quit school to go live with the Pygmies in Africa. He returned shortly thereafter.

2. Use a period after initials and many abbreviations.

Examples W. B. Yeats, 12 A.M., Dr., etc., M.A.

3. Only one period is necessary if the sentence ends with an abbreviation.

Examples The elephant was delivered C.O.D.
To find a good job, you should obtain a B.S. or B.A.

THE QUESTION MARK (?)   P

1. Use a question mark after every direct question.

Examples May I borrow your galoshes?
Is the sandstorm over now?

2. No question mark is necessary after an indirect question.

Examples Jean asked why no one makes a paper milk carton
that opens without tearing.
Dave wondered how the television detective always
found a parking place next to the scene of the crime.

THE EXCLAMATION POINT (!)   P

The exclamation point follows words, phrases, or sentences to show strong feelings.

Examples Fire! Call the rescue squad!

THE COMMA (,)   P

1. Use a comma to separate two independent clauses[1] joined by a coordinating conjunction ("but," "and," "or," "nor," "so," "yet," "for").

Examples You can bury your savings in the backyard, but don't
expect Mother Nature to pay interest.
All Sue inherited was a black limousine, so she started
a chauffeur service.
I'm going home tomorrow, and I'm never coming
back.

[1]An independent clause looks like a complete sentence; it contains a subject and a verb, and it makes sense by itself.

Do *not* join two sentences with a comma only; such an error is called a comma splice. Use a comma plus one of the coordinating conjunctions listed previously, a period, a semicolon, or subordination.

Comma splice	Beatrice washes and grooms the chickens, Samantha feeds the spiders.
Correct	Beatrice washes and grooms the chickens, and Samantha feeds the spiders.
Correct	Beatrice washes and grooms the chickens. Samantha feeds the spiders.
Correct	Beatrice washes and grooms the chickens; Samantha feeds the spiders.
Correct	When Beatrice washes and grooms the chickens, Samantha feeds the spiders.
Comma splice	Jack doesn't like double features, he won't go with us to see *Dr. Jekyll and Mr. Hyde.*
Correct	Jack doesn't like double features, so he won't go with us to see *Dr. Jekyll and Mr. Hyde.*
Correct	Jack doesn't like double features. He won't go with us to see *Dr. Jekyll and Mr. Hyde.*
Correct	Jack doesn't like double features; he won't go with us to see *Dr. Jekyll and Mr. Hyde.*
Correct	Because Jack doesn't like double features, he won't go with us to see *Dr. Jekyll and Mr. Hyde.*

(For additional help, see pp. 302–303).

2. Conjunctive adverbs, such as "however," "moreover," "thus," "consequently," and "therefore," are used to show continuity and are frequently set off by commas when they appear in mid-sentence.

Examples	She soon discovered, *however*, that he had stolen her monogrammed towels in addition to her pet avocado plant.
	She felt, *consequently*, that he was not trustworthy.

When a conjunctive adverb occurs at the beginning of a sentence, it may be followed by a comma, especially if a pause is intended. If no pause is intended, you may omit the comma, but inserting the comma is never wrong.

Examples	*Thus*, she resolved never to speak to him again.
	Thus she resolved never to speak to him again.
	Therefore, he resolved never to speak to her again.
	Therefore he resolved never to speak to her again.

Please note that "however" can never, never be used as a coordinating conjunction joining two independent clauses. Incorrect use of "however" most often results in a comma splice.

Comma splice	The police arrested the thief, *however*, they had to release him because the plant wouldn't talk.
Correct	The police arrested the thief; *however*, they had to release him because the plant wouldn't talk.
Also correct	The police arrested the thief. *However*, they had to release him because the plant wouldn't talk.

3. Set off with a comma an introductory phrase or clause.

Examples	After we had finished our laundry, we discovered one sock was missing. According to the owner of the laundromat, customers have conflicting theories about missing laundry. For example, one man claims his socks make a break for freedom when no one is watching the dryers.

4. Set off nonessential phrases and clauses. If the information can be omitted without changing the meaning of the main clause, then the phrase or clause is nonessential. Do *not* set off clauses or phrases that are essential to the meaning of the main clause.

Essential	Mrs. Mungo quickly identified the man *who had sold her the fake birth certificate.* [The "who" clause is essential to explain which man was identified, and why.] The storm *that destroyed Mr. Peartree's outhouse* left him speechless with anger. [The "that" clause is essential to explain why the storm angered Mr. Peartree.] The movie *showing now at the Ritz* is very obscene and very popular. [The participial phrase is essential to identify the movie.]
Nonessential	Joe Medusa, *who won the jalapeno-eating contest last year,* is this year's champion cow-chip tosser. [The "who" clause is nonessential because it only supplies additional information to the main clause.] Black widow spiders, *which eat their spouses after mating,* are easily identifiable by the orange hour glass design on their abdomens. [The "which" clause is nonessential because it only supplies additional information.]

> Bernie Patooka, *playing second base for the Dodgers*, broke his nose yesterday when he swatted a mosquito without letting go of the ball. [The participial phrase is nonessential because it only supplies additional information.]

5. Use commas to separate items in a series of words, phrases, or clauses.

Examples   Julio collects coins, stamps, bottle caps, erasers, and pocket lint.
Mrs. Jones chased her husband out the window, around the ledge, down the fire escape, and into the busy street.

While journalists and some grammarians permit the omission of the last comma before the "and," many authorities believe the comma is necessary for clarity. For example, how many pints of ice cream are listed in the sentence below:

> Please buy the following pints of ice cream: strawberry, peach, coffee, vanilla and chocolate swirl.

Four or five pints? Without a comma before the "and," the reader doesn't know if vanilla and chocolate swirl are (is?) one item or two. By inserting the last comma, you clarify the sentence:

> Please buy the following pints of ice cream: strawberry, peach, coffee, vanilla, and chocolate swirl.

6. Use commas to separate adjectives of equal emphasis that modify the same noun. To determine if a comma should be used, see if you can insert the word "and" between the adjectives; if the phrase still makes proper sense with the substituted "and," use a comma.

Examples   She finally moved out of her cold, dark apartment.
She finally moved out of her cold and dark apartment.

I have a sweet, handsome husband.
I have a sweet and handsome husband.

He called from a convenient telephone booth.
But not: He called from a convenient and telephone booth. ["Convenient" modifies the unit "telephone booth," so there is no comma.]

Hand me some of that homemade pecan pie.

But not: Hand me some of that homemade and pecan pie. ["Homemade" modifies the unit "pecan pie," so there is no comma.]

7. Set off a direct address with commas.

Examples   Gentlemen, keep your seats.
Car fifty-four, where are you?
Not now, Eleanor, I'm busy.

8. Use commas to set off items in addresses and dates.

Examples   The sheriff followed me from Austin, Texas, to question me about my uncle.
He found me on February 2, 1978, when I stopped for gas in Fairbanks, Alaska.

9. Use commas to set off a degree or title following a name.

Examples   John Dough, M.D., was audited when he reported only $5.68 in taxable income last year.
The Neanderthal Award went to Samuel Lyle, Ph.D.

10. Use commas to set off dialogue from the speaker.

Examples   Alexander announced, "I don't think I want a second helping of possum."
"Eat hearty," said Marie, "because this is the last of the food."

11. Use commas to set off "yes," "no," "well," and other weak exclamations.

Examples   Yes, I am in the cat condo business.
No, all the units with decks are sold.
Well, perhaps one with a large yard will do.

12. Set off interrupters or parenthetical elements appearing in the midst of a sentence. A parenthetical element is additional information placed as explanation or comment within an already complete sentence. This element may be a word (such as "certainly" or "fortunately"), a phrase ("for example," "in fact"), or a clause ("I believe," "you know"). The word, phrase, or clause is parenthetical if the sentence parts before and after it fit together.

Examples   Jack is, I think, still a compulsive gambler.
Harvey, my brother, sometimes has breakfast with
him.
Jack cannot, for example, resist shuffling the toast or
dealing the pancakes.

Practicing What You've Learned

Errors with Commas, Periods, Question Marks

The sentences below contain errors that may be corrected by
changing, adding, or deleting commas, periods, and question marks.

1. The father decided to recapture his youth, he took his son's
   car keys away.
2. Researchers in Balboa, Panama have discovered that the
   poisonous, yellow-belly, sea snake which descended from the
   cobra, is the most deadly serpent in the world.
3. Yes in fact I have often asked myself why it's always the last
   key on the key ring that fits the lock?
4. Lulu Belle, my cousin, spent the week of Sept 1–7, 1986 in the
   woods near Dimebox, Texas looking for additions to her
   extinct, butterfly collection, however she wasn't at all
   successful in her search.
5. William Faulkner, the famous writer was apparently not such
   a great father, for example, when his daughter Jill begged
   him to stop drinking he asked her who had ever heard of
   Shakespeare's child?
6. "Tom did you realize," said Janie. "That khaki pants first
   gained popularity during Queen Victoria's Afghan campaigns,
   unfortunately, the British soldier's traditional white uniform
   made too good a target"
7. Although ice cream didn't appear in America until the 1700s
   our country now leads the world in ice cream consumption,
   Australia is second I think.
8. Last summer the large friendly family that lives next door
   flew Discount Airlines and visited three cities on their
   vacation, however, their suitcases visited five.
9. According to the Georgia-Pacific Corporation which is a wood
   products company, the phrase "by hook or crook" originated
   in feudal times when all forests belonged to the local lord of
   the manor, peasants could gather only those sticks of wood
   they could cut with a pruning hook, or snare with a
   shepherd's crook.
10. Arthur thought that most of the movies made in Hollywood
    California were too silly, therefore he started a letter writing

campaign urging the film producers to shoot less film and more writers.

THE SEMICOLON (;)   *P*

1. Use a semicolon to link two closely related independent clauses.

Examples Belinda sold shoes as an undergraduate; she earned enough money to buy her own sorority house.
The antique piggybank contained thirty-seven cents; only Jules needed money badly enough to break it.

2. Use a semicolon to avoid a comma splice when connecting two independent clauses with words like "however," "moreover," "thus," "therefore," and "consequently."

Examples All Esmeralda's plants die shortly after she gets them home from the store; consequently, she has the best compost heap in town.
This town is not big enough for both of us; therefore, I suggest we expand the city limits.
I don't like the way she dresses, talks, walks, sings, or smiles; moreover, I dislike girls who are not infatuated with me.

3. Use a semicolon in a series between items that already contain internal punctuation.

Examples Last year the Wildcats suffered enough injuries to keep them from winning the pennant, as Jake Pritchett, third baseman, broke his arm in a fight; Hugh Rosenbloom, starting pitcher, sprained his back on a trampoline; and Boris Baker, star outfielder, ate rotten clams and nearly died.
Her children were born a year apart: Moe, 1936; Curley, 1937; and Larry, 1938.

THE COLON (:)   *P*

1. Use a colon to introduce a long or formal list, but do not use one after "to be" verbs.

Correct Please pick up these items at the store: garlic, wolfbane, mirrors, a prayer book, a hammer, and a wooden stake.

Incorrect Jean is such a bad cook that she thinks the four basic food groups are: canned, frozen, ready-to-mix, and take-out.

Correct Jean is such a bad cook that she thinks the four basic food groups are canned, frozen, ready-to-mix, and take-out.

Avoid needless colons.

Incorrect At the store I couldn't find: wolfbane or a wooden stake.

Correct At the store I couldn't find wolfbane or a wooden stake.

2. A colon may be used to introduce a formal or long quotation.

Examples The ambassador explained that his country could not afford a revolution: "Our nation is in the midst of such an energy crisis that we've lowered the palace thermostats to save money."
The late statesman Hubert Humphrey once jokingly apologized to reporters about his having been born in a small apartment above a drugstore: "They were short on log cabins that year."

3. Use a colon to introduce a word, phrase, or sentence that emphatically explains, summarizes, or amplifies the preceding sentence.

Examples Harriet knew the one ingredient that would improve any diet dinner: chocolate.
Horace made a big mistake at the office party: he kissed his boss's wife hello and his job goodbye.

Practicing What You've Learned

Errors with Semicolons and Colons

Correct the semicolon and colon errors below by adding, deleting, or substituting an appropriate mark of punctuation. Skip over any correct sentences.

    1. My doctor failed in his career as a kidnapper, no one could read his ransom notes.

    2. Some of the cars manufactured between 1907 and 1912 that didn't achieve the popularity of the Model T were: the Black Crow, the Swallow, the Bugmobile, and the Carnation.

3. The highest point in the United States is Mt. McKinley at 20,320 feet, in contrast, the lowest point is Death Valley at 282 feet below sea level.

4. There's only one thing that can make our yard look as good as our neighbor's; snow.

5. In a Thurmont, Maryland, cemetery can be found this epitaph "Here lies an Atheist, all dressed up, and no place to go."

6. According to an 1863 book of etiquette, the perfect hostess will see to it that the works of male and female authors are properly separated on her bookshelves, however, if the authors happen to be married, their proximity may be tolerated.

7. Some inventors who named weapons after themselves include Samuel Colt, the Colt revolver, Henry Deringer, Jr., the derringer pistol, Dr. Richard J. Gatling, the crank machine gun, Col. John T. Thompson, the submachine or "tommy" gun, and Oliver F. Winchester, the repeating rifle.

8. George Bernard Shaw, the famous playwright, claimed he wanted the following epitaph on his tombstone: "I knew if I stayed around long enough, something like this would happen."

9. As we drove down the highway we saw a sign that said "See the World's Largest Prairie Dog Turn Right at this Exit," therefore we stopped to look.

10. The next billboard read "See Live Rattlesnakes Pet Baby Pigs"; making us want to stop again.

THE APOSTROPHE (')   AP

1. Use an apostrophe to indicate a contraction.

Examples   *It's* too bad your car burned.[2]
                 Wouldn't the insurance company believe your story?

2. Add an apostrophe plus "s" to a noun to show possession.

Examples   *Jack's* dog ate the *cat's* dinner.
                 The *veterinarian's* assistant later doctored the *puppy's* wounds.

3. Add only an apostrophe to a plural noun ending in "s" to show possession.

---

[2]Don't confuse the contraction "it's" (for "it is") with the possessive pronoun "its," which never takes an apostrophe (The car was old, but *its* coat of paint was new).

Examples   Goldilocks invaded the *bears'* house.
She ignored her *parents'* warning about breaking and
entering.

4. In some cases you may add an apostrophe plus "s" to a singular
word ending in "s," especially when the word is a proper name.

Examples   Bill Jones's car
Doris's chair
the class's project

5. To avoid confusion, you may use an apostrophe plus "s" to form
the plurals of letters, figures, and words discussed as words; no apostrophe is also acceptable.

Examples   He made four *"C's"* last fall. [or *"Cs"*]
The right to resist the draft was a major issue in the
1960's. [or *1960s*]
You use too many *"and's"* in your sentence. [or
"ands"]

QUOTATION MARKS   *P*

1. Use quotation marks to enclose someone's spoken or written words.

Examples   The daughter wrote, "Remember, Daddy, when you
pass on you can't take your money with you."
"But I've already bought a fireproof money belt,"
answered her father.

2. Use quotation marks around the titles of essays,[3] articles, chapter
headings, short stories, short poems, and songs.

Examples   "How to Paint Ceramic Ashtrays"
"The Fall of the House of Usher"
"Stopping by Woods on a Snowy Evening"
"Moon River"

3. You may either underline or place quotation marks around a
word, phrase, or letter used as the subject of discussion.

Examples   Never use "however" as a coordinating conjunction.
The "which" clause in your sentence is misplaced.

---

[3]Do *not*, however, put quotation marks around your own essay's title on either the
title page or the first page of your paper.

Is your middle initial "X" or "Y"?
Her use of such words as "drab," "bleak," and "musty"
gives the poem a somber tone.

4. Place quotation marks around uncommon nicknames and words
used ironically. Do not, however, try to apologize for slang or clichés
by enclosing them in quotation marks; instead, substitute specific
words.

Examples "Scat-cat" Malone takes candy from babies.
Her "friend" was an old scarecrow in an abandoned
barn.
Slang After work Chuck liked to "simple out" in front of the
T.V.
Specific After work Chuck liked to relax by watching old
movies on T.V.

5. The period and the comma go inside quotation marks; the semicolon and the colon go outside. If the quoted material is a question, the
question mark goes inside; if quoted material is a part of a whole sentence that is a question, the mark goes outside. The same is true for
exclamation points.

Examples According to cartoonist Matt Groenig, "Love is a
snowmobile racing across the tundra; suddenly it flips
over, pins you underneath, and at night the ice
weasels come."
"Love is a snowmobile racing across the tundra;
suddenly it flips over, pins you underneath, and at
night the ice weasels come," says cartoonist Matt
Groening.
According to cartoonist Matt Groening, "Love is a
snowmobile . . . suddenly it flips over, pins you
underneath, and at night the ice weasels come";
Groening also advises that bored friends are one of the
first signs that you're in love.
Did he really say, "At night the ice weasels come"?
Sally asked, "Do you think you're in love or just in a
snowmobile?"

Practicing What You've Learned

Errors with Apostrophes and Quotation Marks

Correct the errors below by adding, changing, or deleting apostrophes
and quotation marks; skip any correct sentences.

1. Its true that when famous wit Dorothy Parker was told that President Coolidge, also known as Silent Cal, was dead, she exclaimed, How can they tell?
2. When a woman seated next to Coolidge at a dinner party once told him she had made a bet with a friend that she could get more than two words out of him, he replied You lose.
3. Twenty-one of Elvis Presleys albums have sold over a million copies; twenty of the Beatles albums have also done so.
4. Cinderellas stepmother wasn't pleased that her daughter received an F in her creative writing class on her poem Seven Guys and a Gal, which she had plagiarized from her friend's Snow White and Dopey.
5. Wasn't it Mae West who said, When choosing between two evils, I always like to try the one I've never tried before? asked Olivia.
6. Horace said Believe me, its to everybodies' advantage to sing the popular song You Stole My Heart and Stomped That Sucker Flat, if thats what the holdup man wants.
7. A scholars research has revealed that the five most commonly used words in written English are the, of, and, a, and to.
8. The triplets mother said that while its' hard for her to choose, O. Henrys famous short story The Ransom of Red Chief is probably her favorite.
9. Despite both her lawyers advice, she used the words terrifying, hideous, and unforgettable to describe her latest flight on Golden Fleece Airways, piloted by Jack One-Eye Marcus.
10. Its clear that Bubba didnt know if the Christmas' tree thrown in the neighbors yard was ours, theirs', or your's.

PARENTHESES ( ) **P**

1. Use parentheses to set off statements that give additional information, explain, or qualify the main thought.

> **Examples** The executive pulled over to the side of the road (a decision he would later regret) and held open the door for the hitchhiker.
> Many states (including Texas) still have laws that prohibit persons from remarrying until their divorces have been final for one month.

2. The period comes inside the close parenthesis if a complete sentence is enclosed; it occurs after the close parenthesis when the enclosed matter comes at the end of the main sentence and is only a part of the main sentence.

Examples The Colorado winters of 1978 and 1979 broke records for low temperatures. (See pages 72–73 for temperature charts.)
Jean hates Colorado winters and would prefer a warmer environment (such as Alaska, the North Pole, or a meat locker in Philadelphia).

3. If you are confused trying to distinguish whether information should be set off by commas, parentheses, or dashes, here are three general guidelines:

a. Use commas to set off information closely related to the rest of the sentence.

Example When Billy Clyde married Maybelle, his brother's young widow, the family was shocked. [The information identifies Maybelle and tells why the family was shocked.]

b. Use parentheses to set off information loosely related to the rest of the sentence or material that would disturb the grammatical structure of the main sentence.

Examples Billy Clyde married Maybelle (his fourth marriage, her second) in Las Vegas on Friday. [The information is merely additional comment not closely related to the meaning of the sentence.]
Billy Clyde married Maybelle (she was previously married to his brother) in Las Vegas on Friday. [The information is an additional comment that would also disturb the grammatical structure of the main sentence were it not enclosed in parentheses.]

c. Use dashes to set off information dramatically or emphatically.

Example Billy Clyde eloped with Maybelle—only three days after her husband's funeral—without saying a word to anyone in the family.

BRACKETS [ ]   *P*

1. Use brackets to set off editorial explanations in quoted material.

Examples According to the old letter, the treasure map could be found "in the library taped to the back of the portrait [of Gertrude the Great] that faces north."
The country singer ended the interview by saying,

"My biggest hit so far is 'You're the Reason Our Kids
are Ugly'" [original version by Lola Jean Dillon].

2. Use brackets to set off editorial corrections in quoted material. By
placing the bracketed word "sic" (meaning "thus") next to an error, you
indicate that the mistake appeared in the original text and that *you* are
not misquoting or misspelling.

Examples   The student wrote, "I think it's unfair for teachers to
count off for speling [sic]."
["Sic" in brackets indicates that the student who is
quoted misspelled the word "spelling."]
The highway advertisement read as follows: "For great
stakes [sic], eat at Joe's, located right behind Daisy's
Glue Factory." [Here, "sic" in brackets indicates an
error in word choice; the restaurant owner incorrectly
advertised "stakes" instead of "steaks."]

THE DASH (—)   P

1. Use a dash to indicate a strong or sudden shift in thought.

Examples   Now let's be reasonable—wait, put down that ice pick!
"It's not athlete's foot—it's deadly coreopsis!" cried Dr.
Mitty.

2. Use dashes to set off parenthetical matter that deserves more
emphasis than parentheses denote.

Examples   Wanda's newest guru—the one who practiced
catatonic hedonism—taught her to rest and play at the
same time.
He was amazed to learn his test score—a pitiful 43.

(To clear up any confusion over the uses of dashes, commas, and
parentheses, see the guidelines on p. 319.)

3. Use a dash before a statement that summarizes or amplifies the
preceding thought.

Examples   Wine, food, someone else picking up the check—the
dinner was perfect.
Not everyone agrees with football coach Vince
Lombardi, who said, "Winning isn't everything—it's
the only thing."

THE HYPHEN (-)   *P*

1. Use a hyphen to join words into a single adjective before the noun.

Examples   a wind-blown wig
the mud-caked sneakers
a made-for-television movie
a well-written essay
a five-year-old boy

Do not use a hyphen when the modifier ends in "ly."

Examples   a highly regarded worker
a beautifully landscaped yard

2. Some compound words use a hyphen; always check your dictionary when you're in doubt.

Examples   mother-in-law
President-elect
runner-up
good-for-nothing
twenty-one

3. Some words with prefixes use a hyphen; again, check your dictionary if necessary.

Examples   all-American
ex-wife
self-esteem
non-English

4. Use a hyphen to mark the separation of syllables when you divide a word at the end of a line. Do not divide one-syllable words; do not leave one or two letters at the end of a line. (In most dictionaries, dots are used to indicate the division of syllables. Example: va·ca·tion)

Examples   In your essays you should avoid using fragment sentences.
Did your father try to help you with your homework?

ITALICS (UNDERLINING) (____)   *Ital*

1. Underline or place quotation marks around a word, phrase, or letter used as the subject of discussion. Whether you underline or use quotation marks, always be consistent. (See also pp. 316–317.)

> **Examples**   No matter how I spell <u>offered,</u> it always looks wrong.
> Is your middle initial <u>X</u> or <u>Y?</u>
> Her use of such words as <u>drab, bleak,</u> and <u>musty</u> give the poem a somber tone.

2. Underline the title of books, magazines, newspapers, movies, works of art, television programs (but use quotation marks for individual episodes), airplanes, trains, and ships.

> **Examples**   <u>Moby Dick</u>
> <u>The Reader's Digest</u>
> <u>Texarkana Gazette</u>
> <u>Gone with the Wind</u>
> <u>Mona Lisa</u>
> <u>Sixty Minutes</u>
> <u>Spirit of St. Louis</u>
> <u>Queen Mary</u>

Exceptions: Do not underline the Bible or the titles of legal documents, including the United States Constitution, or the name of your own essay when it appears on your title page. Do not underline the city in a newspaper title unless the city's name is actually part of the newspaper's title.

3. Underline foreign words that are not commonly regarded as part of the English language.

> **Examples**   He shrugged and said, "<u>C'est la vie.</u>"
> Under the "For Sale" sign on the old rusty truck, the farmer had written the words "<u>caveat emptor,</u>" meaning "let the buyer beware."

4. Use underlining sparingly to show emphasis.

> **Examples**   Everyone was surprised to discover that the butler <u>didn't</u> do it.
> "Do you realize that <u>your</u> son just ate a piece of a priceless Bamzant sculpture?" the man screamed at his wife.

THE ELLIPSIS MARK (. . . or . . . .)   *P*

1. To show an omission in quoted material within a sentence, use three periods, with spaces before and after each one.

> **Example** Every time my father tells the children about having to trudge barefooted to school in the snow, the walk gets longer and the snow gets deeper.
> Every time my father tells the children about having to trudge barefooted to school . . . the snow gets deeper.

2. Three periods with spaces may be used to show an incomplete or interrupted thought.

> **Example** My wife is an intelligent, beautiful woman who wants me to live a long time. On the other hand, Harry's wife . . .

3. If you omit any words at the end of a sentence, use four periods with spaces between each one.

> **Example** "Four score and seven years ago our fathers brought forth upon this continent, a new nation. . . ."

4. If the omission of one or more sentences occurs at the end of a sentence, use four periods with no space before the first dot.

> **Example** "The Lord is my shepherd; I shall not want. . . . he leadeth me in the paths of righteousness for his name's sake."

Practicing What You've Learned

Errors with Parentheses, Brackets, Dashes, Hyphens, Italics, and Ellipses

Correct the errors below by adding, changing, or deleting parentheses, brackets, dashes, hyphens, italics, and ellipses.

> *1.* Many movie goers know that the ape in King Kong the original 1933 version, not the re-make was only an eighteen inch tall animated figure, but not everyone realizes that the Red Sea Moses parted in the 1923 movie of the Ten Commandments was a quivering slab of Jell O sliced down-the-middle.

2. Jean has found a way to keep the oven sparkling clean never turn it on.

3. In a person to person telephone call the twenty five year old starlet promised the hard working gossip columnist that she would "tell the truth . . . and nothing but the truth" about her highly-publicized feud with her exhusband, editor in chief of Meat Eaters' Digest.

4. While sailing across the Atlantic on board the celebrity filled yacht the Princess Diana, Dottie Mae Haskell she's the author of the popular new self help book Finding Wolves to Raise Your Children confided that until recently she thought chutzpah was an Italian side dish.

5. During their twenty four hour sit in at the melt down site, the anti nuclear protestors began to sing, "Oh, say can you see . . ."

6. Few people know that James Arness later Matt Dillon in the long running television series Gunsmoke got his start by playing the vegetable creature in the postwar monster movie The Thing 1951.

7. Similarly, well known T.V. star Michael Landon played the leading role in the 1957 classic I Was a Teenage Werewolf what a terrible movie!

8. A French chemist named Georges Claude invented the first neon sign in 1910. For additional information on his unsuccessful attempts to use seawater to generate electricity, see pp. 200–205.

9. When Lucille Ball, star of I Love Lucy, became pregnant with her first child, the network executives decided that the word expecting could be used on the air to refer to her condition, but not the word pregnant.

10. In mystery stories the detective often advises the police to cherchez la femme. Editor's note: Cherchez la femme means "look for the woman."

A Concise Guide to Mechanics

CAPITALIZATION *Cap*

1. Capitalize the first word of every sentence.

Example The lazy horse leans against a tree all day.

2. Capitalize the proper names of people, places, and products, and also proper adjectives.

Examples John Doe
Austin, Texas
First National Bank
Chevrolets
Japanese cameras
Spanish class

3. Always capitalize the days of the week, the names of the months, and holidays.

Examples Saturday, December 14
Tuesday's meeting
Halloween parties

4. Capitalize titles when they are accompanied by proper names.

Examples President Jones, Major Smith, Governor Brown, Judge Wheeler, Professor Plum, Queen Elizabeth

5. Capitalize all the principal words in titles of books, articles, stories, plays, movies, and poems. Prepositions, articles, and conjunctions are not capitalized unless they begin the title or contain more than four letters.

> **Examples**   "The Face on the Barroom Floor"
> *A Short History of the War Between the States*
> *For Whom the Bell Tolls*

6. Capitalize the first word of a direct quotation.

> **Examples**   Shocked at actor John Barrymore's use of profanity,
> the woman said, "Sir, I'll have you know I'm a lady!"
> Barrymore replied, "Your secret is safe with me."

7. Capitalize "east," "west," "north," and "south" when they refer to particular sections of the country but not when they merely indicate direction.

> **Examples**   The South may or may not rise again. ["South" here
> refers to a section of the country.]
> If you travel south for ten miles, you'll see the papier-
> mâché replica of the world's largest hamburger. [In
> this case, "south" is a direction.]

8. Capitalize a title when referring to a particular person;[1] do not capitalize a title if a pronoun precedes it.

> **Examples**   The President announced that anyone opposing the
> new peace plan would be shot.
> The new car Dad bought is guaranteed for 10,000 miles
> or until something goes wrong.
> His mother was disappointed when the magazine
> editor returned her poems at the junk mail rate.

ABBREVIATIONS   *Ab*

1. Abbreviate the titles "Mr.," "Mrs.," "Ms.," "St.," and "Dr." when they precede names.

> **Examples**   Dr. Scott, Ms. Steinham, Mrs. White, St. Jude

[1]Some authorities disagree; others consider such capitalization optional.

2. Abbreviate titles and degrees when they follow names.

Examples Charles Byrd, Jr.; Andrew Gordon, Ph.D.; Dudley
Carpenter, D.D.S.

3. You may abbreviate the following in even the most formal writing: A.M. (*ante meridiem*, before noon), P.M. (*post meridiem*, after noon), A.D. (*anno Domini*, in the year of our Lord), B.C. (before Christ), etc. (*et cetera*, and others), i.e. (*id est*, that is), and e.g. (*exempli gratia*, for example).

4. In formal writing do *not* abbreviate the names of days, months, centuries, states, countries, or units of measure. Do *not* use an ampersand ("&") unless it is an official part of a title.

Incorrect in formal writing	Tues., Sept., 18th century, Ark., Mex., lbs.
Correct	Tuesday, September, eighteenth century, Arkansas, Mexico, pounds
Incorrect	Tony & Gus went to the store to buy ginseng root.
Correct	Tony *and* Gus went to the A & P to buy ginseng root. [The "&" in "A & P" is correct because it is part of the store's official name.]

5. Do *not* abbreviate the words for page, chapter, volume, and so forth, except in footnotes and bibliographies, which have prescribed rules of abbreviation. (For additional information on proper abbreviation, consult your dictionary.)

NUMBERS

1. Use figures for dates, street numbers, page numbers, telephone numbers, and hours with A.M. and P.M.[2]

Examples April 22, 1946
710 West 14th Street
page 242
476-1423
10 A.M.

2. Some authorities say spell out numbers that can be expressed in one or two words; others say spell out numbers under one hundred.

---

[2] 8 A.M. but *eight* o'clock.

Examples   Ten thousand dollars or $10,000
              Twenty-four hours
              Thirty-nine years
              Five partridges
              $12.99 per pair
              1,294 essays

3. When several numbers are used in a short passage, use figures.

Examples   On the punctuation test, Jennifer made 82, Juan made
              91, Pete made 86, and I made 60.
              The hole in the ground was 12 feet long, 10 feet wide,
              and 21 feet deep.

4. Never begin a sentence with a figure.

Incorrect   50 spectators turned out to watch the surfing
               exhibition at Niagara Falls.
Correct   Fifty spectators turned out to watch the surfing
               exhibition at Niagara Falls.

Practicing What You've Learned

Errors with Capitalization, Abbreviations, and Numbers

Correct the errors below by adding, deleting, or changing capitals,
abbreviations, and numbers. Skip any correct words, letters, or
numbers you may find.

1. According to Abigail Van Buren, newspaper Columnist, in
   1980 handguns killed 4 people in Australia, 8 in Canada, 18 in
   Sweden, 8 in England, 23 in Israel, and 11,522 in the United
   States.
2. My sister, who lives in the east, was amazed to read studies by
   Thomas Radecki, MD, showing that 21-year-olds commit 300
   per cent more murders than did the same age group 30 years
   ago.
3. In sixty-seven A.D. the roman emperor Nero entered the
   chariot race at the olympic games, and although he failed to
   finish the race, the judges unanimously declared him The
   Winner.
4. On p. 21 of *Famous Claims For The Future*, author Sara N.
   Dipity, Ph.d., reminds us that in the 1st decade of the 20th
   century, Grover Cleveland once declared, "sensible and
   responsible women do not want to vote."

5. The official chinese news agency, located in the city of xinhua, estimates that there are ten million guitar players in their country today, an amazing number considering that the instrument had been banned during the cultural revolution that lasted 10 years, from nineteen sixty-six to nineteen seventy-six.

6. 231 electoral votes were cast for James Monroe but only 1 for John Quincy Adams in the 1820 Presidential race.

7. The british soldier T. E. Lawrence, better known as "lawrence of arabia," stood less than 5 ft. 6 in. tall.

8. Drinking a glass of french wine makes me giddy before my 10 a.m. english class, held in wrigley field every other friday except on New Year's day.

9. When a political opponent once called him "two-faced," president Lincoln retorted, "if I had another face, do you think I would wear this one?"

10. In 1883, when american aviator Orville Wright was in the 6th grade, he was expelled from his Richmond, Ind., school for mischievous behavior.

Index